Georgia Vineyards and Wineries

Georgia Vineyards and Wineries

A Historical Guide to
Modern Georgia Wines 2016

Wayne Crawford

B

Alphabetta, GA

No compensation was received by Wayne Crawford or BookLogix for any product in this book. The content of this book is not considered an endorsement of any product, but is intended to make the reader aware of the available wines and vineyards in the state of Georgia in 2016.

ISBN: 978-1-63183-265-9

10 9 8 7 6 5 4 3 2 0 1 1 6 1 8

Printed in the United States of America

⊗ This paper meets the requirements of ANSI/NISO Z39.48-1992 (Permanence of Paper)

To my wife, Kathy, who supported my research, reviewed my writing, and often served as the designated driver.

To all the vineyards and wineries in Georgia operational in 2016 that patiently provided their time and expertise to make this book possible.

Contents

Foreword

GEORGIA IS RENEWING its storied position as a wine producer in the United States. Before Prohibition, which started in Georgia in 1907, Georgia was the sixth-largest grape-growing state in the country.

Beginning in the 1980s, Georgia's wine world began to recover from the devastating effects of Prohibition. Today, some fifty wineries and vineyards that grow grapes but don't produce wine are shaping the state's viticultural future, even as they offer today's widely varied wine experience. With 1,100 acres of muscadines planted, Georgia ranks today as the country's largest producer of that grape.

In addition to classic European varietals—grown chiefly in North Georgia—the state grows Blanc du Bois, Lenoir (which may have originated in Georgia), and Lomanto, developed in Texas by Thomas V. Munson, a famous grape breeder in his day (1843–1913). And these are just a few of the perhaps unfamiliar but worthy grape types that make splendid wines, among them Traminette, Norton, and Seyval Blanc. By the time the reader has delved into this book on Georgia wines, these grape types will be as familiar as Chardonnay.

Wayne Crawford has undertaken the first contemporary global look at Georgia's reemerging wine world and covers the state from top to bottom. His work is important from a variety of perspectives, not only for the newcomer to wine but also for the wine educated who may not be at all aware of what is happening in Georgia winegrowing, the grapes the state is cultivating, and what kind of wines they yield.

The history of winemaking in Georgia begins, as he details, with the arrival of the first English settlers, who were tasked by the Trustees in England with growing grapes and making wine.

For various reasons, the goals they set for the colonists could not be achieved. But that's not the end of the story.

Into the nineteenth century, Georgia grew grapes and made wine—lots of wine. During the later decades of the century, some two hundred Hungarian families came from Pennsylvania to West Georgia and farmed thousands of acres until Prohibition shut that operation down. Now winegrowing is reemerging once again in West Georgia at Little Vine Vineyards near Villa Rica and Trillium Vineyard near Bremen.

In addition, his book examines the soil and climate types that characterize this large state—the largest geographically east of the Mississippi River. Many people, even wine professionals, assume a monochromatic geography, climate, and topography for Georgia, and, as Wayne's book clearly shows, that impression is wholly erroneous.

With this book, the reader who wants to venture into Georgia's ever-expanding wine world can organize that exploration from north to south and have at hand a quick reference to the elements that contribute to making these wines taste the way they do. The technical details help explain why North Georgia can grow Vitis vinifera (the noble European grapes) and why South Georgia needs to find other grape types to grow.

And he doesn't overlook the wonderful fruit wines that Georgians are making, from apple to blueberry. One taste of Sweet Acre Farms' "Bramblin' Sam," a sweet blackberry apple wine, will make the point.

By using Wayne Crawford's book to gain a foundational insight on Georgia winemaking, the reader also will glean insights into the diverse personalities that have taken this plunge that some might consider a fool's errand. Some are young families devoted to growing grapes and making wine (Farmer's Daughter Vineyards in South Georgia and Sweet Acre Farms Winery in North Georgia). Several, like Wayne, are former military professionals (Gary Engel at Engelheim Vineyards and Eric Seifarth at Crane Creek Vineyards).

Once-practicing physicians John Ezzard (Tiger Mountain Vineyards) and Carl Fackler (Stonewall Creek Vineyards) craft estate-grown wines that take Georgia winemaking to its next level, especially with their respective Petit Manseng wines. Originating in southwest France, this Vitis vinifera grape is spreading its influence across North Georgia.

This book bestows on Georgia winegrowing a seriousness that it deserves by taking the subject through a rigorous examination of all the components that have brought the state's once-thriving but decimated industry back to life in a relatively short time.

—Jane F. Garvey
Wine Writer

Acknowledgments

THIS BOOK WAS made possible through countless hours visiting every winery in Georgia and the patience and time their owners, winemakers, and vineyard-and-tasting-room managers devoted to answering my questions and tasting their wines. Particularly valuable were my interviews with the early pioneers in the Georgia wine community to include Tom Slick, owner of Habersham Vineyards and Winery, Dr. Donald Panoz, founder of Château Élan, Patty Prouty, daughter of Dr. Maurice Rawlings, founder of Georgia Winery, and David Harris, the former owner of Blackstock Vineyards and Winery. Special recognition to Tom Slick, who patiently reviewed the post-Prohibition history once written for accuracy and clarity.

Special thanks to Parks Redwine, owner of the Atlanta Improvement Company, a wine importer, and a former wine writer for the *Atlanta Journal-Constitution*. Parks's old Georgia wine bottle collection and exceptional early knowledge were invaluable in capturing wine history and photos, particularly following Prohibition. Thanks to Jane Garvey, another former wine writer for the *Atlanta Journal-Constitution* and the resident Georgia senior wine writer, for her expertise in validating and locating vineyards and wineries and for her in-depth Georgia wine knowledge, all of which greatly facilitated my research efforts.

Thanks to Dr. Patrick J. Conner, director of University of Georgia's muscadine-breeding program, for sharing his knowledge and answering questions related to muscadine history in Georgia. His numerous writings on muscadine grapes for UGA were valuable references for this book. University of Florida's Institute of Food and Agricultural Sciences muscadine grape was a valuable reference, along with the UGA's IFAS extension on muscadine grapes. The same is true for the Virginia work on grapevine diseases, Cornell University's grape program, and the team at Penn State's Cooperative Extension, whose sensory program proved invaluable to enhancing my aroma-and-fault detection skills.

There are several key experts whose writing immensely aided my research. Thomas Pinney's *A History of Wine in America: From the Beginnings to Prohibition* is a seminal masterpiece on American wine history. Jancis Robinson, Julia Harding, and José Vouillamoz's *Wine Grapes* was the key go-to reference for validating grape-varietal dates to determine if such a grape grew in a certain time period. James C. Bonner's *A History of Georgia Agriculture 1732–1860* was the best guide available to piece together what was growing in Georgia prior to the Civil War. Finally, Ted Goldammer's *Grape Grower's Handbook: A Complete Viticultural Guide for Wine Production* was a concise reference on grape pests and disease.

Thanks to MyTopo in Billings, Montana, for granting me permission to use their maps as the base map to showcase winery locations in Georgia. Much thanks to Bottoms Nursery and Ison's Nursery and Vineyard for providing muscadine grape photos. Thanks to the Georgia Wine Producers for allowing me to join their growing organization as an associate member and gain insightful knowledge that I might not have been smart enough to ask for.

Final recognition to my two longtime editors at Big Canoe's *Smoke Signals*, Barbara Schneider and Anita Rosen, for their encouragement to write, thoughtful suggestions, and high standards. Barbara was invaluable in assisting with the overall chapter design for the book.

Introduction

Wine is one of the most civilized things in the world and one of the most natural things of the world that has been brought to the greatest perfection, and it offers a greater range for enjoyment and appreciation than, possibly, any other purely sensory thing.

—Ernest Hemingway

When I entered the United States regular army infantry in 1967, my wine experience was limited to that sipped in Episcopal communion—Lancers and Mateus medium-sweet sparkling wines—nothing to stimulate my later passion.

When I arrived in Vietnam as a first lieutenant in 1969, having attended airborne school at Fort Benning in Georgia and advisor school at Fort Bragg in North Carolina, I quickly trained to speak limited Vietnamese. My orders were changed to join a camp team to help convert a special forces A-team with four infantry companies to regional forces in the Vietnamese army. Ironically, I was in Montagnard country, and they did not speak Vietnamese, nor did they have a written language. So much for prior planning!

The good news was, this was like going to war with *National Geographic*. We often lived off the land, and we had a home-court advantage. Every village we encountered was a hometown for one of our fighters. The common practice in those days was to enter a village at the end of a combat mission—seven days, perhaps longer—gather intelligence, and check on the tribe's medical health and overall safety. Hospitality required leaders to share rice wine with village elders.

Rice wine in the Vietnamese highlands was made in great earthen jugs and sipped communally through a long, straw-like funnel. Each village had their own wine customs, much like regional wines. They cooked gluten rice with water, local herbs, and spices, then allowed it to ferment for a month or so in animal skin–covered jugs. We consumed several gallons over several months, always carefully measured with an empty, top-removed Coca-Cola can to ensure we were drinking. I began to adjust my palate to alcohol at 15 percent to 20 percent. Best described as an acquired taste, it has served me well as a wine writer and judge to assess each wine on its own merits and give every wine a chance to shine.

Fifth Special Forces Officers Drinking Rice Wine
The author, a military assistant command Vietnam (MACV) advisor, is second from the left without a cover. In the back is Major Lee Camp, commander with Vietnamese Special Forces Team 1969 II Corp Vietnam

My good fortune was to marry my wife, Kathy, while on leave from Vietnam in Hawaii. A later follow-up assignment brought us to Germany for three years. Like any newlywed couple, we sought out opportunities to enjoy the local food and spirits and travel Europe as time away from my military duties allowed.

Our local beer was delivered to our apartment doorstep two times a week like milk—an excellent way to provide customer satisfaction.

In Germany, my passion for wine and willingness to try all the Rieslings, Frankens, Gewürztraminers, and French, Spanish, and Italian wines inspired me to learn more about each varietal or Bordeaux. My wine epiphany came on a chance evening with the mayor of Gelnhausen, Germany, whose family had deep roots growing grapes and making wine. Invited along with other American commanders to his home, I ended the evening tasting a small glass of his family's most cherished wine. I regret to this day that I did not take notes on this tasting, but it was an aged, late-harvest Riesling, perhaps late 1950s. In my memory it was full bodied with a round, smooth mouthfeel, complex aromas, flavors of honey and fig, and was semisweet with a long finish. This one chance tasting implanted my passion for everything wine.

Over the next few years as we moved around on various military assignments, I had the opportunity to learn the protocols in a British army mess on how to drink and hand port to the left. I also began studying and collecting wine to sharpen my skills and improve my palate. Quickly realizing that this "information thirst" required formal training, I started taking wine certification courses with *Wine Spectator*, among others. On this journey, I completed my Certified Specialist of Wine with the Society of Wine Educators, French Wine Scholar, and Champagne Master Certificates with the French Wine Society (now the Wine Scholar Guild).

Understanding *Vitis vinifera*, the European grape, proved invaluable as I immersed myself in North American wines with the foundational skills provided in these various wine courses. The French certification programs' continued exposure to Master of Wine instructors proved vital. I learned that regardless of your expertise in wine, there is always more room for study.

I am indebted to the American Wine Society, which over the past several years has honed my wine-judging skills with monthly tastings and judging opportunities throughout the Southeast. I was honored to judge in the 2016 and 2017 Georgia Trustees Wine Challenge for the best wines in Georgia.

In 2007, I began writing a monthly wine column, "Wayne on Wine," that appears in the print and online editions of *Smoke Signals*, an award-winning newspaper serving North Georgia and the community of Big Canoe. Each year I've included articles about Georgia wines, winery owners, and winemakers. The number of Georgia wineries in 2007 was twenty-five with a few having planted vines but not yet producing wine.

During my early visits to wineries, it was evident there was limited consolidated state information on Georgia varietals grown, acreage, and overall production, and even less on the economic impact these wineries were having on the Georgia-grown and agritourism movement.

In 2016, except for a handful of muscadine wineries in Central and South Georgia, most wineries were east and north of Atlanta, including Braselton, Dahlonega, Helen, Clayton, Chattanooga, Young Harris, and Ellijay.

The Georgia Farm Winery Bill had been passed and amended over several years, from 1981 to 1984, through the efforts of a small group of wine growers. Fortunately, it has continued to improve over the past twenty-three years. I wrote articles on the challenges with direct-to-consumer shipping rules in Georgia, which were resolved by July 1, 2008. Sunday sales finally adjusted in most of the state on November 20, 2011, when 105 of 127 communities voted for Sunday sales starting at 12:30 p.m.

There were still dry counties, no in-state testing laboratory or viticultural professional skills within the University of Georgia agricultural program, and limited grape expertise among county agents. However, selected county agricultural agents with expertise in other crops and fruits worked hard to learn grapes along with UGA's agricultural staff. At best, this was a hit-or-miss program, and most wineries were shipping laboratory samples to California, New York, and Virginia with many delays in receiving feedback. They were using consultants to fill their knowledge gap.

A decision to add a viticultural expert and open a testing laboratory at UGA was made and finally funded in 2016 with the support of the Georgia Wine Producers and the legislature. The testing laboratory in Athens is now operational with a basic measurement capability, which should continue to improve as demand increases. UGA staffed its first viticultural professor, Dr. Cain Hickey, on March 1, 2017.

By late 2014, the number of Georgia wineries had grown to almost forty-four, yet the absence of combined information on varietals, acreage, and production was still unknown. UGA did produce "Economic Contribution of Georgia Winery & Vineyards" in September 2013. The executive summary in the report concludes, "Georgia wineries and vineyards and related sectors, along with visitor spending contributes up to $81.6 million in output, 655.6 jobs throughout the state's economy, and $4.1 million in state and local tax revenue."[1] These data were drawn from research in the fall of 2012 and the spring of 2013.

Shortage of detailed information as a useful Georgia guide became the catalyst for this book. It was also clear that Georgia investors were briskly adding vineyards each year and varietals were being replaced annually as more experience was gained in vineyards and in wine production to match soil and climate conditions.

This ongoing growth, which I see as continuous, is best served by a book or journal updated at least every two years. This would include new entries based on impacts from the weather, disease, animal damage, and crop changes, along with new vineyards, tasting-room openings, and enhanced legislation, all to better the service in what has become a multibillion-dollar economic benefit to the state. Since 2013, when the first economic report

---

1 Kent Wolfe, Sharon P. Kane, and Karen Stubbs, "Economic Contribution of Georgia Wineries & Vineyards," Athens: UGA Center Report, September 2013.

was finalized, eight new vineyards and wineries have started or restarted.

I discussed this writing concept with a dozen or more wine owners, and all provided positive feedback. My aim is to produce a journal that first enhances the wine consumer's knowledge while providing a broader foundation for enjoying Georgia wines. This effort is intended to capture Georgia wine history, geology, climate, weather, plant disease, and pests to better understand what grows where within the state and why. Second, this book intends to provide a guide to consumers, wineries, and growers with quick facts on owners, winemakers, and varietals to enhance travel to wineries and tasting rooms. Third, I hope to provide a reference for wineries to share information on who is growing varietals and what they produce using Georgia-grown grapes and out-of-state grapes or juice brought in for local production.

As 2016 ended, Georgia wine growers were using over seventy-four different varietals within the state across a broad spectrum of grapevine classifications in fifty-six vineyards and wineries and nine grower vineyards that supply grapes to production wineries.

Throughout the book, I will introduce key topics and use supporting appendix material to provide more details to foster easy access to supporting information, tasting tips, and wine ageability. I gathered all the information on each winery from on-location interviews with owners and winemakers over a period of eighteen months. Most photos were taken by me on location at the Georgia vineyards with permission from the owners or, in a few cases, provided by the primary source or a Georgia plant nursery.

I also conducted in-depth interviews with pioneer wine leaders or family members who were important to the rebirth of Georgia wines beginning in 1979 through 1983. If the winery, vineyard, or tasting room was not operational in 2016, it is not in this book.

My passion for Georgia vineyard and winery growth and long-term success is the catalyst for this first in-depth book on Georgia wines. My journey to gather Georgia wine facts has allowed me to interact with exceptional growers, winemakers, vineyard managers, tasting-room managers, and delightful customers who are eager to see more grapes grown and wine produced in Georgia. In summary, I am not a wine critic nor a casual visitor to our Georgia wineries. I interact continuously with our rapidly evolving wine community.

Drink what you like, but do not overlook the award-winning Georgia-grown and produced wines. This book should help guide your safe travels, and please maintain a designated driver.

If food is the body of good living, wine is its soul.
—Clifton Fadiman

Chapter 1

1733–1752
Seeking Comfort and Reward in the New World

NORTH AMERICA IS unique among the world's wine-growing regions given its diversity in grape species. The pilgrims in New England and colonial Virginia and North Carolina noted an abundance of grapevines growing in their New World.

Not yet classified, these native grapes had adapted, for the most part, to the climate, weather, and plant diseases of the region. The "fox grape" concord is one example that would grow into an important grape for the Northeast, while the round-leaf muscadine grapes would flourish in the Carolinas and Georgia.[1]

There are no records in Georgia to indicate that Native Americans used grapes to make wine before 1800. There is a Cherokee recipe for "Possum Grape Drink" (Oo-ni-na-su-ga Oo-ga-ma) using muscadine grapes to produce a hot or cold drink, though not to be confused with possum grape, the weed.[2]

In answering a letter I sent December 14, 2016, to Dr. Patrick Conner, the director of UGA's early muscadine grape–breeding

---

1 Thomas Pinney, *A History of Wine in America: From the Beginnings to Prohibition* (Berkeley: University of California Press, 1989), 6–7.
2 Momfeather Erickson, "25 Cherokee Recipes," Manataka American Indian Council, http://www.manataka.org/page1237.html.

program, he replied that before the year 1700, all the vines in Georgia were native grapevines.

> Even Scuppernong wasn't grown before the mid-1700s . . . Flowers (a muscadine) was not present until early in the nineteenth century. James (a muscadine) [was] discovered in 1866 and Thomas (a muscadine) in 1845.[3]

These four grapes were in the first UGA muscadine-breeding program.

UGA formed the muscadine-breeding program in 1909, and it continues currently under the leadership of Dr. Patrick Conner as the oldest and largest muscadine grape–breeding program in the United States. It is important to note that muscadine grapes have been cultivated in the South for over four hundred years and grow best in fertile, loamy, sandy, and alluvial soils where temperatures seldom drop below 10 degrees Fahrenheit and where there is a long growing season available to ripen grapes.[4]

What is abundantly clear from Georgia's early history is that Spanish, Italian, French, and English explorers to North America were aware of native grapes and likely assumed that the fertile lands of this New World would grow the *Vitis vinifera* grapes indigenous to southeast Europe and the Mediterranean. Such was the report of Giovanni da Verrazano in 1524 when he observed muscadine grapes growing in the Kitty Hawk region of the Carolinas. "Many vines growing naturally, which growing up took hold of the trees."[5] Sir Walter Raleigh's expedition observed abundant native grapes in 1584. The English would continue to believe growing their Old World grapes in the colonies would happen. See Thomas Pinney's two-volume *History of Wine in*

---

3 Patrick J. Conner, letter response to author on December 15, 2016.
4 Patrick J. Conner, *A Century of Muscadine Grape (Vitis rotundifolia Michx.) Breeding at the University of Georgia*, 1.
5 Thomas Pinney, *A History of Wine in America: From the Beginnings to Prohibition*, 11.

America for a more in-depth discussion on efforts to grow and produce wine in early colonial times.

In 1663, still holding out hope for wine in the New World, the Carolina proprietors chartered by Charles II concentrated on "three rich commodities: wine, silk, and oil (olive)."[6]

By the beginning of the eighteenth century, the pursuit of wine, silk, and oil remained essential in colonial development, along with border security. England was willing to establish a new colony south of the Carolinas to protect its holdings from the French and Spanish, but also Native American tribes, which had attacked the Carolina colonists in 1715. Wars with both European countries had placed restrictions on trade, and England desired to become more self-sufficient.

The pamphlet *Reasons for Establishing the Colony of Georgia* by Benjamin Martyn Esq. was written to outline the key economic benefits if a colony began in Georgia. I believe the target audience for this tract was the English Parliament and other key English leaders and noblemen, whose voices might help gain support and funding for a trustee arrangement in Georgia. Much was made on growing silk and flax, but a discussion on wine and vine acquisition also occurred.[7]

> One Article more I shall mention, viz. Wine, of which (as she is about the same Latitude with Madeira) she may faife, with proper Application and Care, sufficient Quantities, not only for Part of Consumption at home but also for the Supply of our other Plantations, instead of their going to Madeira for it. The Country abounds with Variety of Grapes, and the Madeira Vines are known to thrive there extremely well. A Gentleman of great Experience in Botany, who has a salary from the Trustees, by a particular Contribution of some Noblemen and Gentlemen for the Purpose, sailed

---

6 Pinney, 33–34.

7 Benjamin Martyn Esq., *Reasons for Establishing the Colony of Georgia, with Regard to the Trade of Great Britain* (London: W. Meadows, 1732).

> from hence almost five Months ago, to procure the Seeds and Roots of all useful Plants. He has already, I hear, sent from Madeira a great Number of Malmsey, and other Vines to Charles-Town, for the use of Georgia, with proper instructions for cultivating the Vines, and making the wine.[8]

There would be twelve trustee members in the first council meeting, but during the life of the trust, seventy-two members served. The trust's life was short lived (1732–1752) and returned to the British Crown. Georgia would be the last of the British colonies in North America. The charter forbade trustees from holding office or land in Georgia, and they were not paid. James Oglethorpe was the chief founder, and his vision was a place to recover his fellow subjects from a state of misery and oppression and stake them in happiness and freedom.[9] Neither slavery nor strong drink was to be allowed. The first meeting of the trustees was held in London on July 22, 1732, and in another meeting held on September 22, 1732, in London, Sir Gilbert Heathcote announced that His Majesty had granted a charity (trust) for "relieving necessitous people, and by establishing the aforesaid Colony . . . and granting lands between the Savannah and Altamaha rivers . . . Georgia."[10]

The botanist hired by the trust to establish the Trustee Garden in the new colony was Dr. William Houston. He began his travels heading south to the island of Madeira in 1732 to acquire vine cuttings, which he would send along in two tubs to Charles Town in the Carolinas. The grapevines selected are unclear, but Malmsey, likely the malvasia grape, is suggested, and they were available in 1733.[11] Since Madeira was on the same latitude

8 Benjamin Martyn, 1st ed., 13.

9 Benjamin Martyn, 2nd ed., 10.

10 Library of Congress extract, "Establishment of the Colony of Georgia Proceeding of the Trustees July 22 and September 22 1732," 4–6.

11 Jancis Robinson, Julia Harding, and José Vouillamoz, *Wine Grapes* (New York: HarperCollins, 2012), 571.

as Georgia, the choice to use Madeira grapevines was made.[12] It is worth noting that the pamphlet suggests malmsey vines were already growing in the colonies, but not substantiated. These *Vitis vinifera* vines growing on their rootstocks would not survive the subtropical infestation of harmful insects and disease in South Georgia. Dr. Houston, having sent malmsey or some Madeira cuttings to the Carolinas, moved on to Jamaica in search of additional plants for medicinal purposes to grow in the ten-acre Trustee Garden in the new colony. Unfortunately, he died before ever reaching Georgia.[13]

Fortunately, and concurrently, other vines would be collected and sent to the colony in 1733.[14] Phillip Millar, the gardener at Chelsea Botanical Gardens, sent a tub of burgundy grapevines late in 1733. Charles King, a vineyard owner in Brompton, also sent three tubs of burgundy vines to the colony.[15] No records seem to exist on what burgundy grapevines shipped. In early 1700, the main grapes from this region were white Chardonnay (1583) and red Pinot Noir (1375). There were ancillary grapes: white Aligoté (1667), Sacy (1650), Pinot Gris (1711), and red Gamay Noir (1395).[16] Robert Millar, a brother to Phillip Millar, was chosen to replace Dr. Houston.[17] The dates in brackets are taken from *Wine Grapes*, representing the first known date this grape is mentioned in history.[18]

The first selected colonist's journey to Georgia began on Friday, November 17, 1732, from Gravesend, located twenty-one miles east of London center. James Oglethorpe was on board the two-hundred-ton frigate *Ann* along with Captain John Thomas, a crew of 20 sailors, and 114 colonists. They carried ten tons of

12 Thomas Pinney, *A History of Wine in America: From the Beginnings to Prohibition*, 43–44.
13 Thomas Pinney, 44.
14 Thomas Pinney, 44.
15 Thomas Pinney, 43.
16 French Wine Society Study Manual, French Wine Scholar Exam, 2015 (Frenchwinesociety.org), 91.
17 Benjamin Martyn Esq., *Reasons for Establishing the Colony of Georgia, with Regard to the Trade of Great Britain*, 2nd ed., 13.
18 Jancis Robinson, Julia Harding, and José Vouillamoz, *Wine Grapes*.

Alderman Parson's best beer. Traveling with beer on board was a necessity, since water in barrels became stale and less potable over two months, not to mention the fact that the beer likely improved crew morale. During the two-month journey to Madeira, two children died and four children were born.[19] There is colonial history associated with the colonists' departure from Gravesend. Years earlier in 1617, the Indian princess Pocahontas visited London from the Jamestown colony with her English husband, John Rolfe. One day out on her return from London near Gravesend, she became sick and died at age twenty-one and was buried at St. George's Church.[20]

The distance to Madeira from Gravesend is 1,496 nautical miles. From Madeira to Charles Town in the Carolinas takes 3,135 nautical miles and a voyage of sixty-one days.

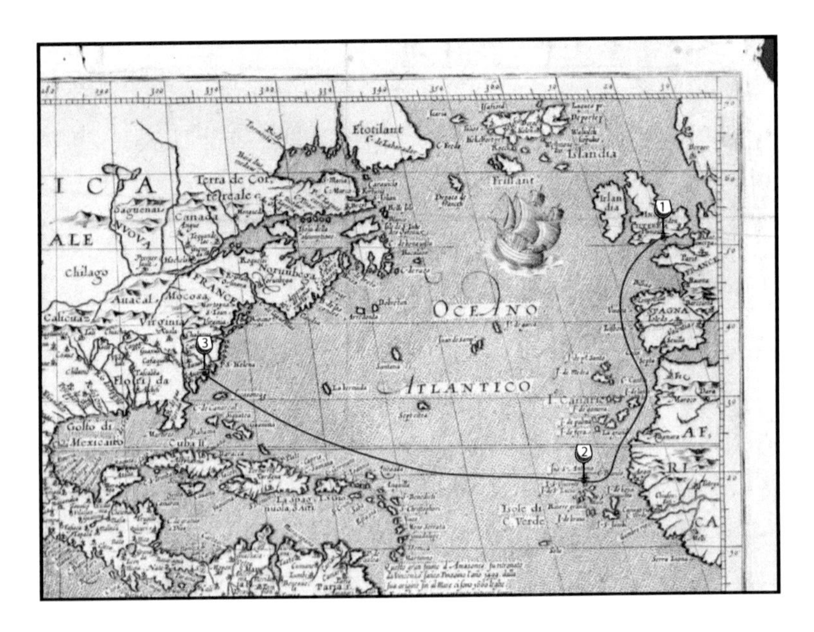

Having made the crossing to Charles Town, arriving on Saturday, January 13, 1733, "James Oglethorpe and the ship *Ann*

---

19 "1772," Georgia's Time Line, gaahgp.genealogyvillage.com.
20 Sarah J. Stebbins, "Pocahontas: Her Life and Legend," National Park Service, August 2010, https://www.nps.gov/jame/learn/historyculture/pocahontas-her-life-and-legend.htm.

came to anchor off our bar. Oglethorpe would come ashore that night to be well received by the Governor of South Carolina." The next day the *Ann* sailed for Port Royal south of Charles Town near what would become Savannah. The colonists were allowed to unload at Trench Island on the twentieth, while Oglethorpe and a small party met with Tomochichi of the Yamacraw Creek Indians at Savannah.[21]

> Mr. Oglethorpe . . . landed at Savannah on the January 18 at 10:00 in the morning; where he found Mr. Wiggan (the interpreter) with the chief men of all the lower Creek nation, were come down to treat of an alliance with the new colony . . . reduce to a tribe of eight towns . . . allied together. They claim from the Savannah River as far as St. Augustine up to the Flint River which falls into the Gulf of Mexico. Much discussion went on related to each town and a treaty was signed on January 21, 1733, and gifts were exchanged.[22]

The treaty was transmitted to the trustees and formally ratified on the eighteenth of October 1733 in England.[23]

Given the original charter that authorized trustee land between the Savannah and Altamaha Rivers, this first treaty signed in 1733 covered only limited territory in Georgia. The following map highlights this initial treaty area and subsequent land cessions with the Creek and Cherokee Indians in Georgia through 1836.

Once the agreement was signed, the colonists relocated to the site Oglethorpe selected for Savannah and began

---

21 Library of Congress extract, "Establishment of the Colony of Georgia Arrival of First Colonists, at Charleston, South Carolina 13 January. 1733 (Charleston Jan 20th)," 9–10.
22 Library of Congress, Conference with the Indians, 10–13.
23 "Georgia Indian Land Cessions," Native American Nations website, accessed September 8, 2017, http://www.nanations.com/land/georgia_land_cessions.htm.

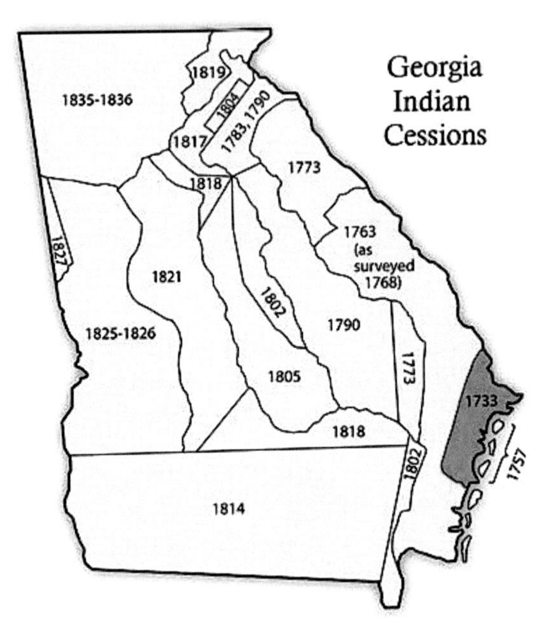

Map by GeorgiaINFO, an online Georgia Almanac

constructing a town with ten acres set aside for the Trustee Garden, considered the first agricultural experiment station in America.[24] Photos of the garden, a one-acre plan for the Trustee Garden, and contact information are in Appendix A.

Notes from an educated Scotsman named Hugh Anderson detail "poor site selection on poor soil with the site exposed to wind and the sun. It would do well to grow mulberry trees, for silk worms, but to grow vines, the trustees need windbreaks, raise hedges, drain the swampland, build a greenhouse, dig a well, and set up a laboratory and a library."[25] More grapevines were shipped to Georgia for the garden, but Anderson's notes tell the story. The growth of *Vitis vinifera* grapes in Georgia had no success, and the trustee program was over by 1754.

England declared war on Spain in the War of Jenkins' Ear, part of the War of the Austrian Succession, and Oglethorpe would

24 Thomas Pinney, *A History of Wine in America: From the Beginnings to Prohibition*, 43.
25 Thomas Pinney, 44.

go on to spend most of his time leading military operations in Georgia, successfully defeating the Spanish at the Battle of Bloody Marsh. He returned to London on July 23, 1743, on the *Success*.[26] Oglethorpe served in the ranks of the British army before retiring as a general. Active to the end, he died on July 1, 1785. Appendix B contains inscriptions from the monumental tablet in Granham Church, England. He would never return to Georgia.

> *It is the wine that leads me on, the wild wine that sets the wisest man to sing at the top of his lungs, laugh like a fool— it drives the man to dancing . . . it even tempts him to blurt out stories better never told.*
>
> —Homer

26 Harriet C. Cooper, *James Oglethorpe: The Founder of Georgia*, Illustrated (New York: D. Appleton and Company, 1904), 186.

Chapter 2

1753–1860
Native Vines

THE TRUSTEE GARDEN experience was not a success for *Vitis vinifera* grapes, but the Royal Province of Georgia began. Spanish rule of Florida transferred to British hands in 1763, and Georgia could stop being a military colony.[1]

As the Georgia Indian Cessions map from the previous chapter illustrates, as a royal province, Georgia was able to expand into an L-shaped figure with Savannah as the apex. Further expansion would not occur until after the American Revolution.

The trustee experience opened farming along the Savannah River, and villages, such as the Austrian colonists' at Ebenezer, were self-sustaining and willing to experiment with wild grapes and other indigenous plants.[2] Following the American Revolution, Georgia's settlement of veterans' claims was the most pressing concern. Land grants promised for those serving in the war would reached 287.5 acres per veteran by 1784.[3]

The most challenging event in Georgia history in the thirty years following 1802 was the removal of Indians from the

---

1 James C. Bonner, *A History of Georgia Agriculture 1732–1860* (Athens: University of Georgia Press, 1964), 8.
2 James C. Bonner, 23.
3 James C. Bonner, 33.

western and northern portion of the state.[4] Gold discovered in Dahlonega in 1828 put further pressure on moving Indians out of the state.[5]

In 1831, Malthus A. Ward was appointed professor of natural history and botany at the University of Georgia.[6] Over the next two decades, he would focus on new fruits and flowers. Peaches, apples, and pears dominated, but unlike new arrivals such as the pear tree, grapevines were indigenous to the South and grew almost everywhere. Early Georgia farmers described the native or wild grape as being of two types: a fox grape—having large, dark, round berries in single or small clusters, often called the bull or bullace grape—and the cluster grape, which bore black clusters, and the fruit was a small berry with a thick skin tasting somewhat like a red bordeaux grape from France. Later this grape would be called a fox grape, taking the original name given to the muscadine or bullace grape.[7]

A third grape found on St. Simons Island was a white grape common to Europe but with a different leaf, likely a scuppernong originally discovered in North Carolina.[8] Scuppernong is a bronze grape cultivar of *Vitis rotundifolia* muscadine and the dominant grape cultivar from 1750 to 1947. Several variations likely exist.[9] These muscadine grapes were the first domesticated American grapes.[10]

As reported from early expeditions to the South, these muscadine grapes grew high into trees and were difficult to cultivate. They were a good source of food for birds and other animals as they ripened.[11] There were, however, several progressive farmers who experimented with native grapes given the high cost and scarcity of wine in Georgia.

---

4 James C. Bonner, 40.
5 James C. Bonner, 43.
6 James C. Bonner, 150.
7 James C. Bonner, 159.
8 James C. Bonner, 159.
9 Dr. Patrick Conner, *Botany and History of Muscadine Grapes* (Athens: University of Georgia seminar, 2009).
10 Patrick Conner, briefing slide.
11 James C. Bonner, *A History of Georgia Agriculture 1732–1860*, 159.

Thomas McCall from Laurens County, who served as surveyor general of Georgia from 1786 to 1795, began in 1816 a systematic experimentation with grape culture and winemaking. By 1826, he was considered one of the best winemakers in Georgia and produced 860 gallons of wine off two acres of vines. His skills were rare and not easily passed along.[12] McCall was familiar with Andrew Estave, a Frenchman who, in the 1770s, had directed at Williamsburg a public vineyard that failed. He was also familiar with St. Pierre's *Art of Planting and Cultivating the Vine*. He would help bridge the gap between the early failures with *Vitis viniferous* and his successful development of hybrid grapes with native grapes.[13]

Other farmers were attempting to reproduce Thomas McCall wine without much success or with limited demand for their product. In 1846, this included James Camak, Iverson Harris, and Camille le Hardy. James Horsley of Upson County made large quantities of scuppernong. The bottom line was that the wine industry in Georgia and the South remained a home enterprise, with no market for the unskilled Southern vintners.[14]

Georgia did have an abundance of summer grapes for table use, all of which had undergone some modifications by 1860. The most popular were the Warren and Devereaux grapes. There was also a Harris grape. Georgia had no system for naming grapes, so often a grape was known by several names. Other grapes of Southern origin included Catawba, Isabella, Lenoir, and Herbemont.[15] The Southern Vine Growers meeting held in Aiken, South Carolina, in 1860 had the grape-naming convention as one key topic. The recommended name solution was first the name of the state in which the grape grew; the town name, river, or locality; and last, the private name or brand of the producer. They also agreed to allow a moderate amount

---

12 James C. Bonner, 160.

13 Thomas Pinney, *A History of Wine in America: From the Beginnings to Prohibition*, 153.

14 James C. Bonner, 160.

15 James C. Bonner, 162.

of brandy or concentration of grape sugar to go into the wine during production.[16]

One last surge in grape cultivation occurred prior to the Civil War. In 1848, Charles Axe, a German immigrant, felt he could successfully grow vines north of Augusta. By 1855 he had acquired the confidence of several other growers to manage their vines. At the Atlanta Fair in 1855, his wines scored a silver cup for his work using Catawba grapes. His success lead to the forming of the Vine Growers Association of Georgia in 1857. Catawba became the most famous wine grape produced in Georgia during the antebellum period.[17] One continuing problem was the lack of transportation to get fruit to market.

Wine is the most healthful and most hygienic of beverages.
—Louis Pasteur

16 James C. Bonner, 163.
17 James C. Bonner, 165.

Chapter 3

1870–1935
Tallapoosa Wine Experience and Prohibition

The most compelling and largest vineyards and wine-production activity in the late-nineteenth century was positioned around Tallapoosa, a city in the Piedmont region of West Georgia in Haralson County.

An investment group centered in the Northeast with Ralph L. Spencer from Connecticut, a guiding force, saw Tallapoosa becoming an industrial center.[1] Spencer and other members of his team began obtaining charters in 1887 for electric and water companies. In 1889, they opened Mountain City Glass Works, and in 1893 they chartered the Georgia Fruit Growing and Winery Association.[2] All were positioned to allow both growth in the community and sustainment of winery operations.

In the same year, the Georgia Fruit Growing Company started. Spencer visited Pennsylvania to recruit four hundred Hungarian immigrants, who knew and understood vine production, to relocate to Tallapoosa to grow and produce wine. To facilitate this recruiting effort, he located a Catholic priest, Father Francis Janisek, to assist in recruiting and relocating the Hungarian families. In turn, Janisek would receive land and a house, and

1 Carole E. Scott, "Tallapoosa," Archives of Haralson County, 1999, http://roadsidegeorgia.com/city/tallapoosa.html.
2 Carole E. Scott, 2–7.

each of the more than two hundred families recruited would be allocated ten acres.[3] Two thousand acres were initially devoted to this effort. By 1896, there were 12,726 vineyard acres of land in Haralson County. The 1900 census on agriculture in Haralson County reported 665,885 grapevines and produced 1,593,536 pounds of grapes.[4]

Even with the big production of grapes in Haralson County and a sister operation in Sidonia, Alabama, later called Fruithurst, there is limited information on what grape varietals were planted. There are notes that 25 percent of the grapes were table grapes and the remainder were used for wine production. The wine and grapes produced were sold in the North. One account indicates that to get the right grapes, plant cuttings were brought in from Hungary.[5]

Speculating on what might have been grown, given the subtropical climate conditions in Georgia, it is possible that Catawba was in the production mix. If the grapes were going to the North, as reported, then Concord might have been included along with Herbemont and Lenoir, which were available in this period.

Grape cuttings from Hungary may have been planted at this time, as well. Hungary is an old wine-growing country that was hit heavily in 1882 with the phylloxera epidemic, so the availability of newly grafted rootstock from America for Hungarian grape stock was problematic. There are, however, several Hungarian varietals that were well known and could have been cut and sent to Georgia for grafting. Potential candidates are the white grape Furmint (1571), a key grape in the making of the sweet wines from the Tokaji region. Blaufrãnkish or Kekfrankos, a dark-skinned grape (1862), is one alternative.[6] The white grape Hárslevelű (1744), an offspring of Furmint, is another candidate.[7]

3 "Vineyards & Winery," Tallapoosa, GA, Google site, https://sites.google.com/site/tallapoosaga/history/winery.
4 "Vineyards & Winery."
5 "Vineyards & Winery."
6 Jancis Robinson, 116.
7 Jancis Robinson, 455.

My examination of the sparse accounts on the Tallapoosa vineyards does not offer an accounting on the varietals grown.

The Tallapoosa vineyard experience made Georgia one of the leading wine-production states in America before 1900. Unfortunately, this was short-lived with the rise of Prohibition.

One historical note from the Longstreet Society is General James Longstreet, a Southern general and second in command under General Robert E. Lee of the Army of Northern Virginia during the American Civil War, purchased a 160-acre property in Gainesville, Georgia, in 1875 to build his home and, in part, to raise muscadine grapes.[8]

Wine makes daily living easier, less hurried, with fewer tensions and more tolerance.

—Benjamin Franklin

8 "Gainesville," The Longstreet Society, accessed September 8, 2017, http://www.longstreetsociety.org/gainesville-.html.

Chapter 4

1936–2016
End of Prohibition and the Modern Renaissance

Georgia's commercial-wine history came to a complete stop with Prohibition. Vineyards and winery operations went out of business, taking along wine expertise and vineyard skills not easily renewable. The Georgia State legislature enacted mandatory statewide Prohibition in 1907, and the law was effective in 1908. Georgia would not come out of Prohibition until 1935, when it agreed to repeal its own Prohibition but never ratified the Eighteenth Amendment to the Constitution.

A new start would begin in 1936 with the founding of Monarch Winery of Georgia in Atlanta. Making peach wine and distilled spirits to include peach brandy, the company has a link to the Monarch Wine Company of Brooklyn, New York, which had the contract to produce Manischewitz kosher wine until 1987. It was then purchased by the Centerra Wine portfolio.[1]

I had dinner with Arthur D. Farr in November 2016 at the awards ceremony for the 2016 Georgia Trustees Wine Challenge in Athens. When he graduated from Georgia Tech, he went to

1 "Manischewitz History," Manischewitz Wine Company, 2013, http://manischewitzwine.com/heritage/history.htm.

work for Monarch Winery of Georgia. He indicated they had two locations, one in Atlanta and another in Roberta, Georgia, where he worked as a chemist. He believes the company closed in the early 1980s.

The company filed for numerous trademarks from 1943 through 1976. Their marketing "marks" included Deuce Juice, Mad Dog, King Cotton, Ace-Hi, Bill Robinson's Bojangles, Sweet Peach, and Granny's. They also supported a combination of wine and distilled spirits not exceeding 20 percent alcohol in pints called sliders.[2]

In an interview I conducted September 6, 2016, with Parks Redwine, wine writer for the *Atlanta Journal-Constitution* from 1976 to 1982 and the current owner of Atlanta Improvement Company, a wine importer, he shared additional information on Monarch Winery.

Following Prohibition, peach prices were nearly at rock bottom, so Monarch, working with Governor Eugene Tallmadge, made a deal to purchase peaches at a higher price than the market in exchange for a state tax break. The deal went through, and both buyers and growers benefited. Apparently, Georgia produced little kosher wine. They also contracted with a grower in Gainesville to grow *Vitis labrusca* grapes along with muscadines, but this apparently never produced any wine based on a follow-up interview with Tom Slick on June 12, 2017.

Monarch Winery of Georgia did jumpstart a return to winemaking in Georgia following Prohibition. A commercial winery buying fresh fruit and producing fortified wine is not a model for farm wineries across the state.

A farm winery model would only come when individual entrepreneurs and visionaries were willing to step forward and lead through trial and error, and not until 1979. These women and men became the Georgia Wine Pioneers. Each in their own way contributed to the foundation on which today's Georgia

2 Tom Slick interview, June 2017.

wineries are built. This small pioneer group was central to modern Georgia wine history.

Georgia Pioneers: Modern Renaissance Begins

The modern renaissance for Georgia wines began in 1979 when Gay Pettit Dellinger began planting her Split Rail Vineyard between Dallas and Cartersville in Bartow County. She and her children would later donate sixty acres, including her vineyard property, to the Margaret and Luke Pettit Environmental Preserve in 1999 for an ecosystem in memory of her parents.

My notes on Split Rail Vineyard are from two interviews, the first with Tom Slick, owner of Habersham Vineyard and Winery and a close friend of Dellinger, on April 29, 2016, and the second on November 11, 2016, with David Harris. David was the winemaker both at Chestnut Mountain, owned by Jim Laikam, and Habersham Vineyard and Winery before opening his own Blackstock Vineyard and Winery in Dahlonega. David was a frequent visitor to Split Rail and would later use Dellinger's grapes to produce wine at Chestnut Mountain.

Back label of a Chestnut Mountain Chenin Blanc with a tribute to Gay Dellinger on the eleventh anniversary of her Split Rail Vineyards in 1990

Five years of wines, including a 1989 Chestnut Mountain signed by David Harris from the Mossy Creek Vineyard, now owned by Habersham Vineyard and Winery. The second Chestnut Mountain wine is the 1990 Chenin Blanc, which is the front part of the label showing the tribute to Gay Dellinger. The next three bottles are vintage years, 1991 to 1993, of Château Élan wines, all produced using Georgia Vitis vinifera grapes.

Dellinger's vineyard started with three acres of *Vitis vinifera* along with French and American hybrids to include Riesling, Seyval Blanc, Pinot Blanc, Baco Noir, Chardonnay, and Vidal Blanc white wines, and for the reds, Chambourcin and Cabernet Sauvignon. She added more acreage over time; David Harris believed she had up to six and a half acres. Her vineyard acted as a test bed for what grapes might grow in Georgia, and she shared that information with the few other vineyard growers in North Georgia.

Dellinger and Tom Slick at Habersham Vineyard and Winery were able to plant and grow grapes in Georgia, but needed help in the early days with producing wine. They turned to the Mississippi State University viticultural team for help because the University of Georgia did not have any wine experts on staff. They worked with a small team in Starkville to include Dr. Pat Hegwood, a viticulturalist, and Dr. Dick Vines, an enologist.

Dellinger and Slick had their first wine bottled by Bob Burgin, who is now the chief operating officer at Childress Vineyards in North Carolina after many years as a winemaker.

They used the Thousand Oaks Winery in Starkville, where Bob worked, to make their 1982 wine, and then brought it back to Georgia. The winery was dissolved in 1984. Later, David bought all Dellinger's grapes to make wine at Chestnut Mountain, where he was the winemaker. He estimated that at one point she had ten or more varieties each of *vinifera*, with the French hybrids and American hybrids growing at the same time.

As important as her work was with restarting Georgia vineyard operations, so too was her encouragement in changing the Georgia farm winery laws in the early 1980s with Tom Slick, Chuck Slick (his brother), and others. Some needed changes included a significant reduction in the license costs, from a thousand-dollar fee to fifty dollars, and assistance in opening up dry counties to farm winery sales at the vineyard site and defining the percentage of wine grapes a Georgia winery needed, as a farm winery, to operate 10 percent. The first Farm Winery Bill did not, however, include operating a winery away from the vineyard, which did not correct immediate needs for growers like Tom Slick.

Unfortunately, Dellinger was overcome by cancer and died in November 2009. She is now buried in the grounds near her vineyard.

Three other early pioneers still support the growth of the Georgia farm vineyards and wineries: Tom Slick at Habersham Vineyards and Winery in Helen, Don Panoz at Château Élan in Braselton, and Maurice Rawlings at the Georgia Winery in Ringgold. All three wineries and vineyards continue to produce Georgia wines today.

I was fortunate to interview both Tom and Don for this book; unfortunately, Maurice passed away before I had the chance to speak with him. However, his daughter Patty Prouty, who now runs Georgia Winery, agreed to share her observations on her dad's passion for wine and talk about her winery today.

A Pioneer:
Tom Slick Habersham Vineyard and Winery

Tom Slick, owner of Habersham Vineyard and Winery in Helen, Georgia

Tom is the longtime active veteran of Georgia vineyard and winemaking history since its rebirth in 1979. He and his brother, Chuck, purchased 143 acres for a vineyard, planting their first vines in 1980 at what is now called the Stonepile Vineyards in Habersham County, east of Helen.

Tom's astute accounts provide wide-ranging clarity and insightfulness addressing the first half-century of the new Georgia wine experience, from 1979 to 2016.

Tom was brought to Atlanta by his parents with two years remaining in high school. Upon graduating from Lovett High School, he attended Yale University, where he received a degree in physiological psychology. Later he attended Emory University's medical program, but his keen interest in science and technology moved him to California and onto San Antonio,

Texas. Along the way, he continued advancing his education in business and accounting and working with venture technology.

In the late seventies, he returned to Atlanta to work with his family on a large real estate acquisition. His time in California gave him an opportunity to better appreciate wine along with sparking his desire to buy land for a vineyard and winery in Georgia.

In the beginning—and over the four years before he was ready to harvest and produce wine—he gave credit to a small group of individuals who served as the keystone of expertise for the budding Georgia winery trade. This group included Bill Rosser, a researcher in the geology department at UGA who had a small vineyard near Athens; Gay Dillinger, who was a year in front of Tom growing grapes; Dr. Pat Hegwood; Dr. Dick Vines; and Ed Friedrich, a very well-known German winemaker whom Don Panoz brought into Château Élan as his winemaker and who visited Tom and his team in 1982.

Additional legislative support was provided by J. R. (Jake) Cullens, a lawyer in Cartersville who had served in the Pacific with the infantry in World War II. Upon returning, he graduated from the University of Georgia School of Law, having served as the editor and chief of the *Georgia Bar Journal.* He served in the Georgia House of Representatives from 1963 to 1965, and he was a key member of the State Bar Legislative Advisory Committee from 1968 to 1978.

This period covered the years in which the various Georgia farm winery bills were under development with a priority to allow growers to sell their wine in a tasting room better located for customers and not just at a vineyard site.

Tom credits the hard work and advice provided by Pat Hegwood as instrumental in first providing him guidelines for selecting a vineyard site in Georgia and then laying out the vineyard at Stonepile. Pat's guidance was multifaceted: find a property at or above one thousand feet in elevation; seek out well-drained soil at higher altitudes with loamy sand and clay, and stay north of the V formed by I-75 to the northwest of

Atlanta, I-85 to the northeast, and the line between Gainesville and Rome, Georgia. Tom and his brother, Chuck, covered ten thousand miles or more traveling around North Georgia with realtors looking for a site matching Pat's guidance. Tom added that staying north was also essential, as land prices in the north were more affordable. Ultimately, he found 143 acres with an abandoned farmhouse that would become the Stockpile Vineyard. Thinking ahead, he had already purchased from a grower in Rhode Island vine cuttings, which he maintained in his basement in Atlanta for several weeks.

Once purchased, the land was immediately laid out on four acres with 543 vines per acre. Pat Hegwood drove the tractor and subsoiler to outline the vineyard contours. The team from Mississippi State that had already helped Gay Dellinger also shared their expertise with Tom. They used Geneva Double Curtain as the first trellis system, eight by twelve.

The grapes planted were Pinot Blanc, Sauvignon Blanc, Pinot Noir, Cabernet Franc, and Chenin Blanc, and Tom said he would have added more plants but what he had were the only cuttings available. Later, Tom would buy the seven- or eight-acre Mossy Creek Vineyard property owned by Dr. Don Chambers, who was then growing Cabernet Sauvignon, Merlot, and Chardonnay. Today, Tom has over forty-two acres under vine and plans to add more.

Concurrent to planting, growing, and harvesting grapes, Tom, Chuck, Gay, and Bill Rosser worked on legislative changes to the Farm Winery Bill. During the years 1980 to 1984, there were additions to the Farm Winery Bill almost each year. At first it was not a unified effort. Of the few vineyards that existed in Georgia, perhaps a half dozen were in varying stages of development. Some needed immediate attention just to sell wine, others were a year away from selling, and others complained that license fees were too high.

Additionally, the Georgia legislature only met for forty days each year, so there was dependence on elected legislators to move a legislative bill through the House and Senate, where certainly cotton or peanuts would have a much higher priority than a handful of yet unproven vineyard growers.

Notwithstanding, in 1976, two wineries in California proved their wines had equal or greater quality than French wines. This "Judgment in Paris" competition made national and global news that would serve as a major catalyst for the American wine industry to grow and, perhaps, stimulate new Georgia wineries to enhance their vision for the future.

One of the first farm winery bills passed was used in Forsyth County to allow the Happy B Farm Winery, owned by Tomas Bun, to sell tomato and honey wine at his farm. Thomas had worked to push this bill through, but it wasn't comprehensive enough to meet other winery needs. Other key farm-wine successes include the 1985 measure that dictated winery tasting rooms could sell wine on Sundays. Another success was at the state level, wherein a winery could sell up to ten thousand gallons of wine in a year.

Old Fashion tomato wine produced by Happy B Farm Winery in Forsyth, Georgia.

Over the next few years there were changes to the Farm Winery Bill. Tom recounted that he and Chuck spent days in Atlanta, with the help of Jake Cullens, working on changes to the bill. Don Panoz at Château Élan was working with his legislator toward a similar objective.

Tom has been the father of Georgia wine since he and Gay Dellinger started growing wines in 1979 and 1980 and bottling together in Starkville, Mississippi. He served as a leader and mentor to many of the first winery associations in the state. Just as important, he also encouraged his general managers at Habersham, Steve Gibson and Emily DeFoor, to take active leadership roles in the Winegrowers Association of Georgia (WAG), serving North Georgia, and the newer Georgia Wine Producers, serving the entire state.

In an interview with the first WAG president, Steve Gibson, on June 29, 2017, he detailed that their goal in forming a collaborative group in North Georgia centered on enhancing marketing and information exchange among the wineries. The group formed in 2002 included Habersham Vineyards and Winery, Château Élan, Frogtown Cellars, Tiger Mountain Vineyards, Three Sisters Vineyards and Winery, Wolf Mountain Vineyard and Winery, and Blackstock Vineyards and Winery. Membership requirements in 2002 included bottling one thousand cases of *Vitis vinifera* or French-American, or growing five acres in a growing season using these varietals. Muscadine growers were not included since the marketing goal focused on North Georgia wine growers.

A Pioneer:
Dr. Donald Panoz, Château Élan

My interview with Dr. Donald Panoz was on August 31, 2016, at his offices near Château Élan in Braselton. In 1961, Don and Milan Puskar formed Milan Pharmaceuticals, later named Mylan, located in White Sulphur Springs, West Virginia. The research group he headed developed the transdermal patch for release medication.

Don left Mylan in 1969, moving his family to Ireland where he formed the Elan Corporation, a company that is now an industry leader in drug technology and delivery products and holds the worldwide patent for the nicotine patch.

In the late 1970s, Don and Nancy returned to Georgia part time. He knew Tom Slick at Habersham, and he met Gay Dellinger; however, he does not recall ever meeting Dr. Maurice Rawlings from Georgia Winery.

By 1981, Don had visited over seventy countries. During his travels, he always took notes on the hotels he visited, paying attention to how they could be improved. He would later use this information when building Château Élan Winery and Resort in Braselton in 1992. It was also during this time that he questioned why no one was making wine in Georgia.

Don owned one hundred acres in Gainesville, Georgia, where his pharmaceutical company was located. It had high powerlines over part of the property with some open land underneath. In 1981, he traveled to the University of California, Davis Department of Viticulture and Enology and asked them if they could come to Georgia and check to see if he could grow grapes on his land.

A team was sent to conduct an assessment, including degree days and soil. The decision was made to plant a one-acre experimental plot under the powerlines in Gainesville. Chardonnay and cabernet sauvignon were planted along with a few other varietals, and lo and behold, they thrived. When I asked about Pierce's disease, he said it did not come up, and the team from Davis did not seem to be aware of the disease that would ultimately be the reason for removing all the *Vitis vinifera* and hybrids from Château Élan and replacing them with muscadine grapes.

Altitude and Disease

Pierce's disease (PD) is a bacterial disease spread by glassy-winged sharpshooters, or leaf-hopper insects, that kills susceptible bunch-grape varieties. It is very common in the Piedmont and Coastal Plain regions of Georgia. PD has not been a significant problem in areas of Georgia above 1,300 ft. in elevation (high mountain area). Between 1,000 and 1,300 ft. (upper Piedmont area), disease pressure varies greatly from site to site. Between 700–1,000 ft. in elevation, PD will often destroy the vines of susceptible cultivars within five years. Below 700 ft. in elevation, PD often destroys the vineyard within three years. These boundaries can shift with climate variation from year to year. Below 1,000 ft. in elevation, plant primarily PD-resistant cultivars. Château Élan is at 957 ft., so it is well within the high-risk spectrum for this disease. As the Georgia climate has grown warmer, there has been an increase of PD at higher elevations.

With the test-site success, Don talked with Gamer Cray at the bank in Gainesville, Georgia, about the availability of land, and he suggested reaching out to Henry Braselton. Don said his vision at the time was a winery with thirty to fifty acres and a conference motel resort. Henry agreed to sell him one hundred acres off I-85 at an exit near a truck stop. Don then went looking for a winemaker and was fortunate to hire Ed Fredrick, a brilliant winemaker who would go on to work at the Chateau for seventeen months and do the initial planting and design of the winery.

It was Dick Vines from Mississippi State who linked Don to Ed. Dick had written a book on winemaking. During this time, a market study was completed resulting in the recommendation to add more land. Thus, Don bought 780 additional acres, allowing him to establish vineyards in 1984 and a resort starting in 1985.

Groundbreaking with Don Panoz and Governor Joe Frank Harris in 1985. (Photo provided by Château Élan)

A Pioneer:
Maurice Rawlings, Georgia Winery

Dr. Maurice Rawlings
(Photo provided by Georgia Winery)

Dr. Maurice Rawlings was a Chattanooga cardiologist who wanted to buy land to farm. He acquired fifty-two acres in 1982 at an auction, sight unseen, at $1,000 per acre.

I interviewed Patty Prouty, Maurice's daughter, on September 9, 2016, for background on her father and the winery. She has run the winery since 1996 and has a background in marine geochemistry. She served as the winemaker for many years.

Maurice was born in 1922 in Washington, DC. He graduated from Georgetown University School of Medicine in 1976 and completed a residency at George Washington University Hospital. Dr. Rawlings also specialized in surgical oncology before his death in 2010.

Having bought the land, he had it tested to determine what could grow on the property, and the only answer was grapes. In the early days, they planted a variety of grapes to include muscadines. He did this as a hobby and came down every weekend with high school students helping him. He never intended to make it a business, but when Patty took it over in 1996, it had indeed become a business. The vineyard is not located at the winery, so selling wine from there proved to be less than practical.

"Initially, we needed a farm winery bill approved," said Patty, "to allow us to sell wine either at the vineyard on in a tasting room."

Maurice lifted the California farm bill and rewrote the bill to submit to the legislature. Patty does not recall Maurice working with other vineyards at the time, and in my interviews with Tom Slick and Don Panoz, they may not have been aware that Maurice was also working on the farm winery bill with his local legislative representative.

Patty did say that in the early years there was limited contact with other wine growers, so, for the most part, they were on their own. Georgia Winery was the first winery in Northwest Georgia to get a farm winery license.

Recognizing they needed to move their tasting room to a better location with more access to the public, Georgia Winery relocated to the KOA store in 1986, which was property located just west of Hwy 75 near Chattanooga that Maurice already owned with another doctor. Concurrently, they discovered that muscadine grapes were the only grapes doing well in their vineyard, so they began removing and replacing *Vitis vinifera* and hybrids. They also were selling more sweet wine than dry, so the muscadines helped sustain these wines.

The muscadine grapes planted included Regal, Fry, Supreme, Carlos, Noble, and Hunt. In 2003, the muscadines allowed the vineyard to become natural, which led to an organic certification—the first in the state. While they still practice organic growing techniques, Georgia Winery found it too time-consuming to maintain the certification.

Like the other early vineyard and winery growers, there was trial and error as they progressed. Surprisingly, they had more success with muscadines than any other grapes. Muscadine grapes are their only homegrown grapes today.

Of all things known to mortals wine is the most powerful and effectual for exciting and inflaming the passions of mankind, being common fuel to them all.

—Francis Bacon

Chapter 5

Georgia Wine Lessons Learned from History

THE EARLIEST COLONISTS accompanying James Oglethorpe came with a plan to grow grapes and other fruits and vegetables with the help of a botanist who had selected what to plant. Unfortunately, the Old World notions on what would grow in the New World did not provide an awareness of the significant adaptations muscadines had made to survive in a subtropical climate, nor the impact of disease and plant pests in the region. Nor did they choose the right land for growing grapes. The Trustee Garden and the Royal Charter were ended within twenty years.

In the period that followed, from 1753 to 1870, there were small groups of winemakers producing wine. However, it proved to be difficult to share newly acquired winemaking skills among the few dispersed winemakers making wines with native grapes or to replicate their successes. Moreover, there was no market for their grapes. Also challenging was the lack of standardization in a naming convention for grapes. The best example is the fox grape; the name applied to many different varietals depending on location. The Revolutionary War and the Dahlonega Gold Rush—with the rapid displacement of native peoples—contributed to migrations into West and Northwest Georgia.

The wine was a long way from proving itself as an agricultural cash crop. There was still only limited transportation assets available to move fresh grapes to market outside the state. The Tallapoosa wine-venture success after 1870 was remarkable and placed Georgia among the top-tier states in wine production nationally. However, the success was short lived once the state voted to go into Prohibition. All commercial winegrowing stopped for twenty-seven years with a concomitant loss of vineyard and winemaking expertise. With the end of Prohibition, it was a slow start to rebuild a Georgia wine program. In 1936, with only one winery operating in the state focused on fruit and fortified wine, it seemed unlikely to be a model to move the Georgia wine program forward.

The arrival of Gay Dellinger and Split Rail vineyards in 1979 saw new challenges, including planting, gaining legislative support to legalize farm-wine sales, reducing costs, and opening dry counties. Georgia wine visionaries were the growers themselves. The state lacked both the viticultural and enology expertise to complement their needs, and it would be thirty-seven years before a testing laboratory or viticulturist was available to provide expert support. More challenging was the legal framework each winery confronted in dry counties.

As Tom Slick highlighted in his interview, the challenge Georgia vineyards and wineries were experiencing was so many "dry counties." Georgia leaders then—and perhaps now—did not appreciate the value wine could bring to the state through agritourism and excise tax revenue and employment opportunities. Nor was the state staffed to assist in gaining farm winery licenses to help support wine sales, when the best land to grow was likely in a dry county with no laws to address winery operations.

Today, Georgia has 159 counties, second only to Texas with 254, but only 32 contain a vineyard, winery, or tasting room. The state has challenges to efficiently support winery expansion into a county where laws for a farm winery never have existed. Flash back thirty-seven years: In Tom's case, the Stonepile Vineyard was in a dry county, and he, along with other early vineyard owners, was unable to co-locate a tasting room on the vineyard site without new legislation in a dry county.

One reason changing the Farm Winery Bill was essential was to let these small businesses grow and prosper. Today, an advocate at the state level to champion this multibillion-dollar business would be invaluable. More often, the winery owner has to help create the new laws before approved farm wineries can open. The suggestion among several winery owners is to have an office in Atlanta supported by the state to rapidly simplify establishing new Georgia wineries legally and to help guide statewide and national marketing to enrich a fuller awareness about the many award-winning wines already produced in the state (see Appendix F for the 2017 Georgia Trustees Wine Challenge results). Georgia Grown is a marketing and economic-development program for the Georgia Department of Agriculture. They are helping to get the word out about the numerous activities wineries and counties offer in agriculture.

By carefully examining history, we can assess past performance and adjust strategic and tactical solutions to provide a new roadmap forward. Vineyard operations farm with geology, soil, climate, weather, plant disease, and pests, directly or indirectly influencing why grapes perform better in one location over another.

The next chapter will provide a broader understanding of how these factors are important to vineyard selection and operations in Georgia.

> *Wine is constant proof that God loves us and loves to see us happy.*
>
> —Benjamin Franklin

Part 2

Georgia Geology, Soil, Climate, Weather, Plant Diseases, and Pests

Wine is bottled poetry.
—Robert Louis Stevenson

Chapter 6

Terroir

THE FRENCH HAVE a word that ties together all aspects linked with grape growing in the vineyard to ensure unique flavors are expressed in wine from their region: *terroir*. Terroir, as defined by the Wine Scholar Guild (formerly the French Wine Society), "embodies the totality of everything that impacts the grape and its final flavors such as elevation, aspect, climate, soil, grape-growing practices, and topographical features."[1]

These physical elements are relatively easy to understand, yet French winemakers also have a divine association when reflecting on their terroir: a passion for the history of the land and how they, as winemakers, impart a regional quality to their wine, much like a fingerprint. In France, these are all important concerns in their Appellation d'Origine Protégée, or AOP system, which replaced the older AOC as the highest-rated and most restrictive control measures to uphold quality and territorial branding. Champagne is an AOP with high vineyard and winemaking standards to maintain a unique luxury brand.

In the United States, the Alcohol and Tobacco Tax and Trade Bureau (TTB), in Title 27, Part 9, establishes application

1 Glossary of French Wine Scholar, Wine Scholar Guild, accessed September 8, 2017, https://www.winescholarguild.org/uploads/scholar/Glossary_Appendix.pdf.

requirements for approving an Amcrican Viticultural Area (AVA). These standards take a similar approach to the French AOP protocols.

> For purposes of this section, information relating to distinguishing features affecting viticulture include the following: climate, temperature, precipitation, wind, fog, solar orientation, radiation, and other climate information; Geology. Underlying formations, landforms, and such geophysical events as earthquakes, eruptions, and major floods; Soils. Soil series or phases of a soil series, denoting parent material, texture, slope, permeability, soil reaction, drainage, and fertility; Physical features. Flat, hilly, or mountainous topography, geographical formations, bodies of water, watersheds, irrigation resources, and other physical features; Elevation. Minimum and maximum elevations . . .[2]

There are other climate components that influence outcomes in the vineyard. Collectively, they are macroclimates, mesoclimates, and microclimates. The Upper Hiwassee Highlands AVA was approved by the TTB on August 18, 2014, as the first Georgia AVA. The four Georgia vineyards contained within this 690-square mile AVA—shared with vineyards in North Carolina—are positioned collectively in one or more macroclimates. For example, Crane Creek Vineyard and Winery outside Young Harris has its own mesoclimate and, given its altitude of 1,918 ft. above sea level and forty-acre property, has numerous microclimates impacting vine vigor and grape production.

2 Electronic Code of Federal Regulations, US Government Publishing Office, updated August 25, 2017, https://www.ecfr.gov/cgi-bin/text-idx?c=ecfr&sid=057f99d792668247a3c45b4699417291&rgn=div5&view=text&node=27:1.0.1.1.7&idno=27.

Understanding how these climate components contribute to final wine quality is the strength one looks for in a good vineyard manager and how important they are in aiding grape quality when fruit is presented to the winemaker for wine production. In smaller wineries, these duties are usually performed by the same person.

Part II of this book is designed to help readers better understand how the factors mentioned above influence where grape varietals are grown across Georgia, and why some are more successful than others.

Wine is sunlight, held together by water.

—Galileo

Chapter 7

Georgia Geology and Soil

"Best evidence reveals the earth is 4.6 billion years old. . . . Understanding the age of the Earth is conceivable only by scaling . . . if the whole of the Earth history were a twenty-four-hour day, modern humans, who evolved about 200,000 years ago, would not appear until four seconds before midnight." This reference is taken from *Roadside Geology of Georgia*.[1]

If you are traveling within Georgia and looking for historic and unique geological formations or are checking out vineyard topography, this is a one-stop shop for details.

Recalling from chapter 1, James Oglethorpe landed near what is today Savannah on the Atlantic Ocean seacoast. The Georgia coastline is ninety-seven miles wide at sea level. Moving across the southern half of Georgia and crossing the lower and upper coastal plain to the Fall Line or Sand Hills provinces (see maps below), the elevation rises to roughly five hundred feet above sea level. The fall line crosses Georgia at a point where the major rivers flowing south drop over rapids, limiting both south and north navigation by boat.

1 Pamela J. W. Gore and William Witherspoon, *Roadside Geology of Georgia* (Missoula, Montana: Mountain Press Publishing Company, 2013), 12.

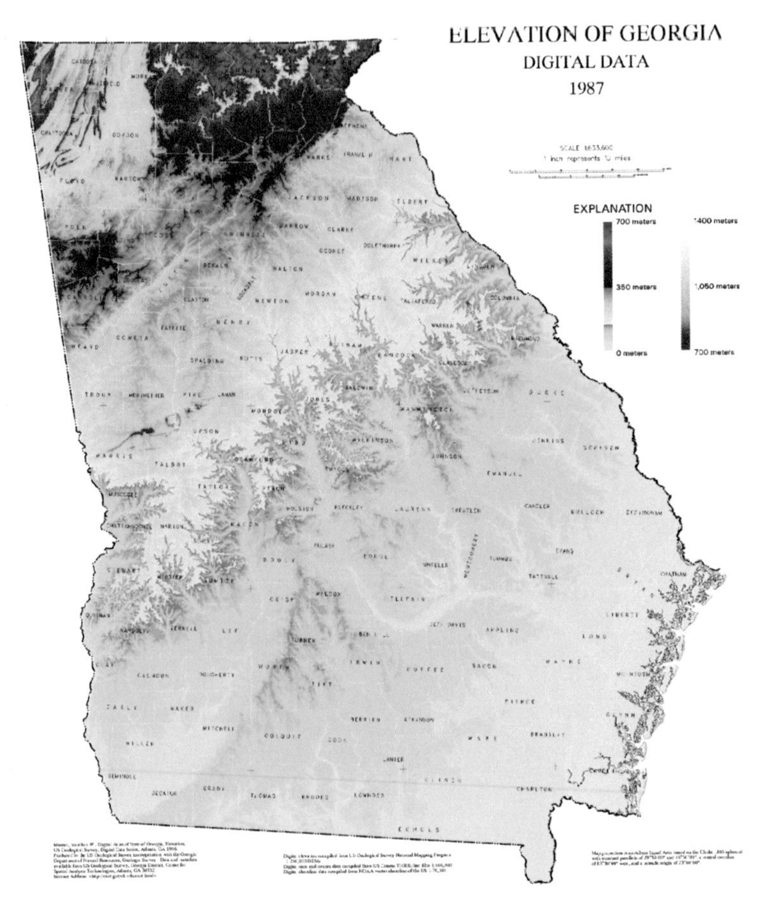

Map by GeorgiaINFO, an online Georgia Almanac

Georgia Elevation

Progressing northwest across the Piedmont region, the elevation rises to one thousand feet. Pushing further north, traversing the Chattahoochee River toward the Blue Ridge and Appalachian Mountains, the altitude ascends to nearly five thousand feet.

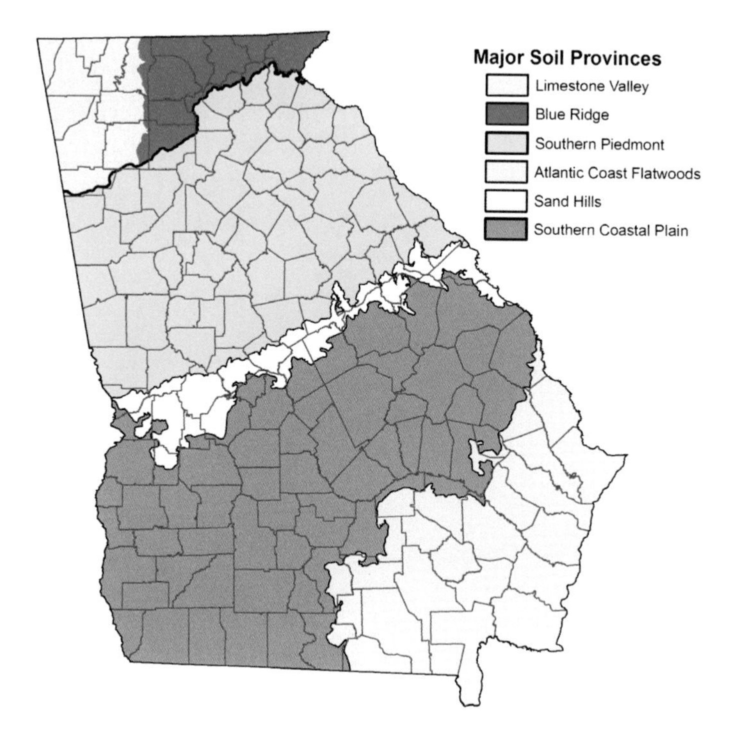

Map by UGA College of Agricultural and Environmental Sciences

Major Soil Provinces with Sand Hills along the Fall Line

The landscape of Georgia is divided into five physiographic regions. In the South, the lower and upper Coastal Plain combine to make this the largest geographical region within Georgia, covering almost 60 percent of the state. The soil is soft and sandy on limestone with some clay in the upper Coastal Plain with gentle slopes and better drainage than in the lower plain. There are ten wineries in this region with a few grower vineyards (grower vineyards sell their grapes to a winery).

GEORGIA PHYSIOGRAPHIC REGIONS

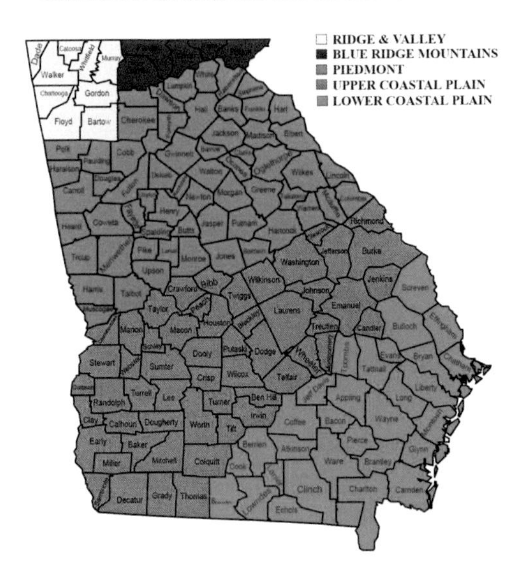

Map by Georgia Department of Natural Resources

The second-largest physiographic region of Georgia is the Piedmont, the largest population center in the state. Elevations range from 500 ft. to 1,700 ft. as it approaches the Blue Ridge Mountains. The most common soil feature of this region is "Georgia red clay," created by water mixing with iron breaking down from exposed rocks. The underlying stone in this region is granite, gneiss, and marble.

Rolling hills provide good drainage, and you still encounter loamy, sandy, and clay soils. This is a productive agricultural growing area containing twenty-nine wineries with multiple grower vineyards.

Georgia's highest mountain is in the Blue Ridge region at Brasstown Bald, which reaches 4,784 ft. in elevation. The highest rainfall in Georgia occurs in this region along with cooler air currents. The growing period in this low agricultural-producing area is 180 to 210 days. There are fifteen wineries in this region along with several grower vineyards.

The Ridge and Valley region, located in Georgia's northwest corner, has predominately soft sedimentary rock with limestone and shale in the valley and the ridges made with sandstone. The growing season is 210 to 220 days. Two wineries and several grower vineyards are in this region.

> *It is no coincidence that, on all four sides, in all four corners, the borders of the Roman Empire stopped where wine could no longer be made.*
>
> —Neel Burton

Chapter 8

Georgia Climate and Weather

NASA EXPLAINS THE difference between climate and weather in these terms: "Climate is how the atmosphere behaves over relatively long periods of time. Weather is what conditions of the atmosphere are over a short period of time."[1]

Georgia's Coastal Plain and Piedmont regions have a humid, subtropical climate, given low elevation and their closeness to the warm Atlantic and Gulf waters. This climate can be characterized by long, hot summers; short, mild winters; and year-round rainfall.

In North Georgia, near the state boundary, the climate is humid continental covering the Blue Ridge and the Ridge and Valley regions. This northern region is cooler, with colder winters accumulating some snow and the most precipitation. The average yearly rain in Georgia is about fifty inches.

The annual Georgia climate summary for 2016 was released on January 8, 2017, by Dr. Pam Knox, who tracks agricultural weather for Georgia growers from UGA. The key highlights:

1 Nasa Content Administrator, ed., "NASA – What's the Difference Between Weather and Climate?" February 1, 2005, NASA.gov, https://www.nasa.gov/mission_pages/noaa-n/climate/climate_weather.html.

> High Plains Regional Climate Center shows that for most of the Southeast, temperatures for 2016 as a whole were well above normal. The only exception was a small patch of four counties in southwest Georgia that were cooler than normal. . . . The warm temperatures were especially apparent in the July through September period in the second half of the growing season. . . . Every month except January and May were above the 20th century average temperature, most months by several degrees. . . . Drought conditions across the year grew dramatically as the warm and dry conditions affected local climate. The drought started in northeast Georgia but expanded rapidly westward so that the worst impacts occurred in northwest Georgia.[2]

Growers in the South have to rely on irrigation to sustain plant growth. The good news for many Georgia winegrowers is the warm weather just before and during harvest, providing high-quality grapes for wine. The 2016 harvest may prove to be one of the best vintage years for Georgia grapes.

The 2012 United States Department of Agriculture (USDA) Plant Hardiness Zone Map is the standard by which gardeners and growers can determine which plants are most likely to thrive at a location. The map is based on the average annual minimum winter temperature, divided into 10-degree Fahrenheit zones. The zones represent the average extreme minimum temperatures from 1976 to 2005. Significantly, when you compare the following map, which helps growers better understand where plants will grow, you see a close parallel to the Georgia physiographic zones.

---

2 Pam Knox, "2016 annual climate summary for Georgia," January 8, 2017, *UGA Extension,* http://blog.extension.uga.edu/climate/2017/01/2016-annual-climate-summary-for-georgia/.

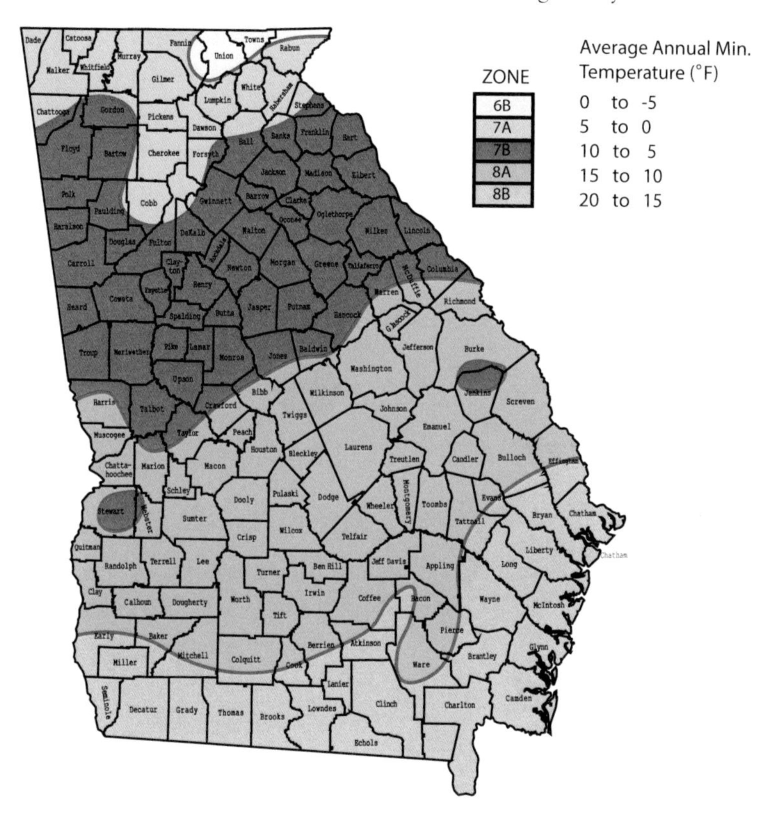

As highlighted in the first chapter, the British believed that grapes grown on the same latitude as Charles Town (original spelling), South Carolina, had a high probability to grow in the new Georgia Trustee Garden planted in Savannah. Accordingly, they selected cuttings from Madeira and Burgundy, France. As illustrated on the following chart, wines generally have the best chance to succeed from 50 to 30 north and south latitude.

This does not mean, as we already know, that the geology, soil, climate, weather, local pests, and disease would allow wines to succeed—which they did not, for most of the early Georgia wine history. *Vitis vinifera* cuttings need to be grafted onto American rootstock for these grapes to flourish throughout the United States. Selecting the right rootstocks is still a work in progress across the state.

10° C = 50° F and 20° C = 68° F

Georgia became the fourth state in the United States on January 2, 1788. The land area of the state is 57,513 square miles,

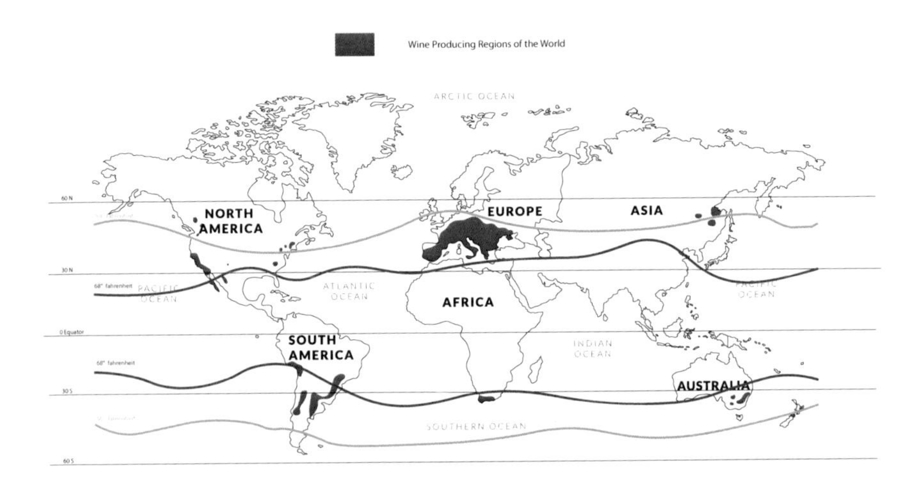

making it the largest state east of the Mississippi River. The latitude is 30° 31' N to 35° and longitude is 81° W to 85° 53'W. The state is 300 miles long and 230 miles wide. Average temperatures in Blairsville in 2016 include a high of 92.5° F to a low of 9° F.

With a brief history on how Georgia evolved with vineyard and winery operations and with additional clarity on geology and climate, a more detailed discussion of vineyard, winery, and grape varietals follows.

> *Someone said drink the water, but I will drink the wine /*
> *Someone said take a poor man, the rich don't have a dime /*
> *Go fool yourself, if you will, I just haven't got the time /*
> *I'll give you back your water, and I will take the wine.*
>
> —Frank Sinatra

Chapter 9

Georgia Plant Diseases and Pests

In chapter 1, we detailed how a single trustee garden in Savannah in 1733 with *Vitis vinifera* grapes failed in part because their European grapes were not adaptable to the subtropical climate and natural diseases found in South Georgia. Fast forward 284 years and Georgia, with sixty-three grape vineyards, still must contend with plant pests and diseases. Fortunately, growers supported by the University of Georgia College of Agricultural and Environmental Sciences, along with county field agents and other private consultants, have the facts and tools to confront these diseases when vigilance is applied.

Dr. Phillip Brannen, a plant pathologist at UGA, pointed out in March 2017 that Pierce's disease is the primary disease to limit European grapes in Georgia.[1] This disease was discussed in detail in chapter 6 as a major challenge confronting Château Élan, eventually leading to its vineyard's *Vitis vinifera* removal and replacement with muscadine grapes.

Georgia has seventy-four different cultivars planted in vineyards across the state. *Vitis vinifera* (European and Mediterranean) accounts for thirty-three grape varietals; *Vitis*

1 Clint Thompson, "Despite potential for disease, Georgia's grape industry is thriving," March 30, 2017, University of Georgia College of Agricultural and Environmental Sciences, http://www.caes.uga.edu/news/story.html?storyid=6160&story=Georgia%27s-Grape-Industry.

rotundifolia (muscadine) accounts for twenty-four grape varietals; American and French hybrids account for fifteen grape varietals; and Norton and Catawba are two other species. Each species contains different thresholds against disease.

Major Georgia Diseases Impacting Grape Production

Powdery mildew impacts vineyards worldwide but especially those in eastern North America. *Vitis vinifera* is exceedingly vulnerable, particularly Chardonnay and Cabernet Sauvignon, along with selected French American hybrids like Seyval and Vignoles. The powdery mildew is primarily caused by a fungus and can spread pores across a vineyard, inhibiting or preventing fruit set and resulting in crop loss.[2]

Downey mildew is a disease native to North America caused by a fungus that impacts young leaves, flowers, and fruit clusters. This disease is common to warm, humid climates like those found in the eastern United States. *Vitis vinifera*, particularly pinot noir, is more at risk than American and French hybrids. Left uncontrolled, defoliation is an outcome impacting fruit ripening and winter vine hardiness.[3]

Black rot is a severe fungal disease that effects the eastern United States. The fungus attacks new plant growth including leaves, petioles, shoots, tendrils, and berries. Black rot can severely damage the fruit, causing the berries to shrivel and mummify. The disease will overwinter, allowing it to return next year. Sanitation is the key to controlling black rot.[4]

Bitter rot and sour rot also impact fruit performance and, ultimately, wine quality. Georgia grape growers have the added challenge that much of the state is in a subtropical climate. In 2016, no vineyard in Georgia was able to pursue organic farming practices.

---

2 Ted Goldammer, *Grape Grower's Handbook: A Guide to Viticulture for Wine Production*, 2nd ed. (Centreville, VA: APEX, 2015), 373.

3 Ted Goldammer, 361–362.

4 Ted Goldammer, 355–357.

Animal Pests

Mother Nature's interface with grape growers also includes animal pests. In my travels across the state, the number-one animal pest is birds. They arrive as the grapes mature near harvest and, if left unattended, can significantly reduce grape tonnage. Birds are particularly a challenge to small vineyards, where one vine row lost to birds is substantial. Birds' impact on the larger vineyards may be just the cost of doing business where the option to net the entire vineyard is prohibitive both in purchase cost and manpower. There are several methods used to overcome bird damage, including netting, noisemakers, and even dogs. Netting is the preferred solution in the small to medium-size vineyards.

Netting Sharp Mountain, August 2016

Deer also present themselves as a challenge to Georgia vineyards. Much like birds, they arrive as grapes ripen. Depending on the location, encroaching deer can be a daily occurrence, especially when tree lines are adjacent to the vineyard. Fencing is one solution, but fence pricing may become cost prohibitive. Other partial solutions are dogs and hunters.

Deer fence surrounding two-acre vineyard at 12 Spies.

Additional animal pests in Georgia include bears, turkeys, raccoons, squirrels, opossums, and feral hogs.

Insect Pests

The first challenge insect pests bring to the vineyard is feeding on leaves, shoots, roots, and grapes. Secondly, pests transport bacterial, viral, or fungal diseases across the vineyard. Insect pests common to the East Coast and Georgia include grape berry moth, grape cane borer, grape flea beetle, grape leafroller, grape phylloxera, grape root borer, green June beetle, Japanese beetle, Asian lady beetle, glassy-winged sharpshooter, mites, and more recently, the spotted wing drosophila.[5]

Life is too short to drink bad wine.

—Anonymous

5 Ted Goldammer, 389–424.

Part 3
Wineries

Beer is made by men, wine by God.
—Martin Luther

Chapter 10

Wineries and Vineyards

THIS CHAPTER SHOULD prove useful when traveling throughout Georgia visiting wineries and tasting rooms.

Georgia wineries are listed first by American Viticultural Areas (AVAs), which include the Upper Hiwassee Highlands and the Dahlonega Plateau (pending), in alphabetic order. Most readers are likely unfamiliar with AVA as a term and what value it brings to the wine professional community and consumers. A formal definition follows:

> American Viticultural Area (AVA): "A viticultural area for American wine is a delimited grape-growing region having distinguishing features as described in the Code of Federal Regulations. . . . These designations allow vintners and consumers to attribute a given quality, reputation, or other characteristics of wine made from grapes grown in an area to its geographic origin.
>
> "The establishment of viticultural areas allows vintners to describe more accurately the origin of

their wines to consumers and helps consumers to identify wines they may purchase."[1]

What Is the Value of Belonging to an AVA?

An AVA exists mainly to create consistency in product and build a reputation for quality based on that reliability. For example, most wine drinkers reading a Napa label understand that AVA represents quality wine. Given a choice to select one wine over another, they may elect to choose a Napa wine, expecting quality consistency.

This geographic pedigree collectively allows an AVA to coordinate promotion and branding in their marketing by sharing advertising costs and special events. An AVA represents shared soil, climate, growing conditions, and often similar varietals, setting consumer expectations on wine quality and choice. For the consumer, an AVA wine must contain at least 85 percent of the varietal listed on the wine.

As of November 30, 2016, there are 239 AVAs approved in the United States, with 138 in California.[2] The first AVA was Augusta AVA, established on June 20, 1980, in Missouri.

I think it is a great error to consider a heavy tax on wine as a tax on luxury. On the contrary, it is a tax on the health of our citizens.

—Thomas Jefferson

1 Regulations and Rulings Division, "American Viticultural Area," updated October 27, 2016, Alcohol and Tobacco Tax and Trade Bureau, https://ttb.gov/wine/ava.shtml.
2 Regulations and Rulings Division, "Established American Viticultural Areas," updated April 13, 2017, Alcohol and Tobacco Tax and Trade Bureau, https://ttb.gov/wine/us_by_ava.shtml.

Chapter 11

Upper Hiwassee Highlands AVA

On July 18, 2014, the Alcohol and Tobacco Tax and Trade Bureau established the Upper Hiwassee Highlands American Viticultural Area. The area is approximately 690 square miles in Cherokee and Clay Counties in North Carolina and Towns, Union, and Fannin Counties in Georgia. Thus, not all of Fannin County is within the AVA. The AVA contains twenty-six commercially producing vineyards, growing approximately fifty-four acres of French American hybrids, American grape varieties, and *Vitis vinifera*. The distinguishing features include topography, temperature, and soils. Four Georgia wineries are within this AVA: Crane Creek Vineyards **(1)**, Hightower Creek Vineyards **(2)**, Odom Springs Vineyards **(3)**, and Paradise Hills Resort and Spa **(4)**.[1] The average annual rainfall in Blairsville, Georgia, is fifty-six inches with 129 rain days.[2]

1 Electronic Code of Federal Regulations, US Government Publishing Office, updated August 25, 2017, http://www.ecfr.gov/cgi-bin/text-idx?SID=32a6e64667ef1e87be277be932419132&node=se27.1.9_1234&rgn=div8.

2 "Average Annual Precipitation for Georgia," Current Results Publishing Ltd., accessed September 11, 2017, https://www.currentresults.com/Weather/Georgia/average-yearly-precipitation.php.

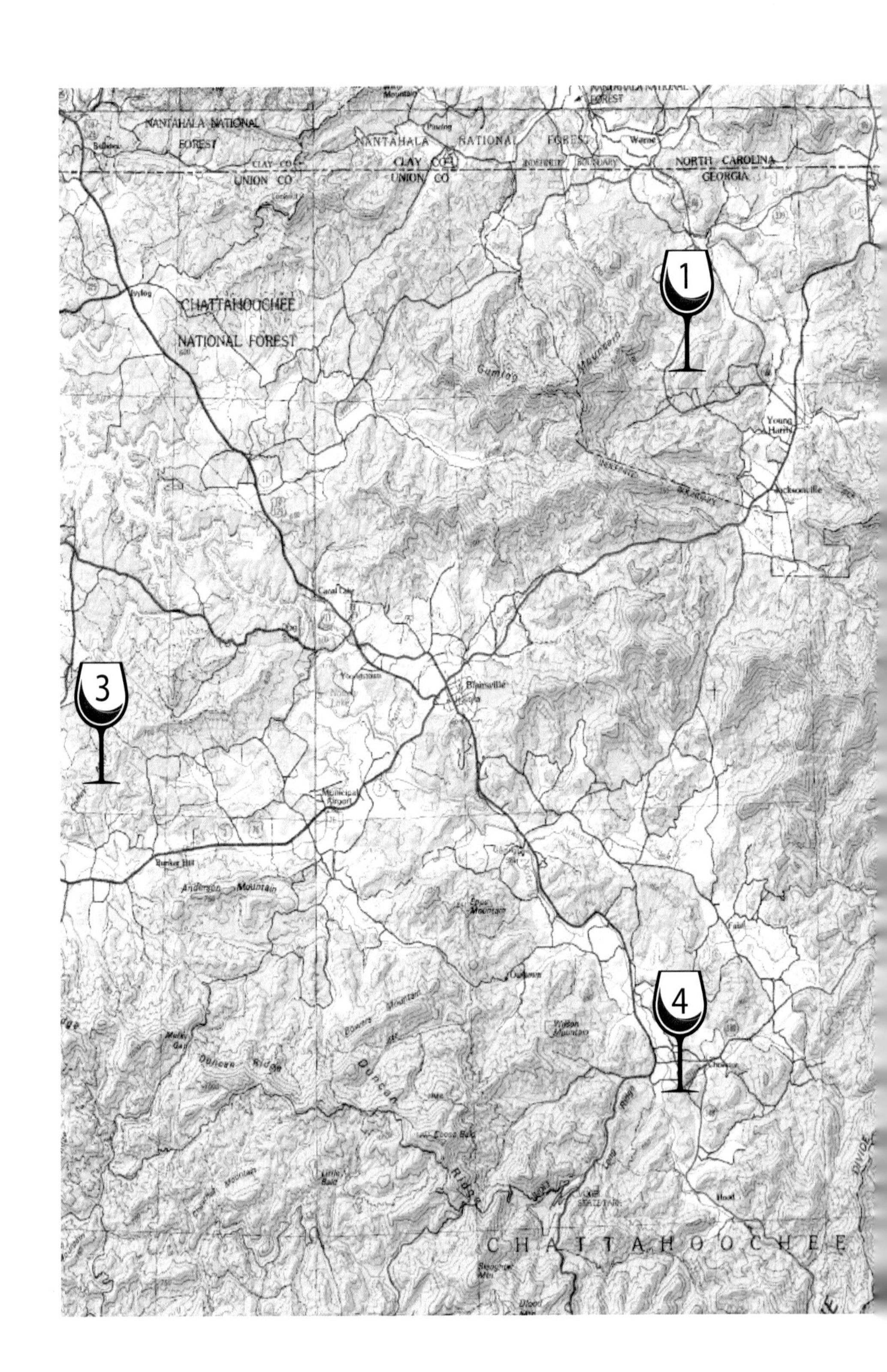

NANTAHALA NATIONAL
FOREST
NANTAHALA NATIONAL FOREST
CLAY CO
UNION CO
NORTH CAROLINA
GEORGIA
CHATTAHOOCHEE
NATIONAL FOREST
1
Young Harris
Jacksonville
Gumlog
Blairsville
3
Municipal Airport
Bunker Hill
Anderson Mountain
4
Duncan Ridge
Bowers Mountain
C H A T T A H O O C H E E
DIVIDE

NANTAHALA
NATIONAL
CLAY CO
TOWNS CO
CHATUGE
LAKE
RIDGE
BLUE
DIVIDE
VALLEY
TOWNS CO
RABUN CO
TENNESSEE
UNION CO
TOWNS CO
WHITE CO
2
Burton
Lake
ATIONAL
FOREST

1

Crane Creek Vineyards

916 Crane Creek Road, Young Harris, GA 30582

Passion for Wine Blossomed in Italy

ERIC AND DEANNE Seifarth met and married in the US Army where Eric was an artillery officer having graduated from the US Military Academy West Point. DeAnne was an army veterinarian. Their passion for wine grew with military service in Italy, where wine is a way of life. In selecting their vineyard, they desired to be in hardiness zone 6 for flexibility to plant Vitis vinifera and other grapes. DeAnne also sought to purchase a veterinarian practice near the vineyard.

Located north of Young Harris, Crane Creek Vineyards is one of the most northern vineyards in Georgia. From their initial planting, they added acreage over twenty-two years, and Eric will be the first to say some grapes, like riesling, did not grow well and required removal.

Eric maintains a diverse selection of varietals to craft his wines. He is particularly proud of Zusa, a delightfully crisp, fresh, blended white wine made with Grüner Veltliner and other white grapes, and Enotah White, made from Chardonel. I also encourage visitors to taste their Hellbender Red made from the Norton grape—one

of the best Nortons produced in Georgia.

Wine prices range from $15.95 to $27.95. Eric is a consummate gentle-man, leader, and veteran winemaker always available to work with and help lead the Georgia wine community. A journey to this North Georgia winery and vineyard is an excellent way to spend a day in the mountains.

Open: Year Round
Tasting Room: At the winery and 94 Public Square North in Dahlonega
Directions:
Northwest from Young Harris
Four miles off GA-66

Owners: Eric and DeAnne Seifarth
Winemaker: : Eric Seifarth
Established: 1995

Altitude: 1,918 ft.
Hardiness zone: 6b 0–5 (F)
Soil: Loamy, a mixture of clay, silt, and sand
Geographical coordinates: 34.960326, -83.882867
Vineyard acreage: 40 acres with 36.3 under vine
Vineyard tonnage, 2016: 27 tons
Varietal grapes: Cabernet Sauvignon, .2 acres; Cabernet Franc, 1.8 acres; Chambourcin, 5 acres; Vidal Blanc, 2.5 acres; Seyval Blanc, 4 acres; Villard Noir, 1.8 acres (rosé wine); Chardonel, 3 acres; Norton, 6 acres; Catawba, 3 acres; Traminette, 3 acres; Blaufrãnkisch, 3 acres; Grüner Veltliner, 3 acres.

(706) 379-1236 / www.cranecreekvineyards.com

2

Hightower Creek Vineyards

Hightower Creek Open Year Round

SANFORD AND LIZ moved from Atlanta to Hiawassee, Georgia, in 1995, where Sanford owned a NAPA parts store. The land was initially used to raise horses. The tasting room and part of the vineyard are on the southside of Hwy 76. The vineyards are on both sides of Hwy 76 about 2,300 ft. apart.

The vineyard produces six premium wines ranging in price from $18 to $26. They also sell a line of sweeter wines called Dueling Banjos, all priced at $15.

This small family winery is open year-round, and the quality of their wines continues to improve each year. Their full-bodied Trillium blended white wine and Deliverance, a red blend, are two wines to taste.

Most of their wines are made from their Georgia-grown grapes or with a small portion from within the North Carolina part of the AVA.

7150 Canaan Drive, Hiawassee, GA 30546

Open: Year Round
Tasting Room: At the vineyard

Directions:
From Hiawassee
Go SE on Hwy 76 for 9 miles.
Vineyard and tasting room are on the right.

Owners: Sanford and Liz Green and son Travis Green
Winemaker: Travis Green
Established: 2009; tasting room opened in 2012

Altitude: 2,146 ft.
Hardiness zone: 7a: 0–5 (F)
Challenges are frost and rain.
Soil: Loamy, sand, silt, clay
Geographical coordinates: 34.926026, -83.632967
Vineyard acreage: 5.65 acres in production; planning to add more acres
Vineyard tonnage, 2016: 11 tons
Varietal grapes: Cabernet Franc, 1.9 acres; Merlot, .75 acres; Pinot Gris, .75 acres; Traminette, .75 acres; Vignoles, .75 acres; Catawba, 100 vines, .25 acres; and Norton, .5 acres.

(706) 896-8963 / www.hightowercreekvineyards.com

3

Odom Springs Vineyards

637 Odom Road, Blairsville, GA 30512

Georgia Farm Family

Steve has several family generations who lived in North Georgia, and the current vineyard land belonged to his father. After graduating from UGA with a degree in agriculture, Steve began planting the vineyard in 2007 in four sections.

Two wines to taste are Homemade Sin, a Chambourcin and Seyval blend, and They Lord, a sweeter wine made with Vidal Blanc. The price range for wines is $16.95 to $22.95. From the tasting-room porch there is a stunning view of the vineyards. The friendly staff will make you feel welcome.

Open: Thursday through Sunday.
Tasting Room: At the vineyard, established 2013

Directions:
Vineyards are one mile inside
Union County near Sharp Top Mountain.

Owners: Steve and Jennifer Odom and sister Shari Odom
Winemaker: Steve Odom and Mark Donahue
Established: Family-owned land; grapes planted in 2007
Altitude: 1,926 ft.
Hardiness zone: 7a 0–5 (F)
Soil: Loamy, clay, silt, and sand
Geographical coordinates: 34.878699, -84.090610
Vineyard acreage: 16-acre property with 7 acres planted
Vineyard tonnage, 2016: 21 tons
Varietal grapes: Chambourcin, 2 acres; Seyval Blanc, 2 acres; Norton, 2 acres; Vidal Blanc, 1 acre.

4

Paradise Hills Resort

TripAdvisor 2015 Excellence Winner for Resort

BOB AND ILKE initially purchased the resort, which included rustic cabins and a spa, as a first step, then started planting grapes in 2012. In 2015, they were awarded a Winner of Excellence award by TripAdvisor.

Bob is the winemaker with two wines made with 100 percent estate-grown grapes: 521 Estate Cabernet Sauvignon and 889 Estate Chardonel, which is their first AVA wine. Prices range from $16 to $28. The number system on the bottles reflects badge numbers both Bob and Ilke had when working with law enforcement, and part of the proceeds from these wines go to a law-enforcement charity. Like most new wineries in Georgia, Paradise Hills purchases additional grapes locally or from other sources until the vineyard produces sufficient fruit to support all of the winery's production needs. Coordinate tastings with the lodge.

366 Paradise Road, Blairsville, GA 30512

Open: See website to confirm tasting room days and hours.
Tasting Room: At the vineyard

Directions:
East of Hwy 19 and ten miles
south of Blairsville, just off Hwy 19

Owners: Robert and Ilke Lander
Winemaker: Robert "Bob" Lander
Established: 2002 as a spa and resort; first planting in 2012

Altitude: 2,001 ft.
Hardiness zone: 7a 0–5 (F)
Soil: Loamy, clay, silt, and sand
Geographical coordinates: 34.828062, -83.920410
Vineyard acreage: 35-acre property with 7.5 acres planted with new plantings in spring 2016
Vineyard tonnage, 2016: 3.5 tons
Varietal grapes: Chardonel, 2.5 acres; Cabernet Sauvignon, .25 acres; Riesling, 2.25 acres; Cabernet Franc, 2.5 acres.

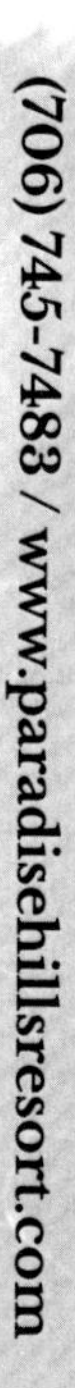

Chapter 12

(Pending) Dahlonega Plateau AVA

On December 2, 2016, the Alcohol and Tobacco Tax and Trade Bureau published a notice of a proposed rulemaking in the Federal Register proposing to establish the approximately 133-square mile "Dahlonega Plateau" AVA in portions of Lumpkin and White Counties in Georgia. On January 31, 2017, the open-comment period ended with no challenges. Normally, this would have led to a final approval several months ago. In my conversations with the Tax Bureau, all AVA approvals are on hold until the appropriate new office holder with the Tax Bureau is approved by Congress. Since this could come at any date, I have chosen to include this pending AVA in this book with the understanding that it is ready now for approval. Included are seven wineries and eight commercial vineyards. They will decide individually if they elect to use the AVA label on their wine bottles. With a long growing season, these vineyards are able to grow an abundance of *Vitis vinifera* grapes.

This hilly country allows for good drainage and wind flow, promoting the production of quality grapes. The temperatures allow the vines to go into dormancy, which helps promote growth. The risks are drought and late frosts in this northern part of the Piedmont region just south of Blue Ridge. The annual average rainfall for Dahlonega, Georgia, is sixty-nine inches.[1]

The seven wineries eligible for inclusion into the AVA are Cavender Creek Vineyards **(5)**, Frogtown Cellars **(6)**, Kaya Vineyard and Winery **(7)**, Montaluce Winery & Restaurant **(8)**, The Cottage Vineyard & Winery **(9)**, Three Sisters Vineyards & Winery **(10)**, and Wolf Mountain Vineyards and Winery **(11)**.

1 U.S. climate data, Climate data for Dahlonega, Georgia, accessed September 11, 2017, http://www.usclimatedata.com/climate/dahlonega/georgia/united-states/usga0155.

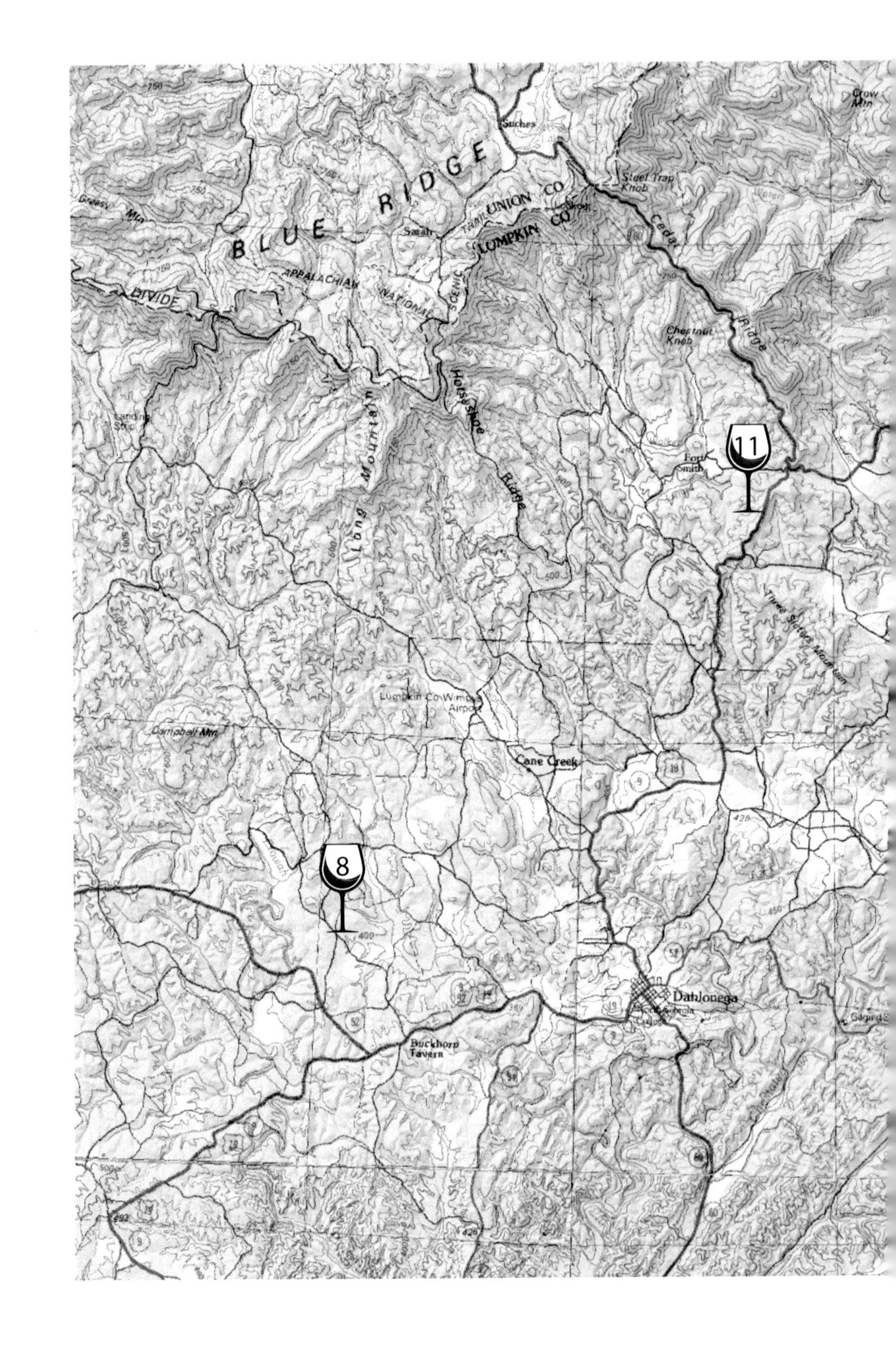

BLUE RIDGE
Suches
Crow Mtn
Steel Trap Knob
UNION CO
LUMPKIN CO
Cedar Ridge
APPALACHIAN NATIONAL SCENIC
DIVIDE
Chestnut Knob
Long Mountain
Horseshoe Ridge
Fort Smith
11
Three Sisters Mountain
Lumpkin Co Wimpy Airport
Campbell Mtn
Cane Creek
8
Dahlonega
Buckhorn Tavern

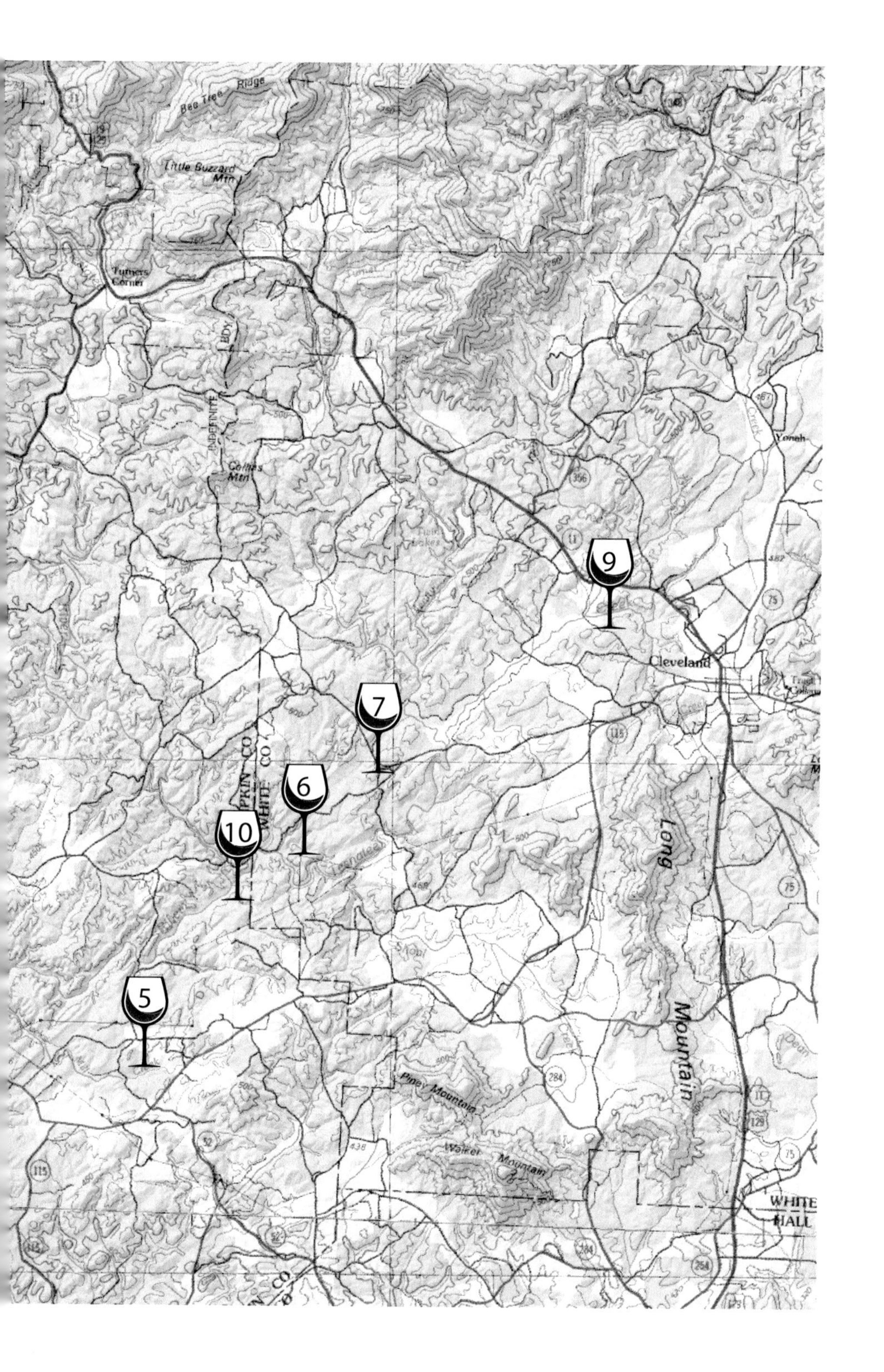

Bee Tree Ridge
Little Buzzard Mtn
Turners Corner
Collins Mtn
Cleveland
Yonah
Long Mountain
Piney Mountain
Walker Mountain
WHITE HALL
WHITE CO
9
7
6
10
5

5

Cavender Creek Vineyards

RAYMOND CASTLEBERRY, US Air Force veteran and retired schoolteacher, originally opened this winery with his first harvest in 2009. In 2015, the winery was bought by Claire Livingston, a retired college professor. Her passion is to make really good wines that customers love to drink, and to provide a friendly, comfortable place to relax and enjoy wine. Today, the winery produces a number of award-winning red, white, and rosé wines, which are single varietal and blends. The wines are created mostly from estate-grown grapes; sometimes grapes from local vineyards are added for blends. Cavender Creek Vineyards boasts that its wines are 100 percent Georgia grown. A family farm winery with a rustic look and down-home and patriotic feel, they proudly fly the American flag. The old barn has been converted into a venue for weddings, receptions, and other events. A two-hundred-year-old log cabin with updated amenities is on the property for vacation rental. Try the Cabernet Sauvignon and Blackjack wines.

3610 Cavender Creek Road, Dahlonega, GA 30533

Open: Year Round
Tasting Room: At vineyard and Canvas and Cork Art Gallery and Tasting Room in downtown Dahlonega

Directions:
From Hwy 9
Go east 3.5 miles. Six miles east from Dahlonega.

Owner(s): Claire Livingston
Winemaker: In-house
Established: 2006

Altitude: 1,578 ft.
Hardiness zone: 7b 5–10 (F)
Soil: Sandy, clay
Geographical coordinates: 34.561714, -83.907612
Vineyard acreage: 15 acres with 3.6 acres planted
Vineyard tonnage, 2016: 6.5 tons
Varietal grapes: Norton, 1 acre; Cabernet Sauvignon, 1 acre; Petit Manseng, 1 acre, 84 plants; Viognier, .20 acres, 84 plants; Cabernet Franc, .20 acres, 84 plants; Touriga Nacional, .20 acres.

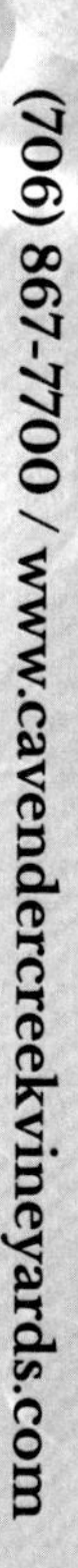

6

Frogtown Cellars

Frogtown Is One of the Oldest and Largest Vineyards in North Georgia

Cydney and Craig both graduated from the University of Florida. Craig acquired a law degree from Emory University, taking an additional year to pursue business and tax law. They moved to Atlanta, where Craig was a partner in a law firm and Cydney was engaged in developing a national-level toddler clothing line. In 1998, Craig wanted to leave the indoor legal practice for outdoor farming and decided growing grapes would help him realize his goal.

Frogtown is one of the oldest winery-and-vineyard operations in the Dahlonega Plateau region. Craig believes the rolling hills and terroir—including soil and climate—are ideal for growing *Vitis vinifera* grapes. In 2012, Frogtown added an additional twenty acres in South Georgia to grow muscadine grapes. Collectively, the two Frogtown vineyards grow thirty-eight varietals used to produce thirty wines. All the grapes are processed and bottled at the Dahlonega trilevel gravity flow winery. The Vitis vinifera wines sell in a price range from $18 to $50, and all the muscadine wines sell at $10. The wines are sold in both the Dahlonega and I-75 Hahira tasting rooms.

700 Ridge Point Drive, Dahlonega, GA 30533

Directions: NE Dahlonega at junction of Hwy 19 and GA 60
Travel 2.43 miles on Hwy 19.
Turn right onto Damascus Church Road.
Go 2.92 miles.
Vineyard on right.
Tasting room: 7495 Union Road, Hahira, GA 31632
(229) 794-1600
Off I-75 at exit 29 go east.
Take Union Road and go 1.4 miles.
Tasting room on left.

Owner: Cydney and Craig Kritzer
Winemaker/Vineyard manager: Craig Kritzer
Established: 1998 with 45 acres (added 12 acres in 2000)

Altitude: 1,675 to 1,825 ft.
Hardiness zone: 7a 0–5 (F)
Soil: Sandy, loam, clay
Geographical coordinates: 34.610316, -83.87870
Vineyard acreage (Dahlonega): 57 acres, 42 planted
Vineyard acreage (Hahira): 20 acres, 18.5 planted
Vineyard tonnage, 2016: Average tonnage is 150–160 tons; down somewhat in 2016.
Varietal grapes (Dahlonega): Cabernet Sauvignon, 4 acres; Cabernet Franc, 3 acres; Sangiovese, 3 acres; Touriga Nacional, 1.5 acres; Tannat, 3.5 acres; Norton, 3 acres; Merlot, 3.5 acres; Seyval Blanc, .5 acres; Viognier, 3.5 acres; Sauvignon Blanc, .5 acres; Chardonnay, 7 acres; Vidal Blanc, .5 acres; Marsanne, 1.5 acres; Roussanne, .5 acres; Petit Manseng, 1 acre; Sauvignon Gris, 1 acre; Carménère, 1 acre; Chambourcin, .5 acres; Malbec, 1 acre; Petit Verdot, 1 acre; Teroldego, .5 acres.
Varietal grapes (Hahira): Noble, 6 acres; Alachua, .25 acres; Black Beauty, .5 acres; Supreme, .5 acres; Creek, 1 acre; Carlos, 2 acres; Doreen, 1.25 acres; Late Fry, .25 acres; Magnolia, 1 acre; Tara, .5 acres; Cowart, .25 acres; Higgins, 1 acre; Welder, 1.25 acres; Jumbo, .25 acres; Southland, .25 acres; Sterling, .25 acres.

(706) 865-0687 / hello@frogtownwine.com

10

Three Sisters Vineyards & Winery

Oldest Family Farm Winery in Dahlonega

Doug and Sharon purchased one hundred acres of land in 1995 and later added eighty-four acres to establish Three Sisters Vineyards & Winery. With first plantings in 1998, they became the oldest family-farm winery in the Dahlonega Plateau. Their background was in TV and radio broadcasting, entertainment promotion, and creative services. Paul led the Cat's Paw sound studio in Atlanta.

With a diverse cross section of varietals over twenty acres, they produce more than twenty separate wines in a price range from $16.95 to $43. In their microclimate, Cynthiana/Norton, Cabernet Franc, Chardonnay, and Vidal Blanc produce some of their best wines. The Fat Boy Red, a blend of Cynthiana, Cabernet Franc, Cabernet Sauvignon, and Merlot, is a well-crafted red blend and best seller. I recommend the two sparkling Cuvee wines produced in the traditional method—a white and a rosé—that offer a crisp, fresh showing, a good mousse, and tiny, persistent bubbles with the right balance and acidity.

439 Vineyard Way, Dahlonega, GA 30533

It was a shock to the Georgia wine community when Doug Paul died in March 2017 at age fifty-nine.

Tasting room: At vineyard

Directions:
10 miles NE of Dahlonega via
Hwy 19 Cavender Creek Road and Town Creek
Church Road

Owner: Sharon Paul
Winemaker: Hezzie Patrick and the Paul family
Vineyard Manager: Ken VanDusen
Established: Purchased 1995, planted 1998, first harvest 2000

Altitude: 1,650 to 1,850 ft.
Hardiness zone: 7b 5–10 (F)
Soil: Clay, loam
Geographical coordinates: 34.609256, -83.879229
Vineyard acreage: 184 acres, 18.8 planted
Vineyard tonnage, 2016: 50–60 tons
Varietal grapes: Cabernet Franc, 3.9 acres; Merlot, 2.9 acres; Cabernet Sauvignon, 1.05 acres; Chardonnay, 3.3 acres; Pinot Blanc, 1.6 acres; Touriga, .5 acres; Cynthiana/Norton, 5.5 acres; Vidal Blanc, 1.6 acres; Pinot Noir, .05 acres.

(706) 865-9463 / www.threesistersvineyards.com

11

Wolf Mountain Vineyards

Full-Service Winery, Tasting Room, and Restaurant

THIS WINERY FIRST opened to the public in 2003 with a primary focus on red grapes, but is well supported by purchasing white grapes from other Georgia vineyards. Karl Boegner and his team have produced many award-winning wines. His unique background in hospitality and vineyard operations include service as the executive vice president at Château Élan, one of the three oldest vineyards and wineries in Georgia.

Wolf Mountain provides both great mountain views and a first-class dining experience. They have long been the leader in sparkling wines in the state. Prices range from $21 to $48. Two excellent wines to consider are the award-winning Private Reserve Cabernet and the Blanc de Blanc Brut sparkling wine.

439 Vineyard Way, Dahlonega, GA 30533

Tasting room: At vineyard

Directions:
5.2 miles from Dahlonega
Northwest on US-19/GA-9

Owner: Karl and Linda Boegner
Winemaker/Vineyard manager: Brandon Boegner
Established: 1999; first planting 2000

Altitude: 1,633 to 1,800 ft.
Hardiness zone: 7b 5–10 (F)
Soil: Sandy loam and clay
Geographical coordinates: 34.594346, -83.978903
Vineyard acreage: 30 acres, 5,000 vines on 11.5 acres
Vineyard tonnage, 2016: 32 tons
Varietal grapes: Cabernet Sauvignon, 3 acres; Syrah, 1 acre; Mourvèdre, 1 acre; Tannat, 3 acres; Petite Verdot, .5 acres; Malbec, 1 acre; Touriga Nacional, 2 acres.

7

Kaya Vineyard and Winery

Rebirth of an Old Winery with Great Character

5400 Town Creek Road, Dahlonega, GA 30533

Kaya opened in 2016 with Bill and Andrea Werkheiser, the new owner having purchased Blackstock Vineyard and Winery. The original vineyard opened in 1997 for vineyard operations and later with a tasting room and winery on April 1, 2006. It closed January 4, 2013. Bill is an entrepreneur who has successfully started several companies. Andrea has a background in medical technology with a keen interest in chemistry.

Ariel Padawer is the vineyard manager and winemaker with Blackstock who returned to Kaya to add continuity to this vineyard and winery restart. What had been around 32.6 acres planted is now 22.7 acres with more on the way. Improvements are also being introduced to the vineyard after being closed for over two years. The new owners are adding a twenty-two-room hotel with a restaurant and fifteen cabins to allow more events to occur on this spacious property.

Kaya Vineyard and Winery produces thirteen wines, all from grapes grown on the property, in a price range from $22 to $36. Wines to enjoy include both the oaked and unoaked Chardonnay, which are well crafted and offer contrasting winemaking styles.

Tasting room: At vineyard

Directions:
11 miles from Dahlonega town square to NE
At junction of Hwy 19 and GA-60,
travel 2.43 miles on Hwy 19.
Turn right onto Damascus Church Road.
Go 4.31 miles.
The vineyards are on your left.

Owner: Bill and Andrea Werkheiser
Winemaker/Vineyard manager: Ariel Padawer
Established: 2016

Altitude: 1642 ft.
Hardiness zone: 7a 0–5 (F)
Soil: Sandy, clay
Geographical coordinates: 34.607888, -83.857899
Vineyard acreage: 90 acres, 22.7 planted
Vineyard tonnage, 2016: 92 tons
Varietal grapes: Merlot, 10.5 acres; Viognier, 1 acre; Chardonnay, 2 acres; Cabernet Sauvignon, 3.5 acres; Touriga, 3.7 acres; Sangiovese, 2 acres.

(706) 219-3514 / info@kayavineyards.com

8

Montaluce Winery & Restaurant

Resort Winery

THE WINERY OFFERS fifteen wines at a price range from $22 to $99. Two wines to consider when you visit are the latest vintage of Petit Verdot and the Pinot Gris. The tasting room and restaurant offer a grand view of the vineyards. This is a majestic location for a wedding.unoaked Chardonnay, which are well crafted and offer contrasting winemaking styles.

501 Hightower Church Road, Dahlonega, GA 30533

Tasting room: At vineyard

Directions:
Five miles NW of Dahlonega town center

Owner: Mountain Field Development
Winemaker: Craig Boyd
Vineyard Manager: Jorge Camacho
Established: 2007; first harvest 2008

Altitude: 1,512 ft.
Hardiness zone: 7a 0–5 (F)
Soil: Red clay, loam, silt, and sand
Geographical coordinates: 34.564413, -84.066881
Vineyard acreage: 35 available; 12.42 acres planted
Vineyard tonnage, 2016: 39 tons
Varietal grapes: Seyval Blanc, 1.38 acres; Sangiovese, .8 acres; Chardonnay, 1.7 acres; Cabernet Franc, .9 acres; Pinot Gris, 1.1 acres; Malbec, .3 acres; Petit Verdot, .36 acres; Merlot, 1.7 acres; Norton, 1.5 acres; Vidal Blanc, 2.38 acres; Chambourcin, 1.1 acres; Teroldego, .5 acres.

9

The Cottage Vineyard & Winery

659 Dock Dorsey Road, Cleveland, GA 30528

European Wines Inspired Winery

JIM ORIGINALLY GREW up in northern New York farm country. He spent twenty-four years in the US Air Force with a tour in Vietnam. However, an assignment to Germany gave Jim wider exposure to European wines and set him on a course to take his wine hobby to the next level with his vineyard and winery. Nathan, Jim's stepson, understudying with Joe Smith, is developing into the primary winemaker. With 6.6 acres of Vitis vinifera in the ground, there are plans to add additional acreage.

The winery offers a wide variety of wines at prices that range from $23 to $45 per bottle. Jim considers his Chardonnay and Merlot as his best-crafted Georgia-grown wines. At the highest elevation in the vineyard, there is a military platform of service flags surrounding a white marble cross. The Cottage Vineyard & Winery offers an exceptional location to pause for a moment of silent thought with a grand view of the surrounding mountains overlooking a war memorial. It is perhaps one of the most scenic views from any winery in Georgia.

Tasting room: At vineyard

Directions:
The winery is 4.9 miles NW of Cleveland, Georgia, on the east side of Hwy 129.

Owner: Jim and Sandra Penner
Winemaker: Joe Smith and Nathan Beasley
Vineyard manager: Jason Keinat
Established: 2012

Altitude: 1,750 ft.
Hardiness zone: 7b 5–10 (F)
Soil: Clay, sandstone
Geographical coordinates: 34.638893, -83.828870
Vineyard acreage: 29 acres, 6.6 planted
Vineyard tonnage, 2016: 3.5 tons
Varietal grapes: Syrah, 1 acre; Merlot, 1 acre; Chardonnay, 1 acre; Viognier, 1 acre; Muscat, .5 acres; Pinot Meunier, 1 acre; Cabernet Franc, .6 acres; Petit Verdot, .5 acres.

Chapter 13

Blue Ridge Mountain Region

THE BLUE RIDGE Mountain region of Northeast Georgia contains the highest mountain in the state with Brasstown Bald at 4,784 ft. elevation. The highest rainfall in Georgia occurs in this region, along with cooler air currents. Clayton receives 135 rain days, averaging annually sixty-nine inches.[1] The growing period in this low agricultural producing area is 180 to 210 days. There are fifteen wineries in this region, to include four in the Upper Hiwassee AVA, along with several grower vineyards. Currently three counties—Rabun, Fannin, and Gilmer—host the wineries and one tasting room within the region. The soil is clay, silt, and sandy alluvial mixture, along with decayed granite and mica.

Four wineries are in Rabun County in the Blue Ridge region: 12 Spies Vineyard **(12)**, Noble Wine Cellar Tasting Room **(13)**, Stonewall Creek Vineyards **(14)**, and Tiger Mountain Vineyards **(15)**.

1 "Average Annual Precipitation for Georgia," Current Results Publishing Ltd., accessed September 11, 2017, https://www.currentresults.com/Weather/Georgia/average-yearly-precipitation.php.

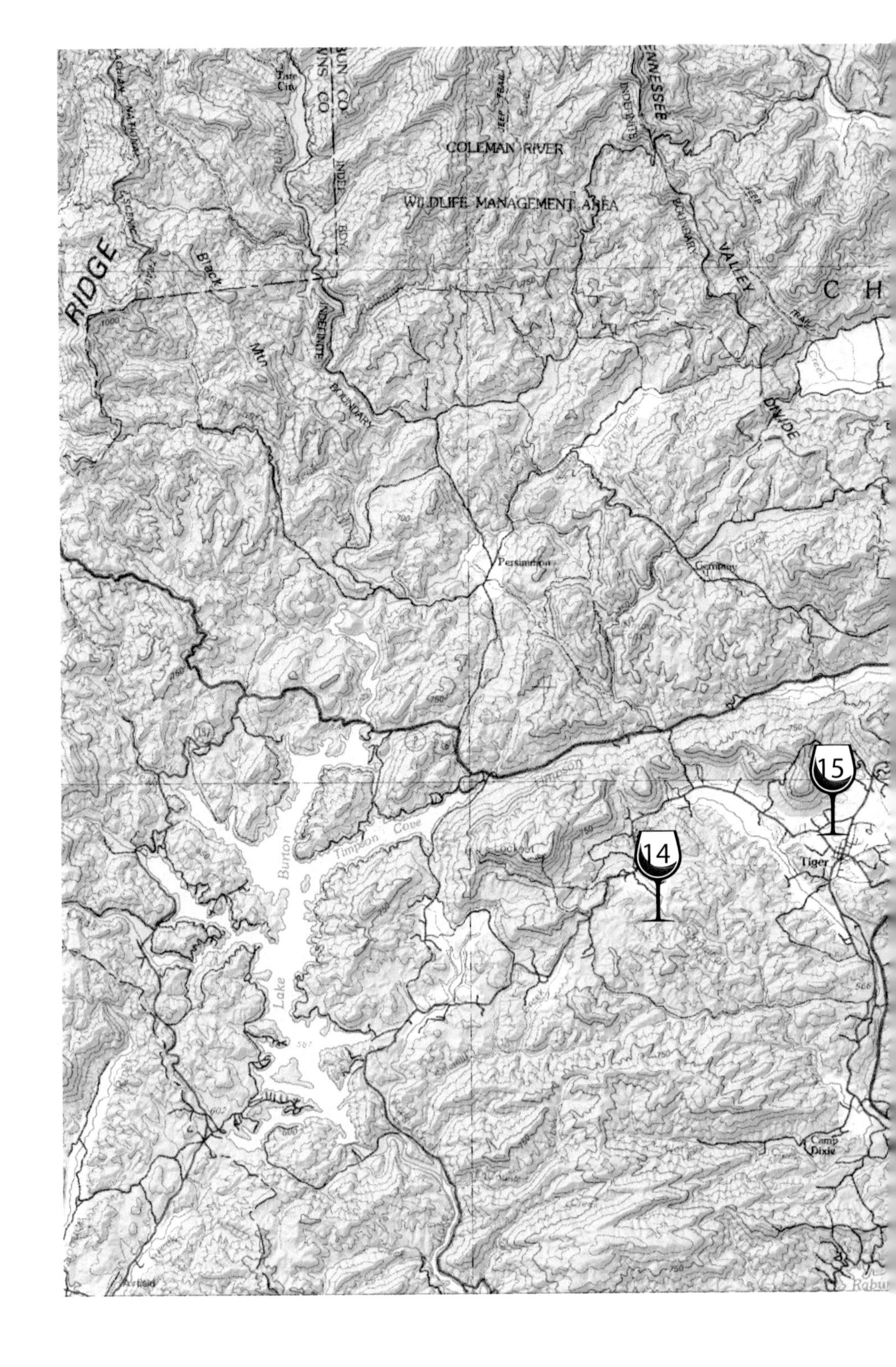

RIDGE
COLEMAN RIVER
WILDLIFE MANAGEMENT AREA
Black
Mtn
BOUNDARY
VALLEY
DIVIDE
C H
Persimmon
Germany
Timpson
Lake
Burton
Timpson Cove
Tiger
Camp
Dixie
14
15

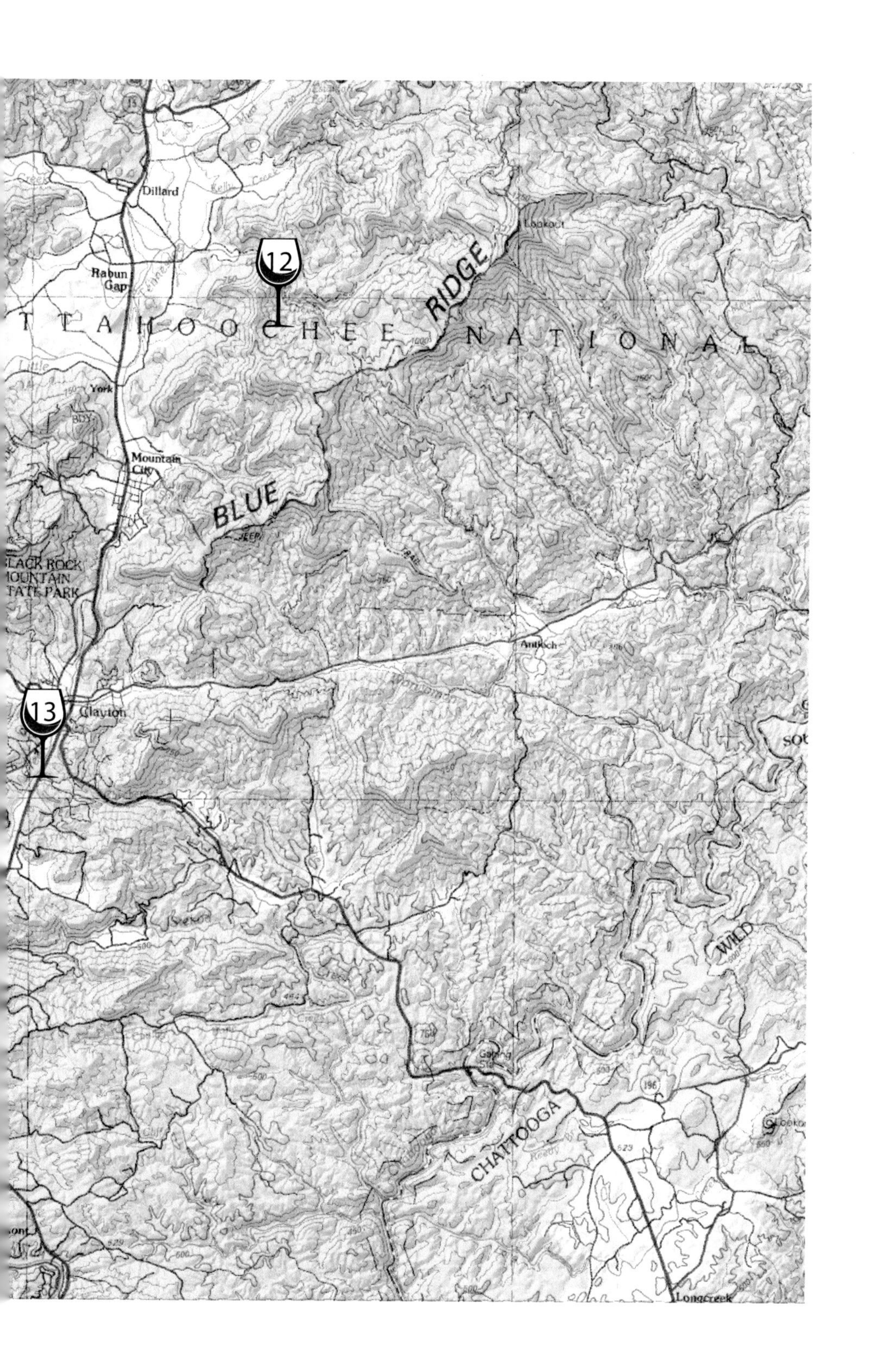

Dillard
Rabun Gap
12
T T A H O O C H E E
N A T I O N A L
RIDGE
Lookout
York
Mountain City
BLUE
JEEP
TRAIL
Antioch
13
Clayton
WILD
CHATTOOGA
196
Longcreek

12

12 Spies Vineyard

A Spot of Heaven on Earth for Mike and Lisa

MIKE AND LISA produce thirteen wines using both their vineyard fruit and other grower fruit. Their wines range in price from $14.50 to $25. Be sure to taste their 12 Spies Cabernet Franc, a medium-body red, and Temptation Traminette, a light, crisp, fresh wine for a warm day. 12 Spies is just 5.5 miles from the North Carolina–Georgia border. They rely on other vineyards to provide Cabernet Sauvignon, Chardonnay, and Seyval Blanc.

550 Black Ranch Road, Rabun Gap, GA 30568

Tasting room: At vineyard

Directions:
North from Clayton
4.1 miles on Hwy 441
Go east on Yorkhouse Rd. 1.4 miles.

Owner: Mike Brown and Lisa Romanello
Winemaker: Mike Brown
Established: 2012

Altitude: 2,279 ft.
Hardiness zone: 7a 0–5 (F)
Soil: Loamy, a mixture of clay, silt, and sand
Geographical coordinates: 34.946052, -83.371132
Vineyard acreage: 9 acres, 1 acre planted
Vineyard tonnage, 2016: 3.5 tons
Varietal grapes: Tannat, 150 vines, .2 acres; Malbec, 200 vines, .25 acres; Cabernet Franc, 250 vines, .35 acres; Traminette, 150 vines, .2 acres.

13

Noble Wine Cellar

New Tasting Room

Jabe Hilson learned growing and making wine in Georgia by working for Tiger Mountain Vineyards and other wineries before he started making his own wine in 2014. Noble Wine Cellar's tasting room is in downtown Clayton. Jabe produces wines with three primary grapes that sell in a price range from $22 to $28. Try the Traminette, a fresh, crisp, white grape that grows well in North Georgia, and the Chambourcin. All the grapes come from a vineyard within the Upper Hiwassee AVA.

58 N. Main Street, Clayton, GA 30525

Tasting room: In Clayton

Directions:
From Hwy 441 in Clayton
Go west onto E. Savannah Street.
Travel 3 blocks and turn right onto N. Main Street.
The tasting room is one block north on the right.

Owner: Jabe and Barbara Hilson
Winemaker: Jabe Hilson
Established: 2014, tasting room in 2015
Hardiness zone: 6b 0–5 (F)
Varietal grapes: Traminette, Gewürztraminer, Chambourcin

14

Stonewall Creek Vineyards

2016 Oglethorpe Trophy Winner

Carl and Carla have family roots tracing back to Germany. Carl is an orthopedic surgeon with residency through Harvard who served as a US Navy medical doctor assigned to the US Marines and later practiced medicine in Atlanta before moving to Rabun County.

Stonewall Creek Vineyards opened in 2012, and the first red grapes were released in 2013. Stonewall Creek has some of the best vineyard canopy control in the state, which contributes to the health of their grapes. Eight wines are available for sale in the tasting rooms.

I encourage visitors to taste the 2015 Boriana, a Petit Manseng white grape, or later vintages. This wine was the 2016 Oglethorpe Trophy winner at the Georgia Trustees Wine Challenge as the top wine of the competition. It is an exceptional wine and may be one of the leading white grapes to grow in Georgia. Their Cabernet Franc is another wine to enjoy with a grape that has adapted well to the rainy weather and soil in the Blue Ridge region.

323 Standing Dear Lane, Tiger, GA 30576

Tasting room: At vineyard and
2454 Highway 17 Sautee, GA, and at
Crane Creek on The Square
4 Public Square North Dahlonega, GA

Directions:
7.2 miles southwest of Clayton Ga

Owner: Carl and Carla Fackler
Winemaker: Carl and son Nate Fackler
Vineyard manager: Miguel Barcemas
Established: Planted in 2005, opened in 2012

Altitude: 2,181 ft.
Hardiness zone: 7a 0–5 (F)
Soil: Decayed granite and mica
Geographical coordinates: 34.839790, -83.477365
Vineyard acreage: 30 acres, 6.5 planted
Vineyard tonnage, 2016: 10 tons
Varietal grapes: Petit Manseng, 1 acre; Cabernet Franc, 2.5 acres; Cabernet Sauvignon, .25 acres; Petit Verdot, .25 acres; Malbec, 1 acre; Tannat, 2 rows, 50 plants; Norton, 1.5 acres; Traminette, 1 acre.

(706) 212-0584 / http://stonewallcreek.com/

15

Tiger Mountain Vineyards

One of Oldest Award-Winning Wineries in Georgia

Tiger is one of the oldest award-winning vineyards and wineries in Georgia, having won the 2015 Oglethorpe Trophy. The farm, now a vineyard, has been in John's family for five generations. John and Martha returned to Georgia from Colorado, where John practiced urology and Martha served as a lawyer, to become early pioneers in Georgia wines.

Martha shifted her legal skills to professional writing for the *Atlanta Journal-Constitution*, while John continued practicing medicine. A delightful, well-written personal account of John and Martha's experience building a farm winery is in Martha's book The Second Bud published in 2013 by Mercer University Press in Macon, Georgia. Her family stories are interlaced with a step-by-step journey building a farm winery, showcasing Northeast Georgia's rural life while laying out the challenges Mother Nature brings to grape farming.

Tiger was the first winery to introduce the white Petit Manseng grape to Georgia, where it has enjoyed considerable success. Tiger produces a dozen or so wines each year, ranging in price from $19 to $42. Their award-

2592 Old Highway 441 South, Tiger, GA 30576

winning Petit Manseng is one of the best white wines produced in Georgia. I highly recommend their Malbec and Cabernet Franc red wines. Twenty years of winemaking have provided John and his team with considerable knowledge on how to obtain the best results from their grapes and the soil.

Tasting room: At vineyard and
Naturally Georgia Public Square Dahlonega

Directions:
2.56 miles south of Clayton on South Main Street,
or 1.75 miles off Hwy 23 using Bridge Creek Road

Owner: John and Martha Ezzard and partners John and Marilyn McMullan
Winemaker/Vineyard manager: John Ezzard
Established: 1995

Altitude: 1,892 ft.
Hardiness Zone: 7b 5–10 (F)
Soil: Clay, granite, sand
Geographical coordinates: 34.8531959, -83.4241050
Vineyard acreage: 10.5 acres
Vineyard tonnage, 2016: 21 tons
Varietal grapes: Petit Manseng, 1.5 acres; Viognier, 2 acres; Touriga Nacional, .5 acres; Malbec, .75 acres; Norton, 2 acres; Tannat, .75 acres; Cabernet Franc, 2.5 acres; Mourvèdre, .5 acres.

(706) 782-4777 / www.tigerwine.com

Fannin County

There are three wine producers in Fannin County: Bear Claw Vineyards **(16)**, Mercer Orchards **(17)**, and Serenberry Vineyards **(18)**. Loamy, clay, silt, and sand dominate the soil in this Blue Ridge region. The city of Blue Ridge, Georgia, has 126 days of rain with an annual rainfall at sixty-one inches.

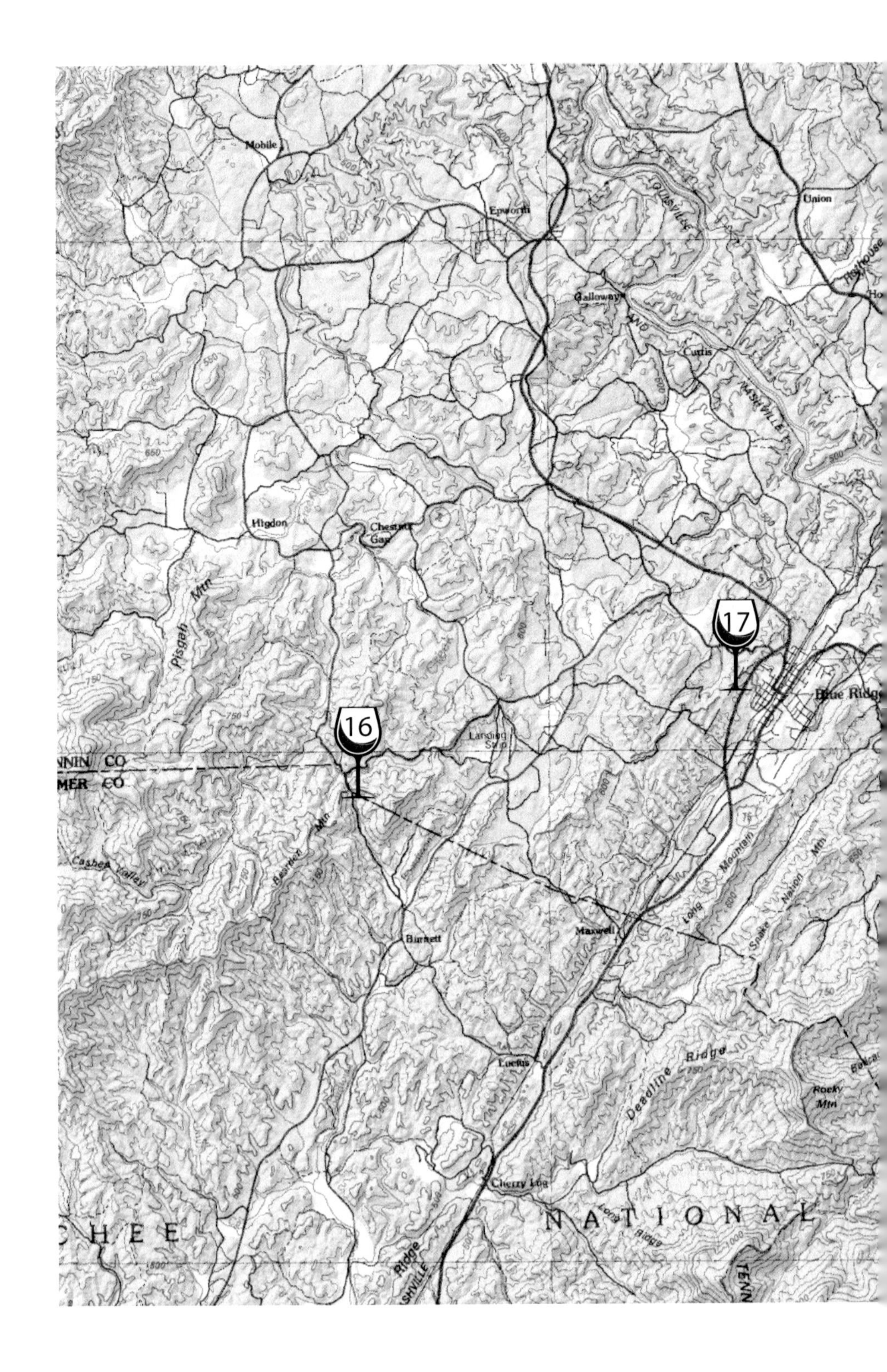

Mobile
Epworth
Union
Galloway
Curtis
Higdon
Chestnut Gap
Pisgah Mtn
17
Blue Ridge
16
Landing Scrip
Long Mountain
Maxwell
Burnett
Lucius
Deadline Ridge
Rocky Mtn
Cherry Log
NATIONAL
Long Ridge
Ridge

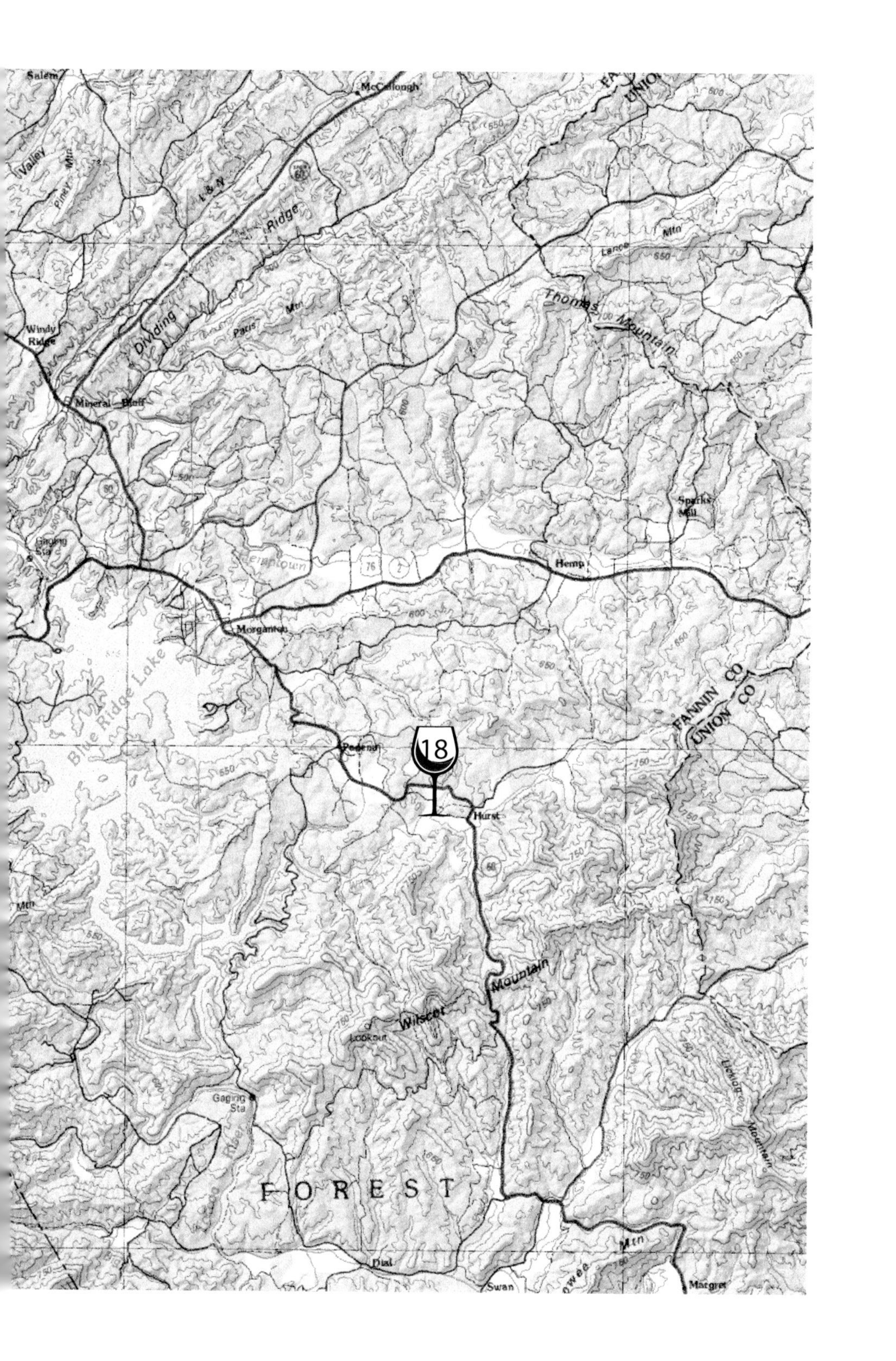

Salem
Valley
Pine Mtn
L & N
Ridge
Dividing
Windy Ridge
Mineral Bluff
Paris Mtn
Lance Mtn
Thomas Mountain
Sparks Mill
Hemp
Morganton
Blue Ridge Lake
18
Hurst
FANNIN CO
UNION CO
Mountain
Wilscot
Lookout
Gaging Sta
FOREST
Dial
Swan
Mtn

16

Bear Claw Vineyards

New Winery Opening

In addition to the farm winery with tasting-room opening in September 2017, Kevin and Michelle Swim also own Blue Ridge Swim & Tennis Club just across the street from the winery. They also built a large treehouse that rents out for special activities and overlooks the vineyards.

2281 Tennis Court Road, Blue Ridge, GA 30513

Tasting room: At vineyard

Directions:
From Blue Ridge
Go west 1 mile on Hwy 5 off of Hwy 515.
Turn left onto Scenic Rd.
Turn left onto Sugar Creek Rd.
Turn right onto Tennis Court Road.
Total distance is 4.8 miles.

Owner: Kevin and Michelle Swim
Winemaker: Kevin Swim and Tom Payette
Vineyard manager: Kevin Swim
Established: 2014

Altitude: 1,832 ft.
Hardiness zone: 7b 5–10 (F)
Soil: Alluvial and sandy loam
Geographical coordinates: 34.879862, -84.372080
Vineyard acreage: 18 acres, 4.5 planted
Vineyard tonnage, 2016: Small amount
Varietal grapes: Chardonnay, 3 acres; Vidal Blanc (two different clones), 1.5 acres.

(706) 223-3750 / https://bearclawvineyards.com/

17

Mercier Orchards

Veteran Orchard Family Now Making Wine

THE ORCHARD WAS started in 1943 by Bill and Adele Mercier and has remained in the family for almost seventy-five years. More recently, they've branched from only making apple cider to making fruit wine.

Mercier is one of the largest apple producers in Georgia. They make three wines from apple, peach, and blackberry fruit: a dry fall-harvest apple wine, a semisweet winter blackberry wine, and a sweet summer peach wine. The tasting room is open daily from 7:00 a.m. to 6:00 p.m. Mercier's attractive and spacious facility is well worth spending time in, enjoying fresh-baked bread, candy, fruits, wine, cider, and a very busy deli.

Tasting room: At vineyard

Directions:
1.5 miles west on Hwy 5 and Hwy 515

Owner: William Mercier family
Winemaker: Justin Gibbs and Ian Flom
Vineyard manager: David Lillard
Established: 1943

Altitude: 1,800 ft.
Hardiness zone: 7b 5–10 (F)
Soil: Sandy, clay loam with good drainage
Geographical coordinates: 34.886278, -84.340536
Vineyard acreage: Started with 25 acres; now 350 acres
Vineyard tonnage, 2016: None, but 5,000 gallons in 2015
Crops grown: Apple, peach, blackberry

(706) 632-2411/ http://www.mercier-orchards.com/

18

Serenberry Vineyards

Family-Owned Land Becomes Farm Winery

SERENBERRY VINEYARDS IS a small, family-owned farm winery located in the Blue Ridge Mountains. The land has been in the family for several generations. Mark's grandparents grew apples, vegetables, and grapes on the property. The love of the land and farming have been carried forward by several generations. Mark and team started renovating the little house on the property as a tasting room, which opened in 2012.

Mark and Janis produce on average of seven or eight different wines each year, ranging in price from $16.95 to $24.95. Two wines to enjoy are Skeenah Red, a blend of Merlot and Cabernet Sauvignon barreled in oak, and Hot House Red, made from Chambourcin with sweet overtones to complement spicy foods.

Tasting room: At vineyard

Directions:
From Blue Ridge on Hwy 515
Travel north to Hwy 60.
Turn right and go 6 miles.

Owner: Mark and Janis Jernigan
Winemaker/Vineyard manager: Mark Jernigan
Established: 2008, with tasting room opening in 2012

Altitude: 2,000 ft.
Hardiness zone: 6b 0–5 (F)
Soil: Loamy, clay, silt, and sand
Geographical coordinates: 34.850562, -84.195002
Vineyard acreage: 37 acres, 1.5 planted
Vineyard tonnage, 2016: 3 tons
Varietal grapes: Chambourcin, .75 acres; Traminette, .75 acres.

(706) 623-8463 / www.serenberryvineyards.com

Gilmer County

There are four vineyards with wineries located in Gilmer County centered around Ellijay, Georgia: Cartecay Vineyards **(19)**, Chateau Meichtry Winery & Vineyards **(20)**, Ellijay River Vineyards **(21)**, and Engelheim Vineyards **(22)**. The average annual rain in Ellijay, Georgia, is 60.9 inches with precipitation for 113 days annually.[1]

1 Ellijay, Georgia, Weatherbase by CantyMedia, accessed September 11, 2017, http://www.weatherbase.com/weather/weather.php3?s=511390&.

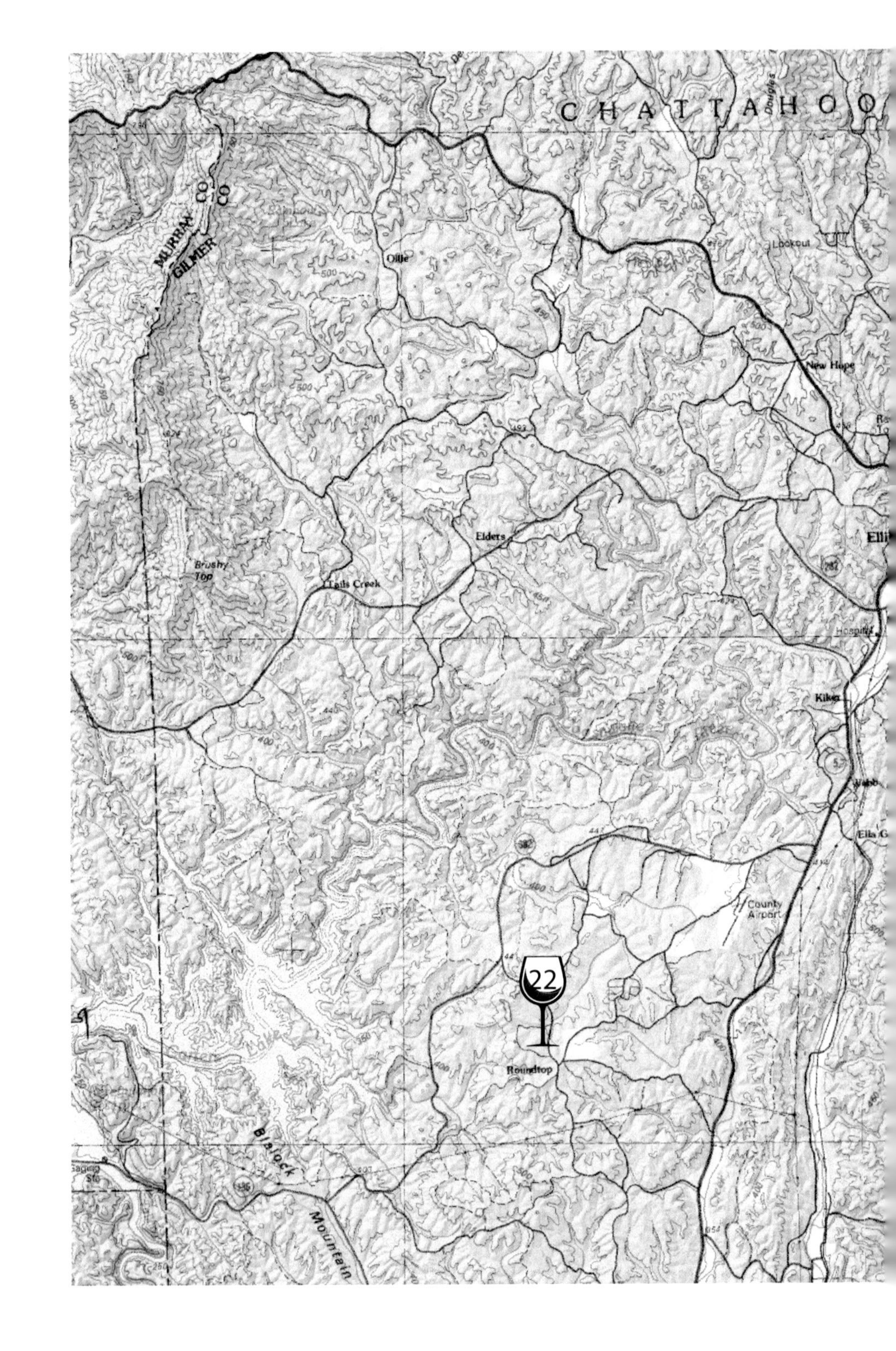

MURRAY CO
GILMER CO
Ollie
Lookout
New Hope
Elders
Tails Creek
Brushy Top
Roundtop
County Airport
22
Blalock
Mountain

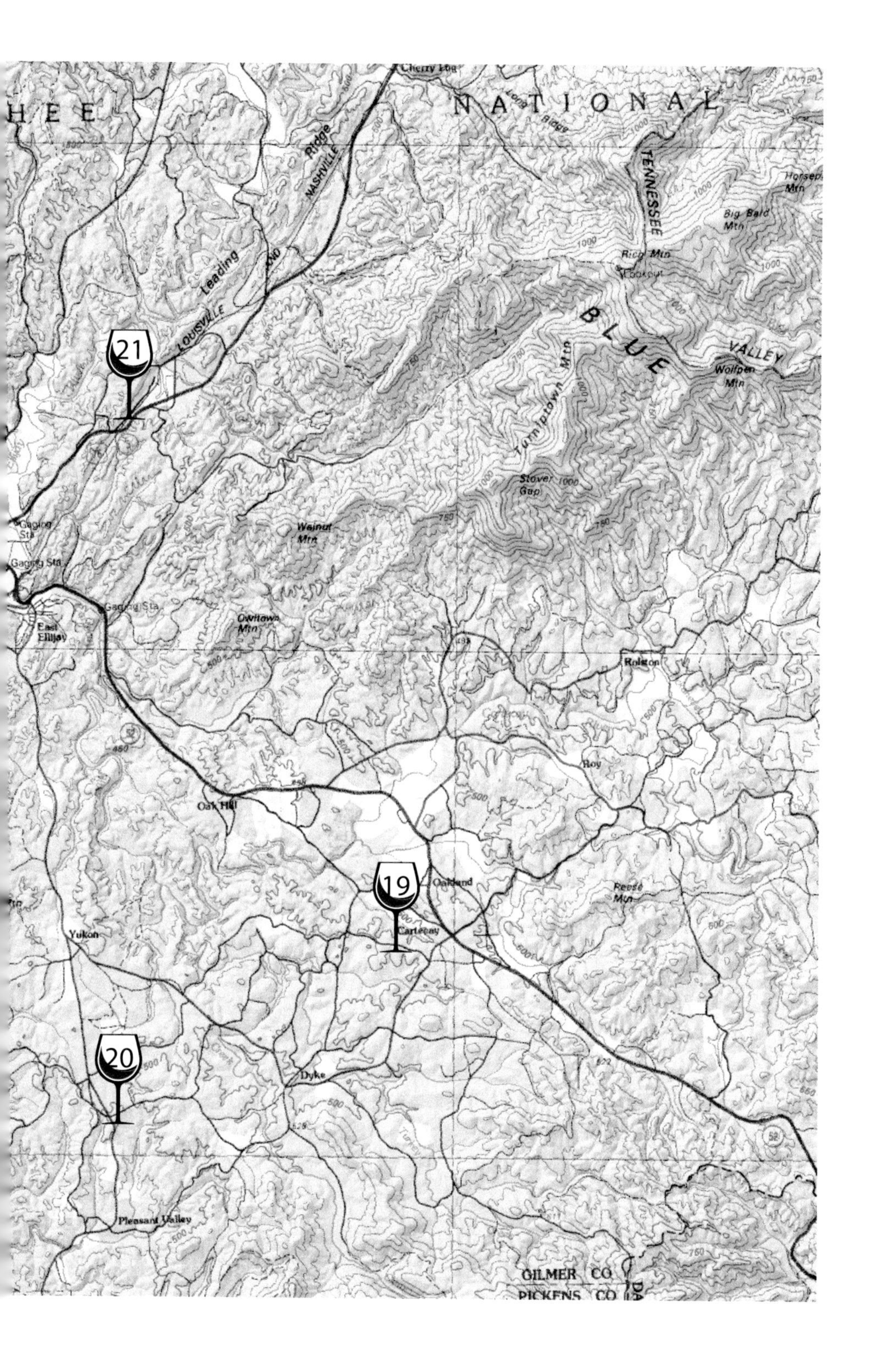

NATIONAL
BLUE
VALLEY
TENNESSEE
Cherry Log
Ridge
NASHVILLE
Leading
LOUISVILLE
21
Big Bald Mtn
Rich Mtn
Lookout
Wolfpen Mtn
Turniptown Mtn
Stover Gap
Walnut Mtn
Owltown Mtn
Gaging Sta
East Ellijay
Rolston
Roy
Oak Hill
Oakland
19
Cartecay
Reese Mtn
Yukon
20
Dyke
Pleasant Valley
GILMER CO
PICKENS CO

19

Cartecay Vineyards

Historic Apple Country Hosting Winery

Larry is a UGA agriculture graduate and served as the first president of the Georgia Wine Producers. He was also a varsity swimmer at UGA. Dr. Shay Lykins is also a UGA graduate with a doctor of dental medicine degree from the Medical College of Georgia. They moved to Ellijay in 2002.

They purchased this old farmland located in Georgia apple country in 2007. The winery produces nine wines using Vitis vinifera, Native American hybrids, and French hybrid grapes in the $19–$28 price range. The crisp, white Vidal Blanc and the medium-bodied Chimney red are two contrasting wines that are both easy drinking, stylish, and great back-porch wines to share with friends.

5704 Clear Creek Road, Ellijay, GA 30536

Tasting room: At vineyard and Wild Berry Cottage
139 E Morgan St., Clarkesville, GA 30523

Directions:
From Hwy 52
Go south on Clear Creek 1 mile.
Vineyard on the left.

Owner: Larry and Shay Lykins
Winemaker: Andrew Beaty and Larry Lykins
Vineyard manager: Larry Lykins and Mike Ott
Established: 2007, planted 2008, first harvest 2010

Altitude: 1,650 to 1,750 ft.
Hardiness Zone: 7b 5–10 (F)
Soil: Loamy clay and sand
Geographical coordinates: 34.6156519, -84.3916736
Vineyard acreage: 50 acres, 13.75 planted
Vineyard tonnage, 2016: 46 tons
Varietal grapes: Merlot, 1.75 acres; Norton, 2.25 acres; Catawba, 1.75 acres; Cabernet Sauvignon, 2.5 acres; Traminette, 2 acres; Vidal Blanc, 2 acres; Petit Manseng, 1.5 acres.

20

Chateau Meichtry Winery & Vineyards

1862 Orchard Lane Talking Rock, GA 30175
2100 Orchard Lane, Talking Rock, GA 30175

Winemaking Roots from Switzerland

THIS FARM WINERY family has a tradition of grape growing from a grandfather who immigrated to America from Switzerland. Considerable time was spent locating a property in North Georgia with good air flow, aspect, and drainage.

Chateau Meichtry makes eleven or twelve wines using both Georgia grapes and grapes brought in from other states. The price range of their wines is $21 to $32. Two wines I particularly recommend are their 100 percent Seyval Blanc and Georges Cuvee, a red-wine blend of Norton and Noiret.

Tasting room: At vineyard

Directions:
4.7 miles from Hwy 52 at Clear Creek Road.
Turn south until you reach Homer Right Rd.
Go left to Orchard Lane.
The vineyard is just south of the road.

Owner: Robert and Karin Meneill
Winemaker/Vineyard manager: Justin Meneill
Established: Purchased in 2010; first planting in 2013; tasting room opened in 2015

Altitude: 1,862 ft.
Hardiness zone: 7b 5–10 (F)
Soil: Loamy clay and sand
Geographical coordinates: 34.5890140, -34.4318683
Vineyard acreage: 50 acres with 2 acres planted
Vineyard tonnage, 2016: 5 tons
Varietal grapes: Norton, 1 acre; Seyval Blanc, .5 acres; Noiret, .5 acres.

21

Ellijay River Vineyards

The Dutch Have Arrived

Marijn is Dutch by birth. He came to Atlanta in 1986 to study at Emory University, but ended up getting his PhD in electronic engineering from Georgia Tech Institute of Technology. He still works in Atlanta but spends as much time as possible at the vineyard.

Currently, he is only bottling one wine: a Seyval Blanc that costs $18. In 2017, he will produce three additional labels, bottling Albariño and Viognier and most likely a red blend.

111 River Birch Lane, Ellijay, GA 30540

Tasting room: At vineyard

Directions:
From Hwy 515 take Whitepath Road,
going west 1.77 miles to vineyard on the right.

Owner: Marijn Brummer
Winemaker/Vineyard manager: Marijn Brummer
Established: Purchased in 2010; planted in 2011

Altitude: 1,387 ft.
Hardiness zone: 7b 5–10 (F)
Soil: Loamy, sandy
Geographical coordinates: 34.7601129, -84.4224736
Vineyard acreage: 19.7 acres, 4.5 acres planted in 2011
Vineyard tonnage, 2016: 10 tons
Varietal grapes: Seyval Blanc, 1 acre; Albariño, .5 acres; Viognier, 1 acre; Merlot, .5 acres; Grüner Veltliner, .5 acres; Cabernet Sauvignon, .5 acres; Chardonnay, .25 acres; Cabernet Franc, .25 acres.

22

Engelheim Vineyards

Farm Boy and Professional Soldier Leads Vineyard-and-Winery Team

GARY GREW UP on a South Alabama farm that raised potatoes and other crops. After spending twenty-nine years in the army, the colonel retired and began looking for the proper ground to establish a vineyard and winery. He selected the land just north and west of Ellijay for the vineyard, as it had the right elevation, drainage, soil, sun exposure, and a great view of the mountains to the north.

Gary and team produce ten to twelve wines. Two 100 percent Georgia-grown and award-winning wines are his Merlot and Sweet Molly, made with Traminette, a fresh, crisp white wine. Engelheim Vineyards boasts a delightful tasting room with a winery downstairs. Be sure to plan ahead and ask for a tour.

127 Lakeview Road, Ellijay, GA 30540

Tasting room: At vineyard

Directions:
From Hwy 515 north of Ellijay
Turn west on Powersports Dr.
Turn immediately left onto Old Hwy 5S.
Go .75 miles and turn right onto Round Top Rd.
At 3.65 miles, turn right onto Knight Rd.
The vineyard is the first road on the left at 3.78 miles from Hwy 515.

Owner: Gary and Jan Engel
Winemaker: Gary Engel
Vineyard manager: Mike Ott
Established: Purchased in 2007; planted in 2009; tasting room opened 2014

Altitude: 1,717 ft.
Hardiness zone: 7b 5–10 (F)
Soil: Loamy, Sandy, clay
Geographical coordinates: 34.6050571, -84.5678685
Vineyard acreage: 62 acres, 8.75 planted
Vineyard tonnage, 2016: 39 tons
Varietal grapes: Traminette, 2 acres; Merlot, 1.5 acres; Cabernet Sauvignon, 1.5 acres; Cabernet Franc, .5 acres; Pinot Gris, .25 acres; Chambourcin, 1.5 acres; Petit Manseng, 1.5 acres; Vidal Blanc, .5 acres; Noiret, .5 acres.

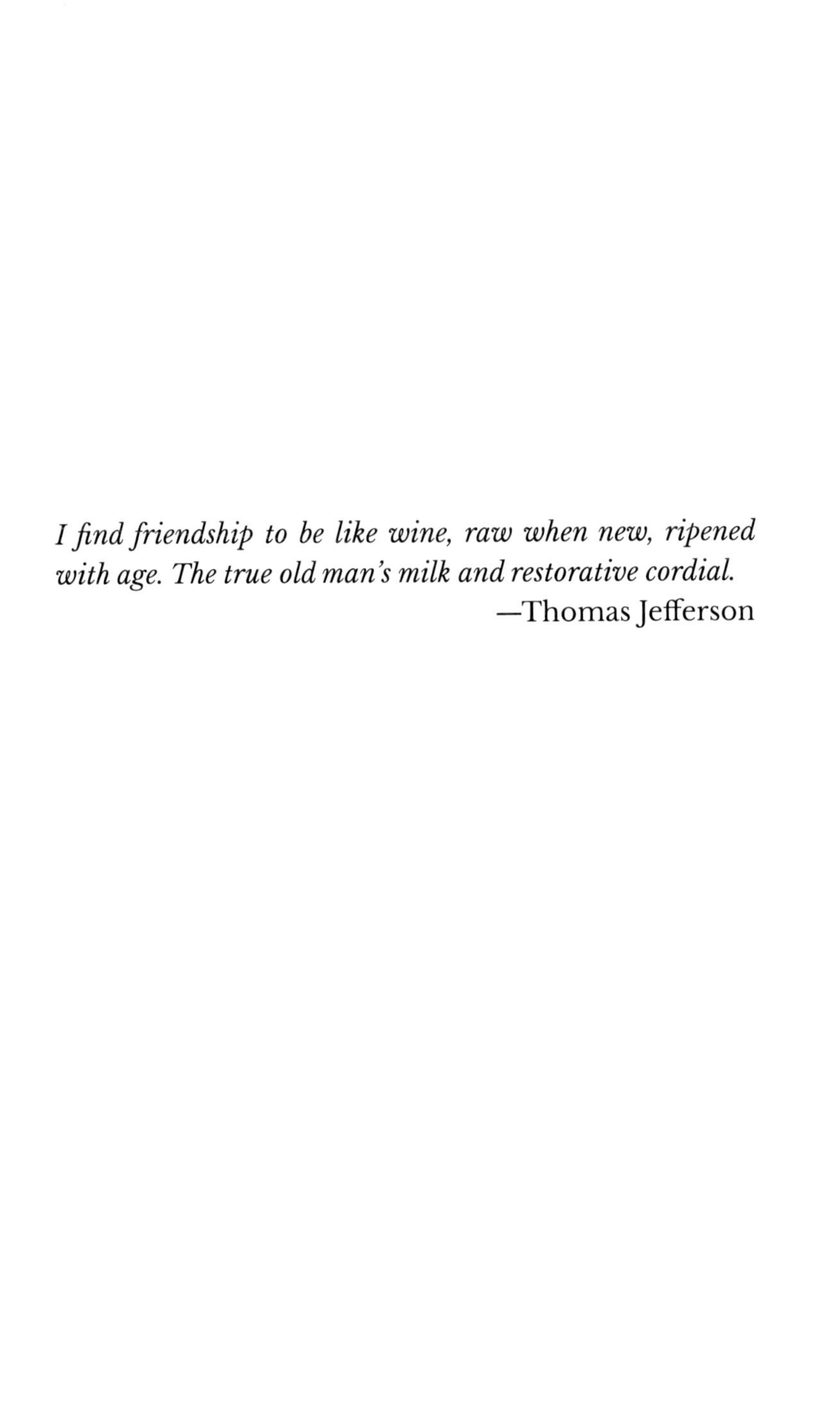

I find friendship to be like wine, raw when new, ripened with age. The true old man's milk and restorative cordial.

—Thomas Jefferson

Chapter 14

Ridge and Valley Region

The Ridge and Valley region, the smallest region in Georgia, is located in the state's northwest corner with predominately soft sedimentary rock, limestone, and shale in the valley and ridges made with sandstone. The growing season is 210 to 220 days. Two wineries and several grower vineyards are in this region, including Catoosa and Walker Counties. Georgia Winery **(23)** is located just south of Chattanooga, Tennessee, west from Ringgold Georgia and Hwy 75. The annual precipitation is 50.6 inches with ninety-five rain days.[1] Debarge Vineyard and Winery **(24)** is located west from LaFayette, Georgia, along Hwy 193. The annual precipitation in LaFayette is 56.3 inches and there are 108 rain days.[2]

1 Ringgold, Georgia, Weatherbase by CantyMedia, accessed September 13, 2017, http://www.weatherbase.com/weather/weather.php3?s=984790.

2 LaFayette, Georgia, Weatherbase by CantyMedia, accessed September 12, 2017, http://www.weatherbase.com/weather/weather.php3?s=149490.

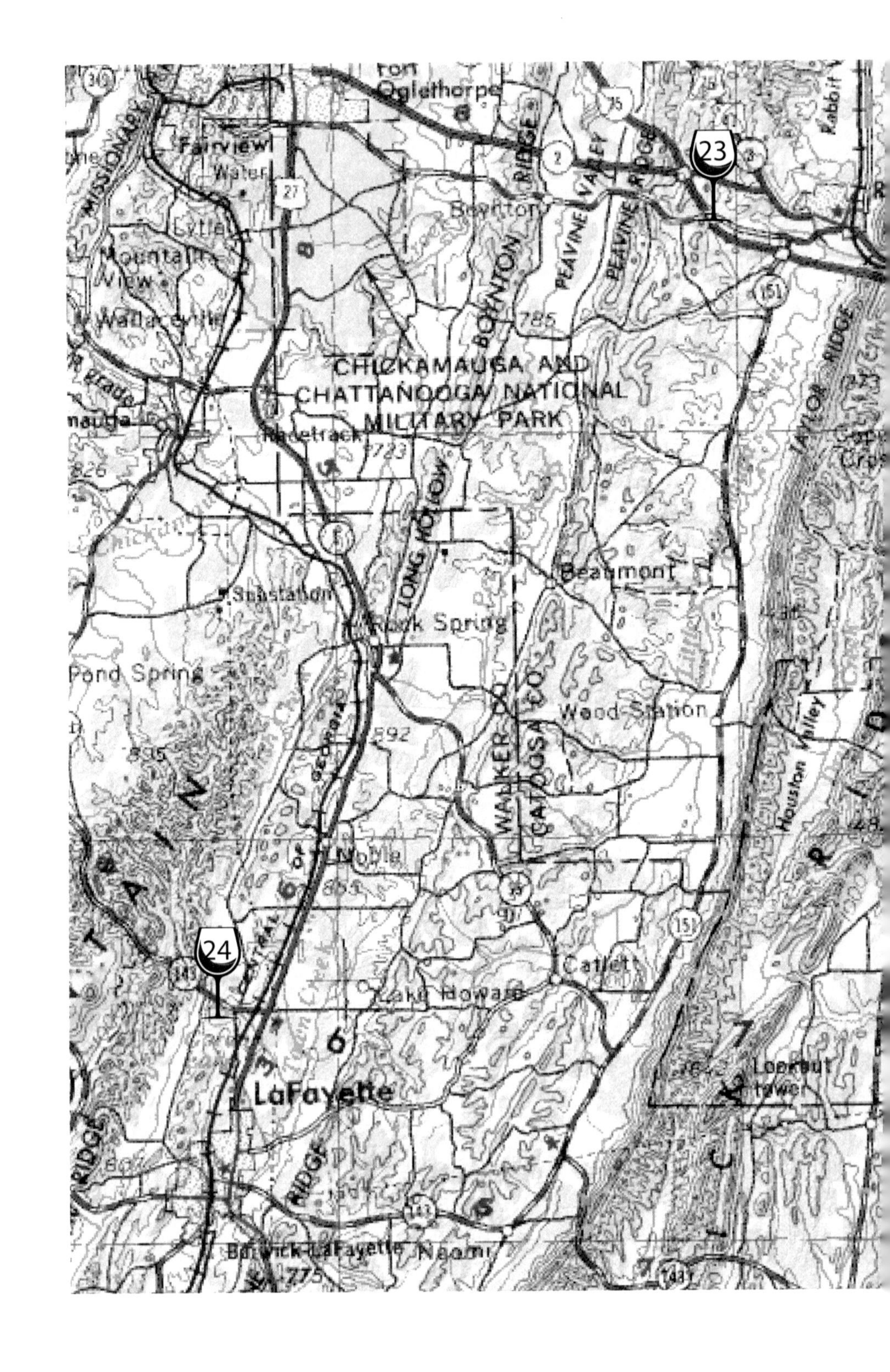

Fort Oglethorpe
Fairview
Lytle
Mountain View
Wallaceville
MISSIONARY
Boynton
BOYNTON
RIDGE
PEAVINE VALLEY
PEAVINE RIDGE
CHICKAMAUGA AND CHATTANOOGA NATIONAL MILITARY PARK
Racetrack
LONG HOLLOW
Beaumont
Rock Spring
Pond Spring
Wood Station
WALKER CO.
CATOOSA CO.
Houston Valley
TAYLOR RIDGE
Catlett
Lake Howard
LaFayette
RIDGE
Naomi
Lookout tower
23
24

NATION
FORE
Catoosa Springs
Keith
Lookout tower
Varnell
Tunnel Hill
Waring
Dawnville
Rocky Face
Dalton
Mill Creek
WALKER CO
LOOPERS BEND
ROCKY FACE MOUNTAIN
Phelps
735

23

Georgia Winery

First Farm Winery Licensed in Northwest Georgia

GEORGIA WINERY WAS purchased in 1982 by Dr. Maurice Rawlings, who secured one of the first farm winery licenses in Georgia in 1983. The operation of the vineyard and winery was passed to his daughter, Patty Prouty, in 1996, and she continues to maintain Georgia Winery as a family-owned winery with the help of her daughter, Tara Taymore, and husband, Jesse, along with Patty's son, Adrian.

The large tasting room with modern production facilities is just off I-75 south of Chattanooga, Tennessee. They produce more than twenty wines annually, with prices ranging from $12.95 to $20.95. Try the Muscadine Gold and the Rawlings Ruby Red. Both are 100 percent Georgia grapes.

6469 Battlefield Parkway, Ringgold, GA 30736

Tasting room: At winery

Directions:
Take exit 350 on I-75.
Go west to KOA Road and turn north 500 ft.

Owner: Patty Prouty and family
Winemaker: Glynn Estes
Vineyard manager: Adrian Prouty
Established: Purchased 1982; farm license 1983

Altitude: 1,100 ft.
Hardiness zone: 7b 5–10 (F)
Soil: Limestone, shale
Geographical coordinates: 34.930170, -85.157075
Vineyard acreage: 52 acres planted 15 acres
Vineyard tonnage, 2016: 17.5 tons
Varietal grapes: Carlos, Noble, Fry, Regale, Jumbo, Magnolia (acreage is variable)

24

Debarge Vineyards & Winery

21058 Hwy 193, LaFayette, GA 30728

First Farm Winery in Walker County

Ray is a practicing ophthalmologist in Chattanooga, Tennessee. He acquired the vineyard property in 1998, and after traveling to Belgium, he decided wine grapes could grow well at 1,350 ft. elevation. He planted a 1.25-acre test plot with eleven Vitis vinifera and hybrids to test out what could grow best in his soil and climate.

Today, there are almost four acres planted with seven varietals. The plan is to add ten acres of vines. Debarge is the first winery in Walker County. For the last several years, Ray maintained a tasting room in Chattanooga, Tennessee, but moved his entire operation to the vineyard northeast of LaFayette. He credits his early success to his contemporary winegrowers in North Georgia who shared their local expertise. Ray produces on average a dozen white and red wines to include one fruit wine and one mead wine each year. He is particularly pleased with a blended white wine, Cloudland, and his mixed red wine, Ridge Runner. The wines range in price from $17 to $30.

The vineyard has a grand view of the mountains to the west and south.

Tasting room: At vineyard

Directions:
From LaFayette, off Hwy 27
Travel NW on Hwy 193 5.8 miles.
Vineyard on the right.

Owner: Raymond and Jane Debarge
Winemaker/Vineyard manager: Ray Debarge
Established: Bought in 1996; first planting in 2000

Altitude: 1,350 ft.
Hardiness zone: 7a 0–5 (F)
Soil: Limestone, shale
Geographical coordinates: 34.739828, -85.329289
Vineyard acreage: 56 acres, 3.4 planted
Vineyard tonnage, 2016: 15 tons
Varietal grapes: Cabernet Franc, .75 acres; Traminette, .25 acres; Cabernet Sauvignon, .4 acres; Chardonel, .5 acres; Alberino, .25 acres; Merlot, .1 acres; Chambourcin, .4 acres; Norton, .75 acres.

http://debargewines.com

Wine from long habit has become an indispensable for my health.

—Thomas Jefferson

Chapter 15

Piedmont Region

THE SECOND-LARGEST REGION in Georgia is the Piedmont, the largest population center in the state. Elevations range from 500 ft. to 1,700 ft. approaching the Blue Ridge Mountains. The most common soil feature of this region is "Georgia red clay," produced by water mixing with iron breaking down from exposed rocks. The underlying stone in this region is granite, gneiss, and marble.

Rolling hills provide good drainage, and one still encounters loamy, sandy, and clay soils. This is a productive agricultural growing area containing twenty-nine wineries with multiple grower vineyards. The distance from Jasper to Gray, Georgia, the upper and lower Piedmont cites, is approximately 125 miles north to south, and the distance from Tallapoosa to Columbia County on the Savannah River, west to east, is 205 miles. Contained within this spacious region are fourteen counties, with vineyards and wineries from over sixty counties. Growing conditions will vary throughout this region, with the most northern wineries surrounding Helen, Georgia, able to grow *Vitis vinifera*. Moving further east and south, vineyards are more likely to grow French and American hybrids or muscadine grapes for wine production. The average rainfall in Toccoa, Georgia, in Stephens County east from Helen is fifty-eight inches over ninety days.[1] Currahee Vineyard & Winery **(25)** is located south from Toccoa along Hwy 123.

---

1 Toccoa, Georgia, Weatherbase by CantyMedia, accessed September 12, 2017, http://www.weatherbase.com/weather/weather.php3?s=20837&.

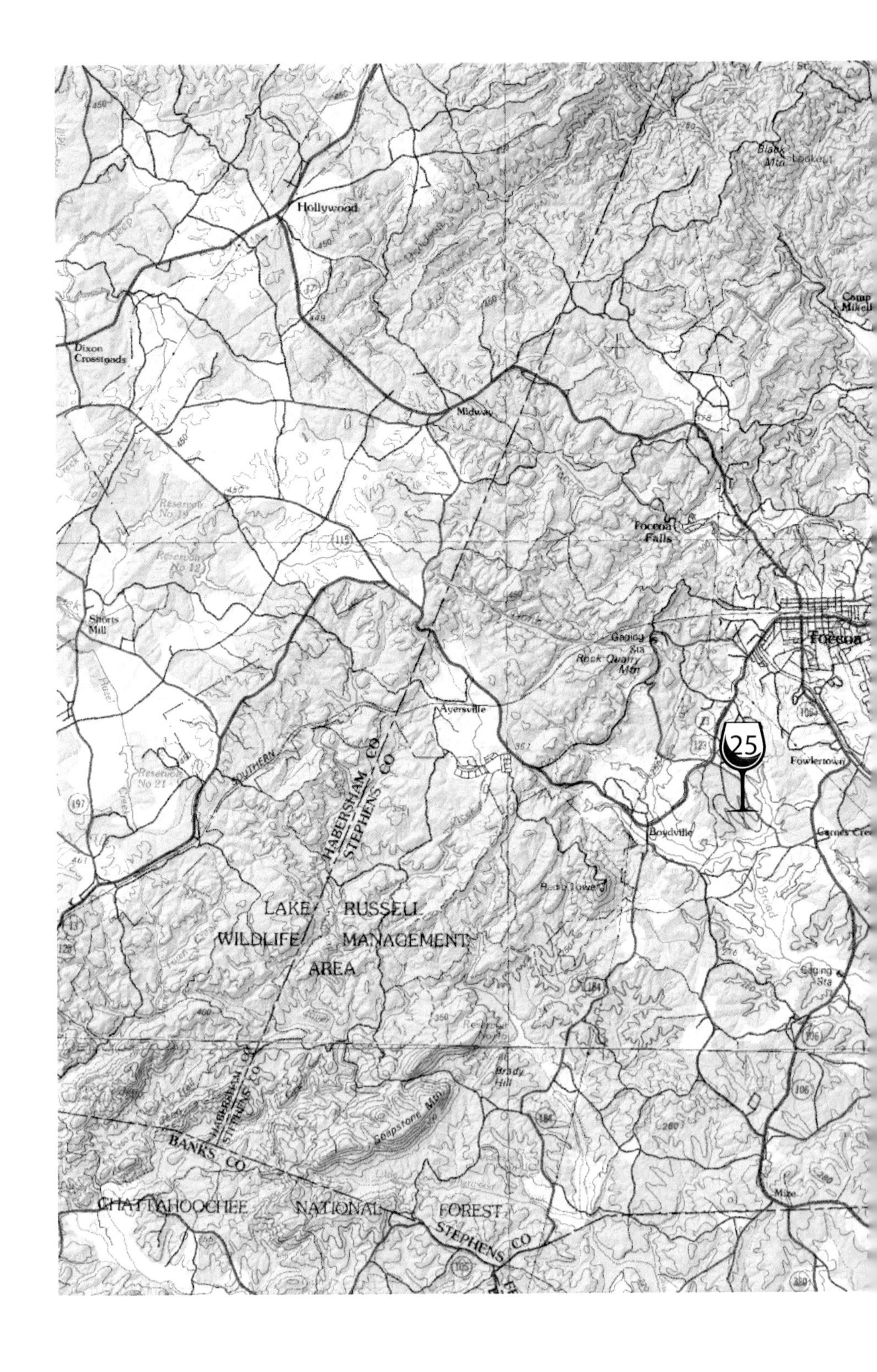

Hollywood
Dixon Crossroads
Midway
Black Mtn
Camp Mikell
Toccoa Falls
Toccoa
Gaging Sta
Rock Quarry Mtn
Shorts Mill
Ayersville
Fowlertown
25
Boydville
HABERSHAM CO
STEPHENS CO
SOUTHERN
LAKE RUSSELL
WILDLIFE MANAGEMENT
AREA
Brady Hill
Soapstone Mtn
BANKS CO
CHATTAHOOCHEE NATIONAL FOREST
STEPHENS CO
Mize

OCONEE CO
STEPHENS CO
Madison
Jarrett
Lake Louise
Old Madison
Dixon Crossroads
Airport
HARTWELL LAKE
SOUTH CAROLINA
GEORGIA
Fighting Pine
Eastanollee
Avalon
Martin
Toms Creek
STEPHENS CO
FRANKLIN CO
SOUTHERN

25

Currahee Vineyard & Winery

Family Orchard Now Hosting Vineyard and Winery

MARVIN'S DAD GREW apples on the property in the seventies and eighties. The family purchased the property in 1946. Marvin spent time in Helen, Georgia, learning about wine, which helped him decide on moving forward with a vineyard to produce wine with the assistance of Joe Smith.

Wine prices range from $14 to $28. Wines named Old Blue and Destiny stand out. Both are red wines and are excellent wines to taste and savor. Marvin plans to add additional acres for hybrid grapes Blanc du Bois and Lenoir.

Currahee Vineyard & Winery is located in the foothills of Currahee Mountain, famous as the training home in WWII for the 506th Airborne Infantry Regiment. There is an airborne museum in Toccoa that is very close to the vineyard, and both are well worth a visit.

3301 W Currahee Street, Toccoa, GA 30577

Tasting room: At vineyard and in Ellijay

Directions:
From intersection Hwy 123 and Hwy 184
Go 500 yards northeast to Hwy 184.
Turn right.
The vineyard is 3 miles from Toccoa.

Owner: Marvin Dunson and Family
Winemaker: Marvin and Joe Smith
Vineyard manager: Marvin, Chris Hansel
Established: 1995; first planted 2009; first harvest 2012

Altitude: 924 ft.
Hardiness Zone: 7b 5–10 (F)
Soil: Loamy, clay
Geographical coordinates: 34.543536, -83.356803
Vineyard acreage: 36 acres, 5 planted
Vineyard tonnage, 2016: 22 tons
Varietal grapes: Muscadine Ison, 1.25 acres; Nobel, 1.25 acres; Carlos, 1.25 acres; Tara, 1.25 acres.

(706) 768-5383 / http://www.curraheevineyards.com/

White County

The average rainfall in Helen, Georgia, in White County is seventy-one inches over 115 days.[1] Five wineries are located close to Helen: CeNita Vineyards **(26)**, Habersham Vineyards and Winery **(27)**, Serenity Cellars **(28)**, Sylvan Valley Lodge and Winery **(29)**, and Yonah Mountain Vineyards **(30)**.

1 Helen, Georgia, Weatherbase by CantyMedia, accessed September 12, 2017, http://www.weatherbase.com/weather/weather.php3?s=32490&.

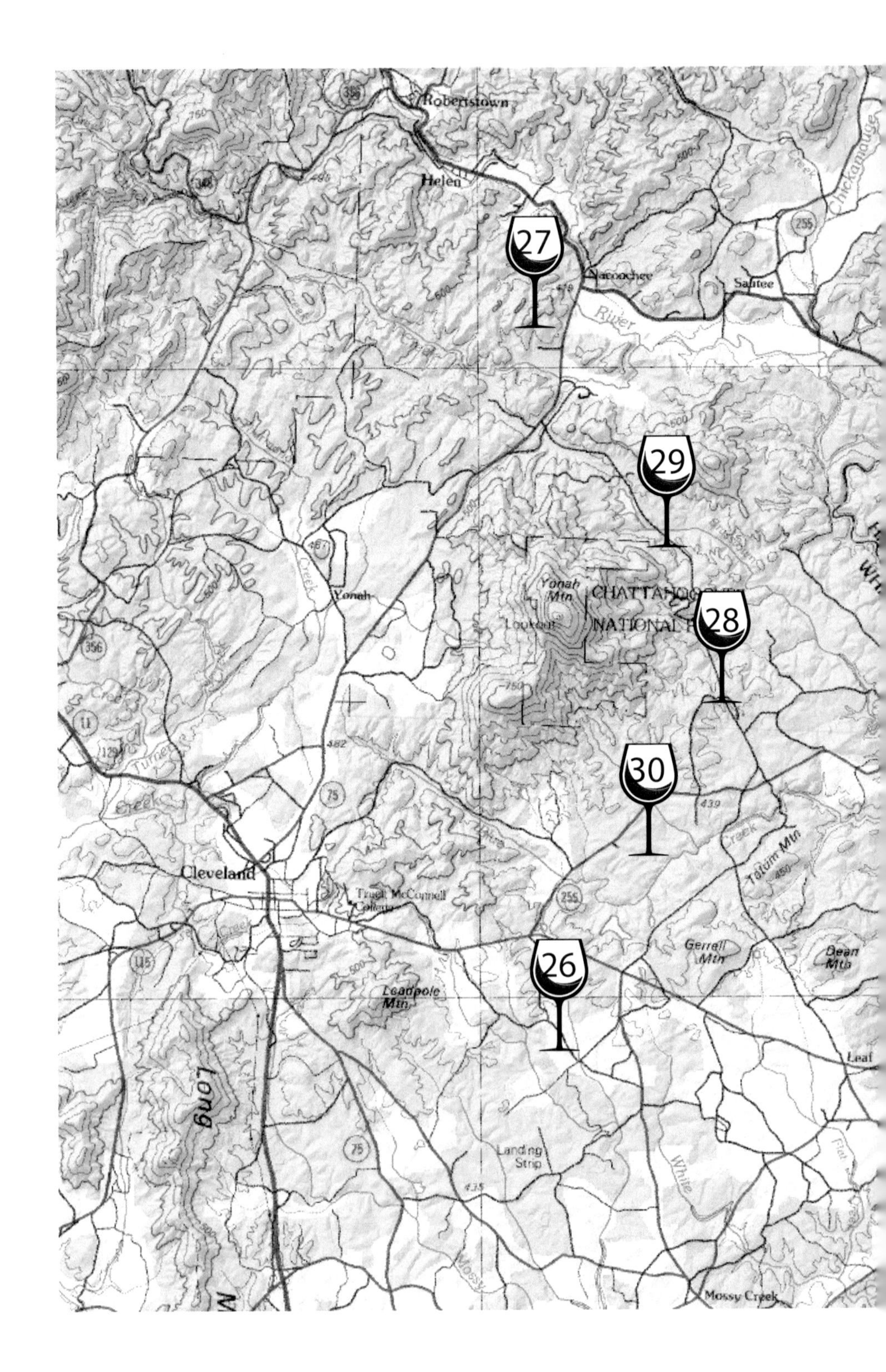

Robertstown
Helen
27
Nacoochee
Sautee
River
29
Yonah
Yonah Mtn
Lookout
CHATTAHOOCHEE
NATIONAL F
28
30
Cleveland
Truett McConnell College
Talum Mtn
Gerrell Mtn
Dean Mtn
26
Leadpole Mtn
Long
Landing Strip
White
Mossy Creek
Leaf
Chickamauga

Seed
Aerial
Harvest Mountain
Harvest
Beaverdam
Stilton
Mill
Landing Strip
Fairview
Clarkesville
Habersham
Habersham Mills Lake
Colson Store
Hospital
Demorest
Mills Ponds
Soquee
River
Creek
Yellow Bank

26

CeNita Vineyards

Two-Hundred-Acre Family Farm Makes Room for Vineyard and Winery

CeNita is on a two-hundred-acre family farm that Joe Chambers, Greg Crumley's brother, continues to farm. Greg is in construction, which provides CeNita with added resources to build and maintain the tasting room and event center, which opened in 2015.

Greg and Carol make six wines that average in price from $17 to $25. Currently, they are the only winery in Georgia growing Barbera grapes. Enjoy the Cabernet Franc and CeNita Red when you visit. The event center offers a splendid view of Yonah Mountain to the north and the luscious farmland surrounding the vineyard to the south.

591 Dock Dorsey Road, Cleveland, GA 30528

Tasting room: At vineyard

Directions:
From Cleveland
Go east on Hwy 115.
After 3 miles, turn south on Dock Dorsey Rd.
Go about half a mile. Vineyard on the left.

Owners: Greg and Carol Crumley and Joe Chambers
Winemaker/Vineyard manager: Greg Crumley
Established: 2008

Altitude: 1,527
Hardiness zone: 7b 5–10 (F)
Soil: Loamy sand, clay
Geographical coordinates: 34.583829, -83.714535
Vineyard acreage: 3.8 acres
Vineyard tonnage, 2016: 12.5 tons
Varietal grapes: Cabernet Franc, 1 acre; Chambourcin, 1 acre; Barbera, .2 acres; Vidal Blanc, 2 acres; Traminette, .6 acres; Norton, 40 plants; Cabernet Sauvignon, .5 acres; Merlot, 250 plants

27

Habersham Vineyards and Winery

Oldest Vineyard and Winery Operation in Georgia

HABERSHAM IS THE oldest winery in Georgia, and Tom Slick is the father of Georgia wines since its rebirth after Prohibition (see profile on Tom in chapter 1). Tom started out in a dry county, so his tasting room is not adjacent to the vineyards. He began planting in 1980 at the Stonepile Vineyard and then later bought the Mossy Creek Vineyard. Tom continues to be a pioneer in adding new grapes to his vineyards, bringing in Aromella recently. Andrew Beaty, a graduate of the University of California, Davis, is the longest serving winemaker in the state.

Today, Habersham produces seventeen wines in multiple categories, including Georgia-grown Vitis vinifera and hybrids, muscadine wines from grapes grown in South Georgia, and their unique Creekstone wines. The price range of these wines is from $14 to $30 per bottle. Two exceptional wines to enjoy when you visit are the Creekstone Chardonnay and Cherokee Rose, both award-winning wines.

7025 S. Main Street, Helen, GA 30545

Tasting room: At vineyard and 16 North Park Street, Public Square, Dahlonega, GA and 430 McCracken Street, Juliette, GA

Directions:
Located 1/2 Mile South of Helen on Hwy 75 on the west side.

Owner: Tom Slick
General manager: Emily DeFoor
Winemaker: Andrew Beaty
Vineyard manager: Matt Chobanian
Established: 1980

Altitude: 1,377
Hardiness zone: 7b 5–10 (F)
Soil: Loamy, sand, clay (two vineyard sites: Stonepile and Mossy Creek)
Geographical coordinates: 34.6895035, -83.7118937
Vineyard acreage: 39.6 acres planted
Vineyard tonnage, 2016: 70 tons
Varietal grapes: Chardonnay, 6.30 acres; Cabernet Sauvignon, 6.30 acres; Merlot, 3.4 acres; Chambourcin, 8.4 acres; Traminette, 2.2 acres; Vidal Blanc, 5.2 acres; Seyval Blanc, 4.25 acres; Cabernet Franc, .75 acres; Chardonel, 1.7 acres; Aromella, 1.1 acres.

28

Serenity Cellars

From Music to Winemaking

We know Joe Smith as a winemaker, but not as a recording engineer, producer, and songwriter mainly associated with Jive Records, a business he was in for twenty years with notables like the Backstreet Boys and Aaron Carter. Yet wine was always Joe's hobby growing up in the Finger Lakes region of New York.

Joe and Tina produce twelve wines on average, ranging in price from $18 to $32. Try the Chardonnay and Cabernet Sauvignon, and count on Joe having great musical entertainment while you enjoy your wines on a weekend or special event. Joe is the winemaker for several other Georgia wineries.

265 Laurel Ridge Road, Cleveland, GA 30528

Tasting room: At vineyard

Directions:
From Hwy 75 linking Cleveland to Helen
Turn east onto Hwy 384.
Travel 3.2 miles to Laurel Ridge Rd.
Turn south .25 miles.
Vineyard on left.

Owners: Joe and Tina Smith
Winemaker/Vineyard manager: Joe Smith
Established: 2013

Altitude: 1,535 ft.
Hardiness zone: 7b 5–10 (F)
Soil: Loamy, sand, clay
Geographical coordinates: 34.6356270, -83.690905
Vineyard acreage: 1.5 acres
Vineyard tonnage, 2016: 3.2 tons
Varietal grapes: Cabernet Sauvignon, 600 plants; Sangiovese, 400 plants.

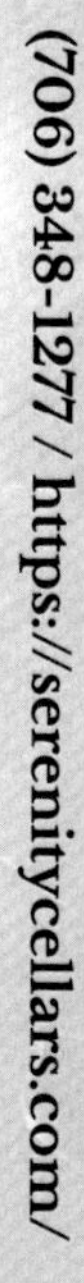

29

Sylvan Valley Lodge and Cellars

A Lodge and Restaurant Transition to Vineyard and Winery

THIS VINEYARD IS currently in the process of removing the Muscat Blanc grapes. John and Ginevra originally bought the lodge and restaurant in 2004. In 2007, they made a decision to convert the restaurant to a tasting room, lodge, and vineyard. They produce nine wines under the Frolicking Faerie label. The two wines to be certain to enjoy are the Frolicking Izzy, a blend of Cabernet Sauvignon and Chambourcin, and the Frolicking Faerie Sybil, a dry rosé wine that is well crafted, light, crisp, and a joy to drink, a blend of Vidal Blanc and Cynthiana. All the grapes are Georgia grown. They are planting more grapevines in the spring of 2017.

747 Duncan Bridge Road, Sautee Nacoochee, GA 30571

Tasting room: At vineyard

Directions:
Go north from Cleveland on Hwy 75.
Turn right onto Hwy 384.
Go 1.12 miles. Vineyard on left.

Owner: John and Ginevra Boyes and John Edgar Boyes
Winemaker/Vineyard manager: John Edgar Boyes
Established: Purchased in 2004; started winery and tasting room in 2007

Altitude: 1,530 ft.
Hardiness zone: 7a 0–5 (F)
Soil: Loamy, sand, clay, granite
Geographical coordinates: 34.661382, -83.707028
Vineyard acreage: 6 acres, entire new planting 2017
Vineyard tonnage, 2016: None
Varietal grapes: Initial planting was Muscat Blanc, .25 acres.

30

Yonah Mountain Vineyards

State-of-the-Art Tasting Room and Event Facilities

Bob's career in financial services trained him well to do his research before making the purchase of his Yonah Mountain vineyard. Today, Bob and Jane have nearly twenty acres planted since they bought the property in 2005. Their focus is on Vitis vinifera grapes, with some grapes being brought in from out of state.

Their wines range in price from $32 to $107 for standard 750 ml bottles. They make eight different wines; I recommend tasting their estate wines. They have one of the most modern tasting rooms and event facilities in Georgia, and they take great pride in the quality of their wines and the hospitality they provide their guests.

1717 Highway 255, Cleveland, GA 30528

Tasting room: At vineyard

Directions:
From Hwy. 75 from Cleveland
Turn right at Hwy 384.
Go 5 miles to Hwy. 255 S.
Turn right. Go 1 mile.
Vineyard on right.

Owners: Bob and Jane Miller
Winemaker: Joe Smith
Vineyard manager: Jeff Parker
Established: 2005

Altitude: 1,420 ft.
Hardiness zone: 7b 5–10 (F)
Soil: Loamy, sand, clay
Geographical coordinates: 34.613160, -83.6929634
Vineyard acreage: 197 acres, 17.28 planted
Vineyard tonnage, 2016: 38 tons
Varietal grapes: Sauvignon Blanc, .33 acres; Chardonnay, 3.6 acres; Petit Manseng, 3.5 acres; Cabernet Sauvignon, 3.5 acres; Merlot, 3 acres; Cabernet Franc, 1.75 acres; Malbec, .2 acres; Petit Verdot, 1.4 acres.

(706) 878-5522 / http://www.yonahmountainvineyards.com/

Pickens and Cherokee Counties are located in the Piedmont region. Jasper is the largest city within Pickens County, with Ball Ground immediately adjacent in Cherokee County. The average rainfall is fifty-seven inches and 104 days with precipitation.[1] Four wineries are located in these two counties: Fainting Goat **(31)**, Sharp Mountain Winery **(32)**, Big Door Vineyards and Winery **(33)**, and Feather's Edge **(34)**.

1 Jasper, Georgia, Weatherbase by CantyMedia, accessed September 12, 2017, http://www.weatherbase.com/weather/weather.php3?s=846490&.

Blaine
Talking Rock
Ranger
Ludville
Jerusalem
TALLY MTN
SHARP TOP MTN
Lookout tower
RICH MTN
32
WHITE MTN
SALACOA VALLEY
EAGLE MTN
OAKEY MTN
PICKENS COUNTY
CHEROKEE COUNTY
Bolivar
GARLAND
Microwave tower
Rydal
Lookout tower
Waleska
BYRD MTN
Keithsburg
33
South Canton
Canton

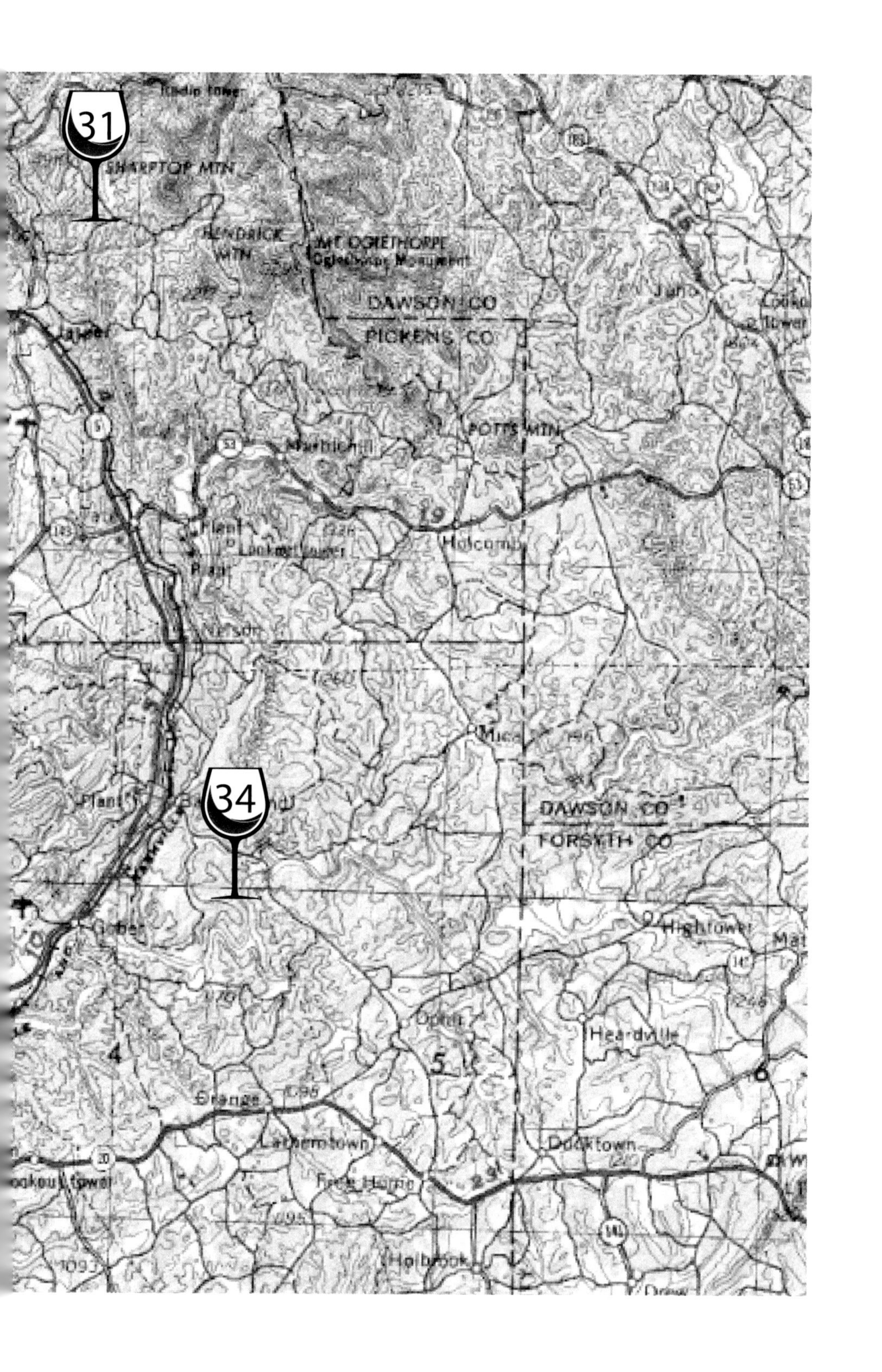

31
SHARPTOP MTN
HENDRICK MTN
MT OGLETHORPE
DAWSON CO
PICKENS CO
POTTS MTN
Nelson
34
DAWSON CO
FORSYTH CO
Hightower
Heardville
Orange
Ducktown
Holbrook

31

Fainting Goat Winery

Experienced Ohio Farmers Establish Vineyard and Winery

Dave and Robin come from a farming background. They grew peaches and raised farm animals in Ohio, later moving to Marietta, Georgia, in 2007.

Today they offer eleven wines ranging in price from $19 to $38. They provide a broad cross section of *Vitis vinifera*, hybrid grapes, and muscadine grapes. The muscadines Carlos and Noble come from Gin Creek in South Georgia. Two wines they are particularly proud to offer include a Cabernet Sauvignon–blended "1812" and a Barbera wine.

201 Vineyard Way, Jasper, GA 30143

Tasting room: At vineyard

Directions:
From Jasper
Take Burnt Mountain road north 3.5 miles.
Turn right. Go 3.4 miles.
Winery on the left.

Owners: Dave and Robin Higginbotham and daughter McKenzie
Winemaker: McKenzie Higginbotham
Vineyard manager: Dave Higginbotham
Established: Purchased in 2010; planted in 2013; opened tasting room in 2015

Altitude: 1,548 ft.
Hardiness zone: 7b 5–10 (F)
Soil: Loamy, sand, clay
Geographical coordinates: 34.4953050, -84.3843519
Vineyard acreage: 2 acres planted
Vineyard tonnage, 2016: 3.5 tons
Varietal grapes: Cabernet Sauvignon, 1.25 acres; Merlot, .75 acres.

(706) 692-9463 / http://www.faintinggoatvineyardsandwinery.com/

32

Sharp Mountain Winery

Veteran Winemaker Going Strong for More Than Twenty Years

RON, WITH HIS Sharp Mountain Vineyards and Winery, is a twenty-year winemaking veteran who grows twelve different varietal *Vitis vinifera* grapes. Sharp Mountain Winery offers great early-evening mountain views to the north.

The winery has its own microclimate west of Jasper, Georgia. Ron and Jody produce fifteen wines ranging in price from $12.95 to $29.95. Two distinctive wines to enjoy are their Gewürztraminer and Collage, a Bordeaux blend of three red grapes.

Tasting room: At vineyard

Directions:
From Hwy 515
Go west at Salem Church Rd. 3.8 miles.
Turn right onto Pettit Rd./Sharp Mountain Parkway .5 miles.
Turn right on Rathgeb Trail.

Owners: Ron and Jody Rathgeb
Winemaker/Vineyard manager: Ron Rathgeb
Established: 1995

Altitude: 1,385 to 1,500 ft.
Hardiness zone: 7b 5–10 (F)
Soil: Loamy, sand, clay
Geographical coordinates: 34.4430350, -84.4868330
Vineyard acreage: 5.15 acres
Vineyard tonnage, 2016: 8 tons
Varietal grapes: Pinot Noir, .2 acres; Gewürztraminer, .75 acres; Pinot Gris, .2 acres; Chardonnay, .75 acres; Sauvignon Blanc, .5 acres; Trebbiano, .5 acres; Viognier, .5 acres; Cabernet Franc, .5 acres; Cabernet Sauvignon, .75 acres; Sangiovese, .1 acres; Primitivo, .25 acres; Merlot, .15 acres.

(770) 735-1210 / http://www.sharpmountainvineyards.com

33

Big Door Vineyards

A New Vineyard and Winery

TASTING ROOM TO open in December 2017. They are harvesting grapes in coordination with Ed Perry at Horse Creek while construction continues.

125 Clearwater Trail NE, White, GA 30184

Tasting room: At vineyard

Directions:
From Knox Bridge Hwy
Turn north on Clearwater Trail.
Travel 1,000 ft.
The vineyard is on the left.

Owners: Rodney Alldredge and Ray Parker
Winemakers: Ed Perry and Travis Green
Vineyard manager: Ray Parker
Established: Purchased in 2012; tasting room opened in 2017

Altitude: 1,000 to 1,100 ft.
Hardiness zone: 7b 5–10 (F)
Soil: Loamy, clay, silt, and sand
Geographical coordinates: 34.215571, -84.650820
Vineyard acreage: 16.5 acres, 10 planted
Vineyard tonnage, 2016: 8 tons
Varietal grapes: Lenoir, 2 acres; Lomanto, 4 acres; Blanc du Bois, 3 acres; Villard Blanc, 1 acre.

(470) 377-2137 / http://www.bigdoorvineyards.com/

34

Feather's Edge Vineyards

10061 Ball Ground Hwy, Ball Ground, GA 30107

First Vineyard and Winery within a City Limit

David and Julie have owned the well-appointed American craft gallery Wild Cat on a Wing for many years. Today the tasting room for Feather's Edge is connected to Wild Cat.

David planted a test vineyard in 2011 to determine what grapes would grow best in this Piedmont soil. Today, he has 5.5 acres and plans to add more. They produce four wines under the Feather's Edge label and, in collaboration with other wineries, offer nine other wines. Wine prices range from $16.50 to $30. Feather's Edge is one of the few wineries and vineyards in Georgia within a city limit.

Tasting room: At vineyard

Direction:
One mile north from Ball Ground on Ball Ground Hwy

Owners: David and Julie Boone
Winemaker/Vineyard manager: David Boone
Established: 1989–1994; planted from 2011 to 2014

Altitude: 1,260 ft.
Hardiness Zone: 7b 5–10 (F)
Soil: Clay, granite base
Geographical coordinates: 34.352673, -84.379682
Vineyard acreage: 24 acres, 5.5 planted
Vineyard tonnage, 2016: 306 gallons
Varietal grapes: Norton, 1.5 acres; Catawba, .75 acres; Blanc du Bois, .75 acres; Tara, 1 acre; Noble, 1.25 acres; Carlos, .25 acres.

(770) 735-6923 / http://feathersedgevineyards.com/

Fulton County has only City Winery **(35)**. Grapes are purchased locally for selected wines sold in this entertainment winery venue. The winery is located in downtown Atlanta.

Samuel Inman
Sch
Henry Grady
High Sch
Empire
BM 884
VIRGINIA
AVE
Park
Parks
GREENWOOD
950
900
Linwo
972
PONCE DE LEON
BM 962
NORTH
35
1000
Parks
Hill
Sch
Parks
Pk
Comm
Tower
Library
Pk
1025
Georgia
Medical Center
HIGHLAND
AVE
10
Mt Zion

Callanwolde
Art Center
Montag
BM 1016
984
SPRINGDALE
OAKDALE
950
896
1019
AVE
PARKS
Ponce
FULTON CO
DE KALB CO
AVENUE
Goldsboro
Park
1000
Mary Lin
Sch
Golf Course
Candler
Park
HIGHLAND
Little
Five Points
AVE
MCLENDON
Mclendon
BM 1024
Park
Pk
Edgewood
Fire
Sta
DE KALB
Comm
Tower

35

City Winery

650 North Avenue, Ponce City Market, Atlanta, GA 30308

Fifth City Winery in America

Michael Dorf founded the city winery concept in New York and then proceeded to open venues in Chicago, Napa, Nashville, and then Atlanta in 2016. The concept is to integrate dining, entertainment, and wine into a place that allows wine production within the facility. David Lecomte, from France, is the chief winemaker in New York, and Travis Green is the Atlanta winemaker. The concept includes purchasing local grapes for their production facility. The first grapes brought into City Winery were from a twenty-year-old winery in North Georgia. Their ice wine–style Vin du Glaçière, Gone with the Vin made from Vidal Blanc, is the only Georgia wine award winner. They won the 2017 Oglethorpe Award for the Best Georgia Wine.

(404) 946-3791 / http://www.citywinery.com/atlanta/

Tasting room: In winery

Directions:
Corner of North Avenue and Glen Iris Drive adjacent to Ponce City Market

Owner: Michael Dorf in New York
Atlanta Winemaker: Travis Green
Established: 2008 in New York

Hall, Madison, and Barrow Counties contain one winery each: Sweet Acre Farms **(36)**, Boutier Vineyards **(37)**, and Château Élan **(38)**. Commerce, Georgia, central to these three wineries, has an annual rainfall at 52.4 inches with an average of 104 precipitation days.[1]

1 Commerce, Georgia, Weatherbase by CantyMedia, accessed September 12, 2017, http://www.weatherbase.com/weather/weather.php3?s=81290&.

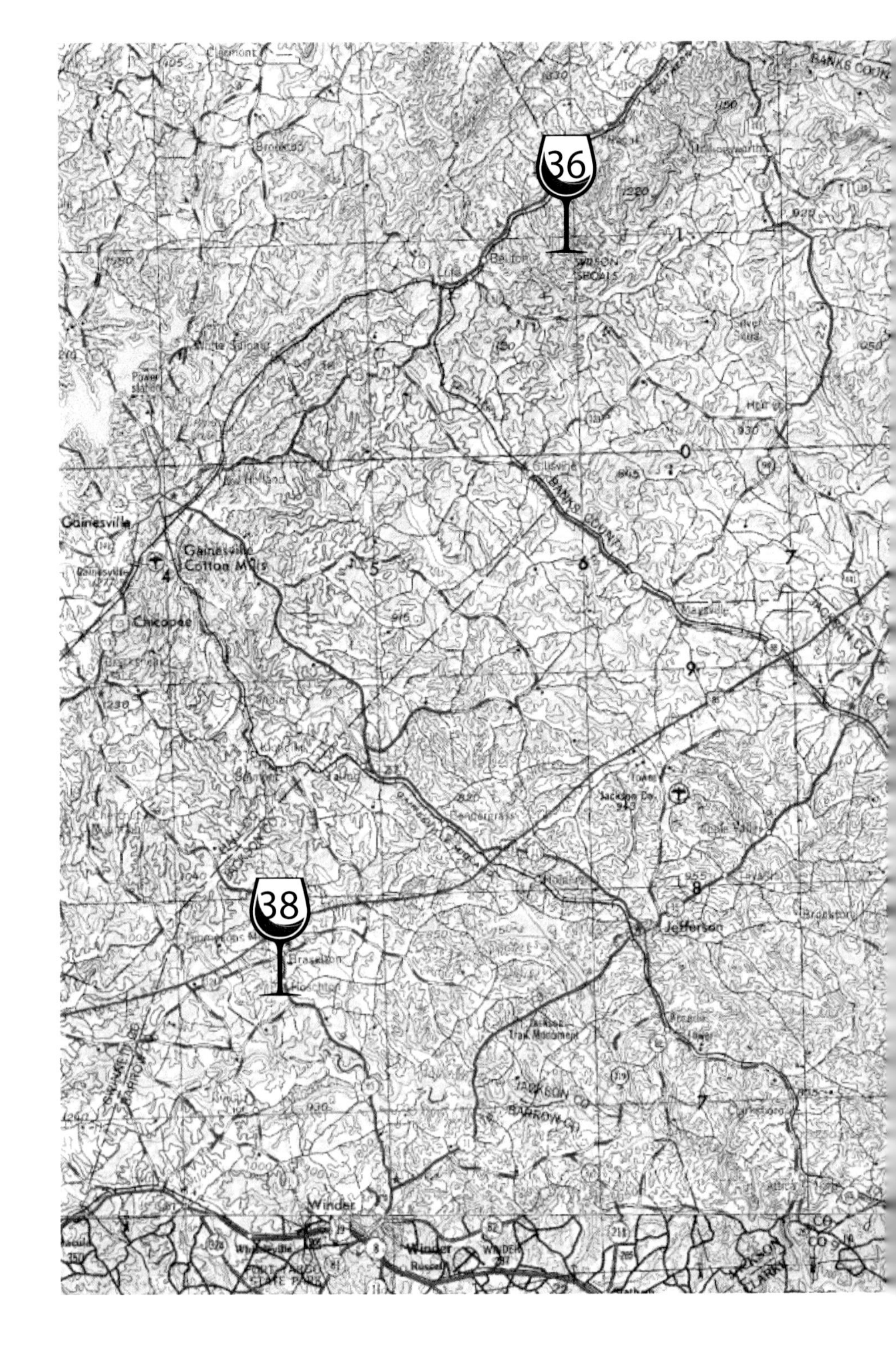

36
38
Gainesville
Gainesville
Cotton Mills
Chicopee
Jefferson
Winder
Braselton
Hoschton
Maysville
BANKS COUNTY
JACKSON CO
BARROW CO
Jackson Co.
Wilson Shoals
Baldwin
Lula
New Holland
White Sulphur
Clermont
Whitesville
Fort Yargo State Park

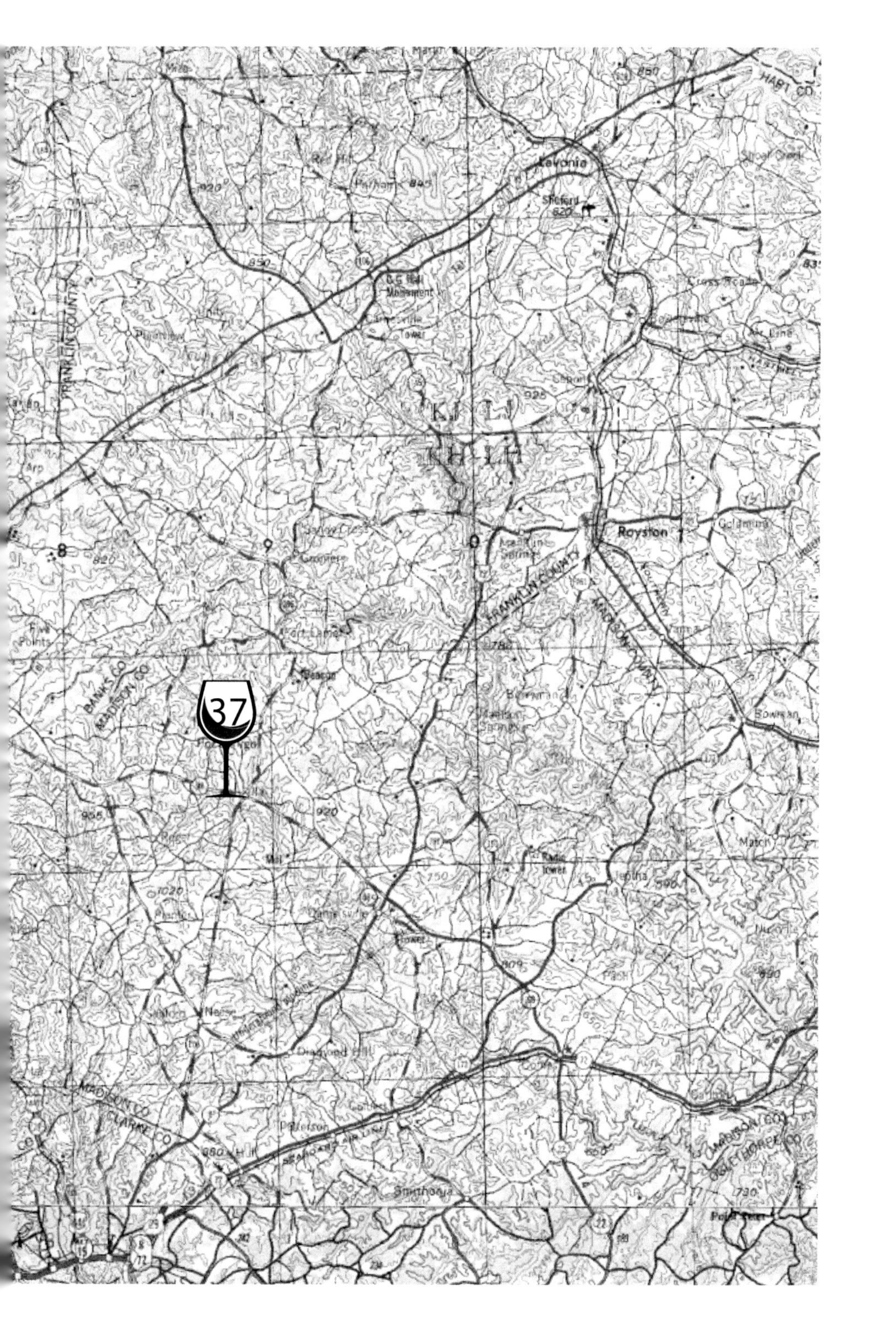
HART CO
Lavonia
Red Hill
Parham
Shirley
FRANKLIN COUNTY
Cross Roads
Royston
FRANKLIN COUNTY
MADISON COUNTY
Five Points
BANKS CO
MADISON CO
37
Bowman
Radio tower
Danielsville
Diamond Hill
Neese
MADISON CO
CLARKE CO
SEABOARD AIR LINE
Smithonia
MADISON CO
OGLETHORPE CO

36

Sweet Acre Farms

Youngest Winery Owners in Georgia

Matthew and Lindsey met at Valdosta State and are the youngest winery owners in the state. Their vineyard land was purchased over several years and now covers forty-six acres. Their expertise is fruit wines without concentrate and bottled unfiltered to reinforce natural fruit flavors.

Currently all the fruit, except for fresh lemons from Texas, is bought in Georgia, along with white and red muscadine grapes. Matt is the winemaker and produces thirteen to fifteen wines annually in a price range from $14 to $29. He particularly recommends his Sweet Ass Peach and Red Muscadine wines as two of his favorites. I would also encourage visitors to give the lemon-based wine a taste. Located fifteen miles north of Gainesville in the Piedmont region, he has the option to grow grapes. There is also a spacious tasting room for a group visit.

7584 Bill Wilson Road, Alto, GA 30510

Tasting room: At vineyard

Direction:
15 miles north of Gainesville on Hwy 985/23
Go NW on Belton Bridge Road 1.6 miles.
Turn right onto Bill Wilson Road.
Go 1.1 miles. Winery on right.

Owners: Matthew and Lindsey Vrahiotes
Winemaker/Farm manager: Matthew Vrahiotes
Established: 2010, 25 acres; 2012, 21 acres

Altitude: 1,269 ft.
Hardiness zone: 7b 5–10 (F)
Soil: Shale, slate, clay, loam
Geographical coordinates: 34.437144, -83.657828
Vineyard acreage: Blackberry, 1 acre; blueberry, .25 acres.

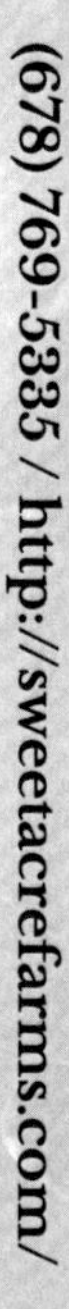

37

Boutier Winery

4506 Hudson River Church Road, Danielsville, GA 30633

Old Vineyards Regained

Victor is originally from the Netherlands and Mary is from Ireland. He came to the USA working in international ocean freight. He already had a keen interest in brewing beer, which set him up to pursue winemaking.

The Boutier Winery has a storied history. It first opened around 1991–1993 as Watermelon Ranch owned by Gene Mara, later becoming Acoustic Vineyard. Victor moved here in 2008. He is also growing blueberries and blackberries.

Victor and Mary make around twenty different wines in a price range from $14.99 to $18.99. Their Georgia Peach Wine Diva Licious and Madison County Norton are two award-winning wines. Also, be sure to try the Riesling when you visit.

Tasting room: At vineyard

Directions:
Take I-75 / 85 North to I-85 North.
Take exit 149 (Tanger Outlet Center).
Turn right on the Hwy 441.
Follow directions on website 11 miles to winery.

Owners: Mary Jakupi Boutier and Victor Boutier
Winemaker/Vineyard manager: Victor Boutier
Established: 2008

Altitude: 787 ft.
Hardiness zone: 7b 5–10 (F)
Soil: Red clay, thinner soil
Geographical coordinates: 34.234472, -83.310966
Vineyard acreage: 4.5 acres planted
Vineyard tonnage, 2016: 4.5 tons
Varietal grapes: Norton, 2 acres; Blanc du Bois, .5 acres; Lenoir, 1 acre; Cabernet Sauvignon, .25 acres; Chardonnay, .25 acres; Cabernet Franc, .25 acres; Villard Blanc, .25 acres.

(706) 789-0059 / http://boutierwinery.com/

38

Château Élan

Oldest Resort Vineyards and Winery in Georgia

Château Élan, one of the three oldest wineries in Georgia, opened in 1984 by Don and Nancy Panoz (see chapter 1 for details on Don). Originally, the vineyard planted *Vitis vinifera* grapes, but the low altitude and heat could not hold off infestation from Pierce's disease. When Simone was brought in as the executive winemaker, he had vast educational and winemaking experience in Italy, and in 2008 he moved to the United States to gain broader experience in East Coast winemaking. He has a degree in oenology and viticulture from Turin University.

After his arrival, the decision was made in 2013 to remove all the old, struggling vines and replace them with thirty acres of muscadines and bring in juice from California. Today, Simone produces twenty-eight wines ranging in price from $11.95 to $49.99. He produces two Muscadry wines, a white and rosé, from grapes grown on the estate, and he is particularly pleased with super premium wines.

100 Rue Charlemagne, Braselton, GA 30517

Tasting room: At vineyard

Directions:
From I-85, take exit 126 North.
The Chateau is immediately on the left.

Owner: Hank Evers
Winemaker/Vineyard manager: Simone Bergese
Established: 1984

Altitude: 957 ft.
Hardiness zone: 7b 5–10 (F)
Soil: Loamy red clay
Geographical coordinates: 34.1020576, -83.8172650
Vineyard acreage: 40+ acres, 33 planted
Vineyard tonnage, 2016: 30 tons from 18 acres
Varietal grapes: Carlos, 23 acres; Noble, 10 acres.

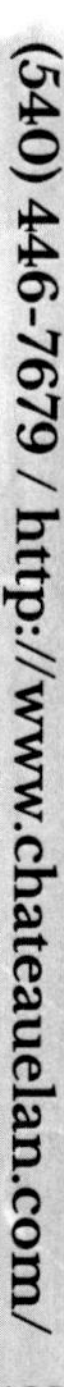

Walton County has one vineyard and winery, Fox Vineyard & Winery **(39)**, in Covington, Georgia. It is nine miles from Social Circle and has an average annual rainfall of 49.2 inches over one hundred days annually.[1]

1 Covington, Georgia, Weatherbase by CantyMedia, accessed September 12, 2017, http://www.weatherbase.com/weather/weather.php3?s=813290.

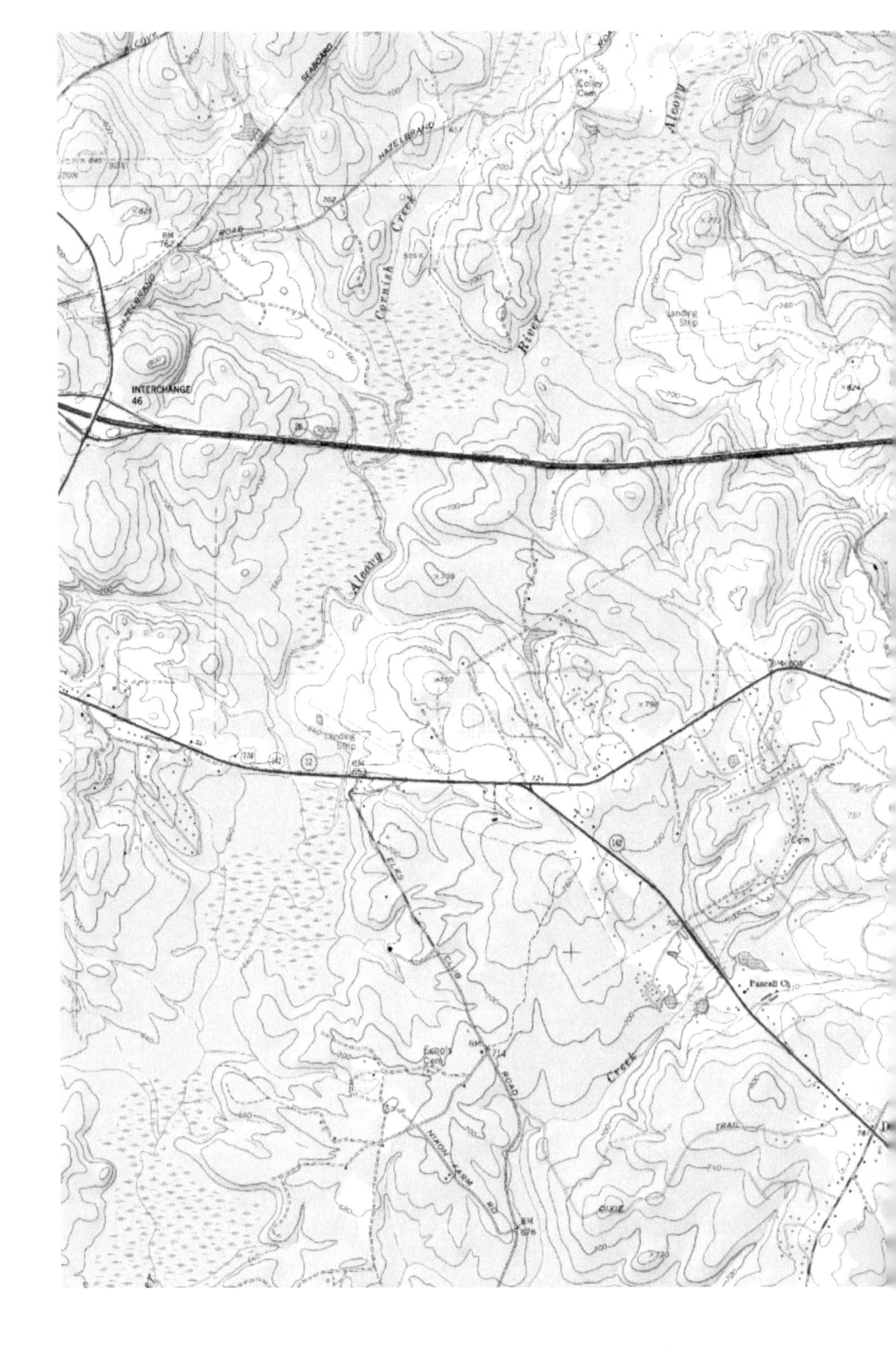

SEABOARD
HAZELBRAND
ROAD
Colley Cem
Alcovy
Cornish
Creek
River
Landing Strip
INTERCHANGE
46
Alcovy
Landing Strip
ELKS
CLUB
ROAD
Echols Cem
NIXON FARM RD
Creek
Pascall Ch
TRAIL
DIXIE
Cem

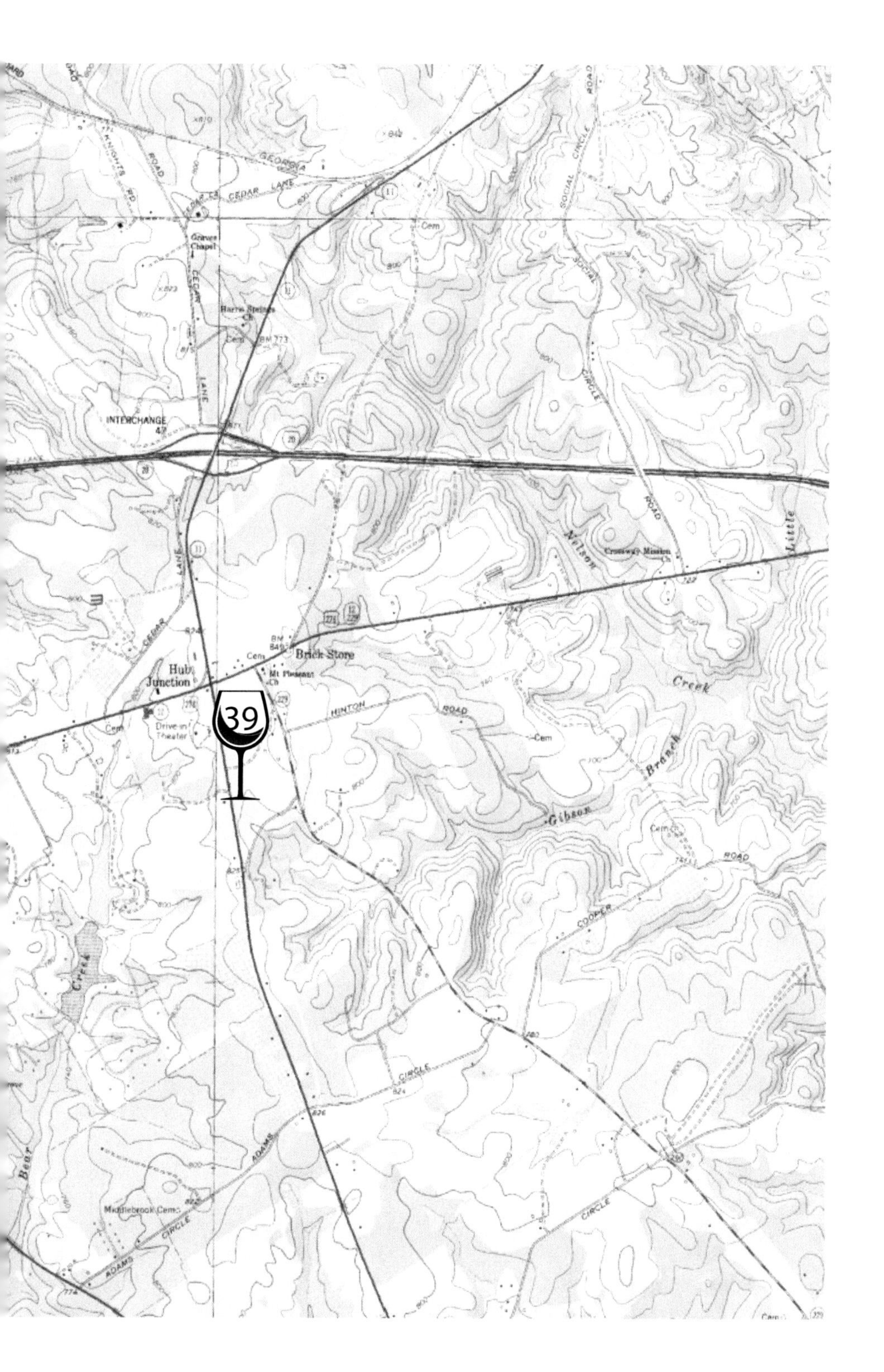

39
Hub Junction
Brick Store
INTERCHANGE 47
Drive-in Theater
HINTON ROAD
Gibson
Branch
Creek
Little
Nelson
CEDAR LANE
SOCIAL CIRCLE ROAD
COOPER ROAD
CIRCLE
ADAMS CIRCLE
Middlebrook Cem
Bear
Creek
Cem
GEORGIA
Graves Chapel
Harris Springs Ch
Crossway Mission Ch
Mt Pleasant Ch
KNIGHTS RD

39

Fox Vineyard & Winery

225 Highway 11 S., Social Circle, GA 30025

An Early Winery in Georgia Challenged by Altitude and Disease

JOHN FUCHS, A former Eastern Airlines pilot, established what would become a fifteen-acre vineyard and winery. Given the low altitude and heat, the Vitis vinifera and hybrids he planted eventually succumbed to Pierce's disease. Apparently, for several years the winery did not take action to replace these vines and finally planted muscadine grapevines indigenous to the region. When I visited the tasting room, John was no longer able to conduct interviews. There were about a dozen wines for sale, and large, full tanks were waiting for bottling. I tasted the Captain's Choice, a red, semisweet wine, 10 percent alcohol, with a nice aroma and taste similar to a dessert wine with a dark, ruby-red color, almost like grape juice.

Tasting room: At vineyard

Directions:
Take I-20 East toward Augusta.
Take exit 98 (Hwy 11).
Turn right on Hwy 11 for approximately 2 miles.
The vineyard is on your left.

Owner: John Fuchs
Winemaker/Vineyard manager: Kenneth Fuchs
Established: 1983

Altitude: 887 ft.
Hardiness zone: 7b 5–10 (F)
Soil: Loamy, clay
Geographical coordinates: 33.593526, -83.748148
Vineyard acreage: 4–5 acres
Vineyard tonnage, 2016: Unknown
Varietal grapes: Carlos, 1.5 acres; Fry, 1 acre; Noble, 1.5 acres; Cowart, .5 acres (estimates).

(770) 787-5402 / http://www.foxvinwinery.com/Home/tabid/56/Default

The West Georgia Piedmont region, including Haralson and Carroll Counties, contains two farm wineries, including a vineyard with a separate tasting room in Villa Rica, Georgia. Historic Tallapoosa, Georgia, averages 51.5 inches annually in rain with precipitation averaging ninety-four days.[1] The Vineyards at Mill Creek's tasting room, Uncorked, is located in Villa Rica **(40)**, Trillium Vineyard **(41)**, and Little Vine Vineyards **(42)**.

1 Tallapoosa, Georgia, Weatherbase by CantyMedia, accessed September 12, 2017, http://www.weatherbase.com/weather/weather.php3?s=745890.

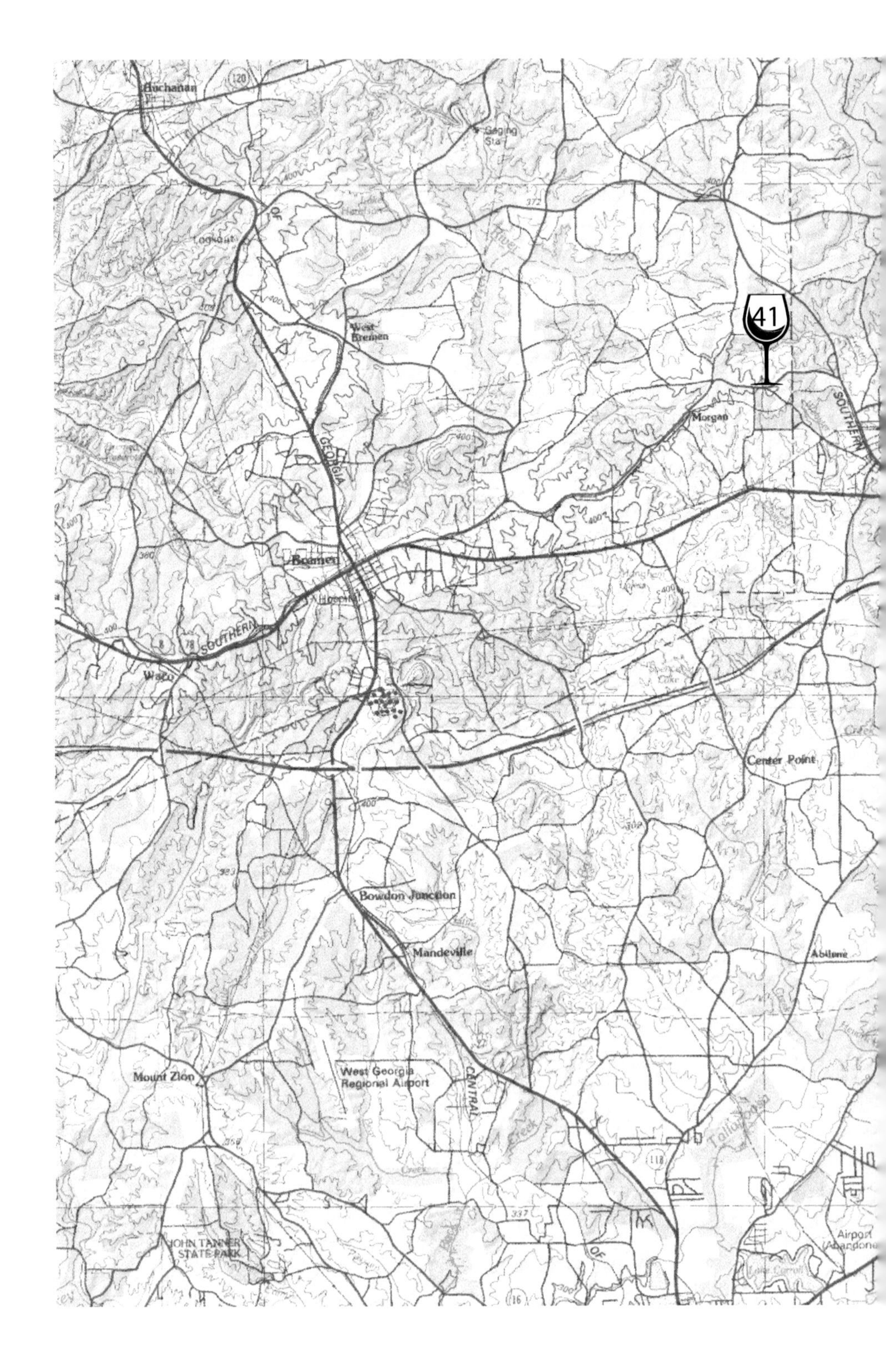

41
Buchanan
West Bremen
Bremen
Morgan
Waco
Center Point
Bowdon Junction
Mandeville
Abilene
Mount Zion
West Georgia Regional Airport
JOHN TANNER STATE PARK

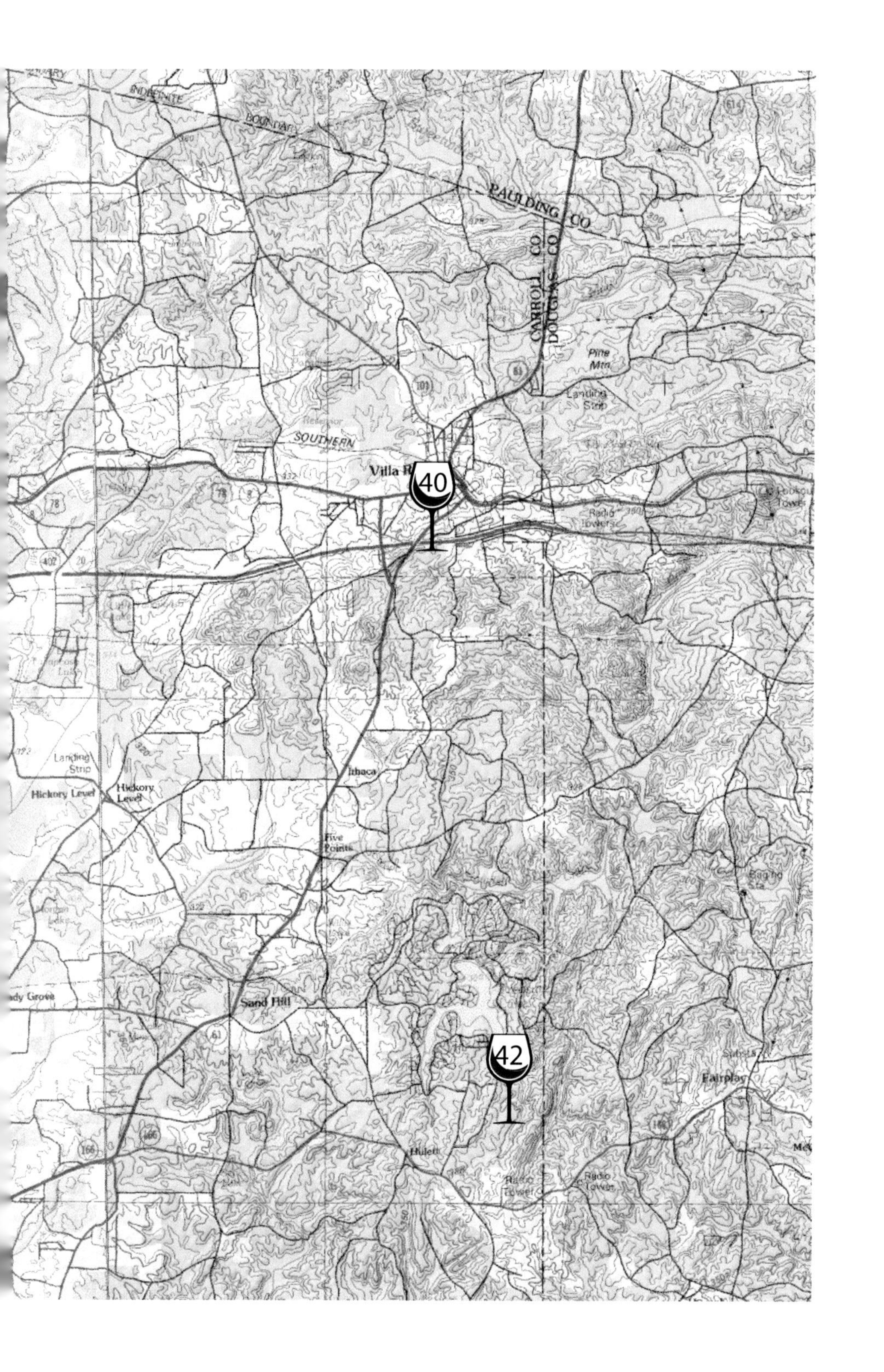

PAULDING CO
CARROLL CO
DOUGLAS CO
Pine Mtn
Landing Strip
SOUTHERN
Villa R
40
Radio towers
Landing Strip
Hickory Level
Hickory Level
Ithaca
Five Points
Sand Hill
42
Fairplay
Hulett
Radio Tower
Radio Tower

40

The Vineyards at Mill Creek

Family Farm Winery

THE LAND, WHICH stretches seventy-nine acres, was purchased in 1981 to farm. Randy came to Georgia from California to build a manufacturing plant. He grew up on a farm in Pennsylvania. Over time, Randy and his family became more interested in growing grapes. In 2012, they planted their first grapes. He hopes to expand by ten to twelve acres.

His tasting room is in Villa Rica just off Hwy 20. Randy installed water-collection tanks to ensure he would have water during the driest months, which serve to supplement small ponds in the vineyard. The water is collected off tin roofs in the vineyard. Randy is also growing his own cuttings to support the expansion of the vineyard. Currently, Randy sells grapes to Ed Perry at Horse Creek and to Marvin Dunson at Currahee Vineyard and Winery. They both produce the wine and then sell the product back to distribute the wine in Villa Rica at Uncorked on Main. I expect they will move to a farm winery license in 2017.

664 Waddell Road, Bremen, GA 30110

Tasting room: 129 Main St, Villa Rica, GA 30180

Owners: Randy and Ann Muller and Joey Muller
Winemaker: Ed Perry at Horse Creek
Vineyard manager: Joey Muller
Established: 2012

Altitude: 1,274 ft.
Hardiness zone: 7b 5–10 (F)
Soil: Loamy, clay
Geographical coordinates: 33.7926248, -850852830
Vineyard acreage: 4.5 acres
Vineyard tonnage, 2016: 13 tons
Varietal grapes: Blanc du Bois, 2.5 acres; Lenoir, 1.5 acres; Lomanto, .25 acres; Villard Blanc, .25 acres.

41

Trillium Vineyard

1968 Old Bush Mill Road, Bremen, GA 30110

Aviator Lets His Sheep Keep the Vineyard Trim

Bruce spent twenty years in the US Navy flying P-3 Orion aircraft before retiring as a commander. The land Trillium Vineyards sits upon was already in Bruce's family and was used as pasture ground for horses, but the setting was ideal for a vineyard. Bruce began raising alpaca on the land but fenced them off from the vineyard when they made the decision to produce wine.

A decision was made two years ago to place a UGA test site on the property testing four grapes. Babydoll Southdown sheep are efficient mowers and trimmers and provide organic fertilizer with their small deposits. Most importantly, they do not harm the fruit. Production will start in 2017.

Under construction

Tasting room: At vineyard

Directions:
Take Hwy 20 North to Waddell Street 3 miles.
Go left 1.8 miles to Old Bush Mill Road.
Go right 1 mile. Vineyard on right.

Owners: Bruce and Karen Cross
Winemakers: Thomas Payette and Bruce Cross
Vineyard manager: Bruce Cross
Established: 2015

Altitude: 1,265 ft.
Hardiness zone: 7b 5–10 (F)
Soil: Loam with gravel capped with clay
Geographical coordinates: 33.753565, -85.181783
Vineyard acreage: 2 acres
Vineyard tonnage, 2016: 8 tons
Varietal grapes: Blanc du Bois, 1.85 acres; Villard Blanc, .05 acres; Lenoir, .05 acres; Norton, .05 acres.

42

Little Vine Vineyards

665 N Hulett Road, Villa Rica, GA 30180

Federal Agent Now Growing Grapes and Producing Wine

JERRY AND SHERRIE bought eleven acres and decided to grow grapes. Jerry was an accounting major at Auburn University who went on to spend twenty-nine years as a federal agent with the IRS and then as an independent consultant.

He made the decision to plant American and French hybrids along with Norton, a *Vitis aestivalis* or native summer grape. He also planted Herbemont, which once grew in South Carolina and Georgia. With his winemaker Joe Smith, Jerry produces seven wines in a price range from $22 to $26. Jerry's award-winning Red Dirt Road white and red, along with his Blanc du Bois, are well worth a trip to Little Vine Vineyards.

Tasting room: At vineyard

Directions:
Take exit 24 off I-20.
Go 4.10 miles south on Hwy 61 onto Moss Ferry Road/Sandhill Hulett Road.
After 4.5 miles, turn left onto Hulett.
Travel 1 mile. Vineyard on the right.

Owners: Jerry and Sherrie Culver
Winemaker: Joe Smith
Vineyard Manager: Jerry Culver
Established: Purchased 2010; first planting 2011; first harvest 2013

Altitude: 1,161 ft.
Hardiness zone: 7b 5–10 (F)
Soil: Loam with granite and clay
Geographical coordinates: 33.625720, -84.920911
Vineyard acreage: 6 acres
Vineyard tonnage, 2016: 25 tons
Varietal grapes: Blanc du Bois, 9,000 plants (2 acres); Norton, 700 plants (1.5 acres), Lenoir, 1,000 plants (2 acres); Villard Blanc, 180 plants in 3 rows (.4 acres); Herbemont, 65 plants.

(770) 851-4454 / http://www.littlevinevineyards.com/

Hancock County has two vineyard wineries centered around Sparta, Georgia: Cedar Green **(43)** and Courson's Winery **(44)**. Sparta's annual rainfall is 45.6 inches with eighty-seven precipitation days.[1]

1 Sparta, Georgia, Weatherbase by CantyMedia, accessed September 12, 2017, http://www.weatherbase.com/weather/weather.php3?s=322890&.

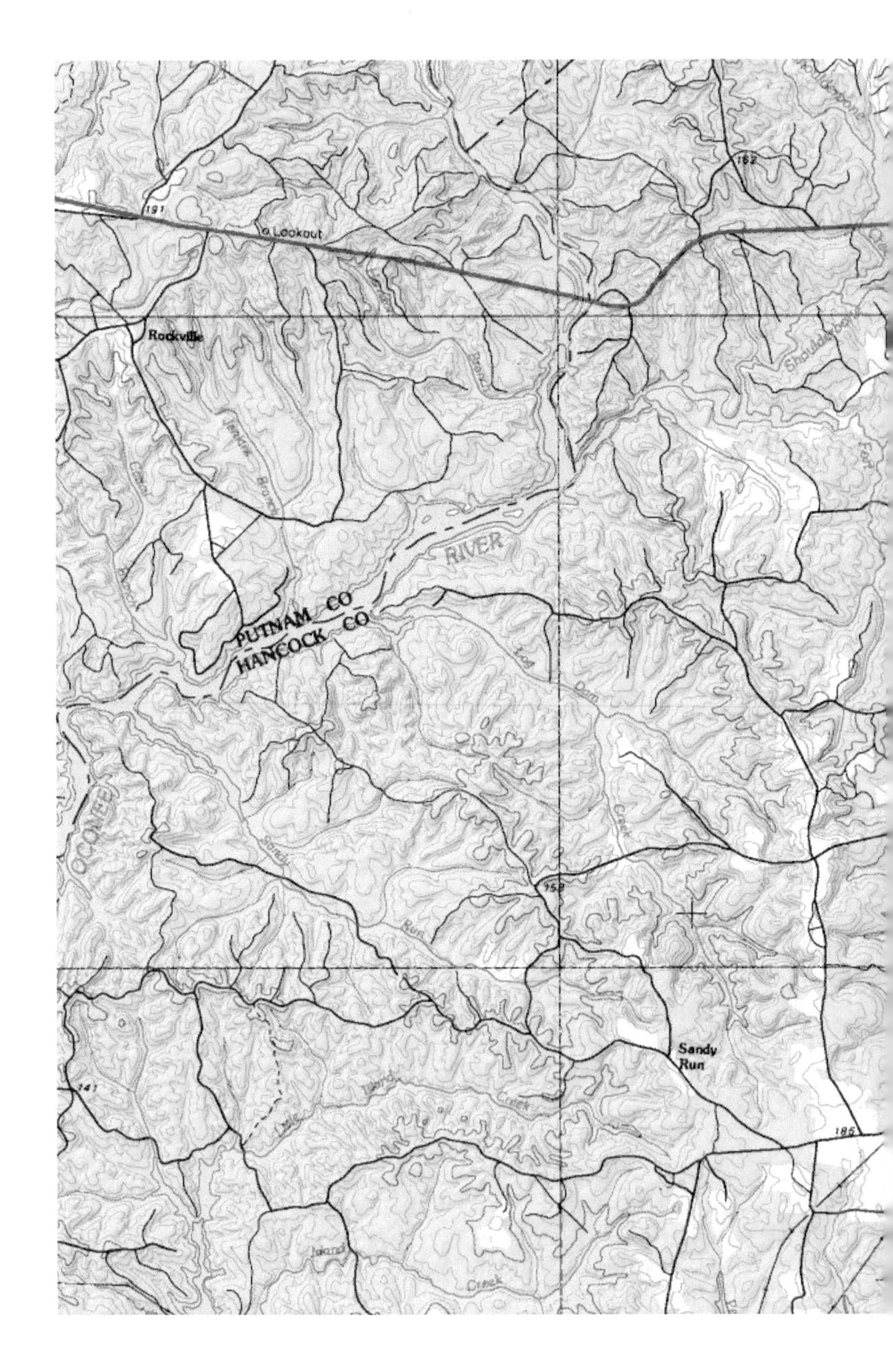

191
Lookout
162
Rockville
Shoulderbone
Branch
Jenkins Branch
RIVER
PUTNAM CO
HANCOCK CO
Log Dam Creek
OCONEE
Sandy Run
159
Sandy Run
141
Creek
185
Island
Creek

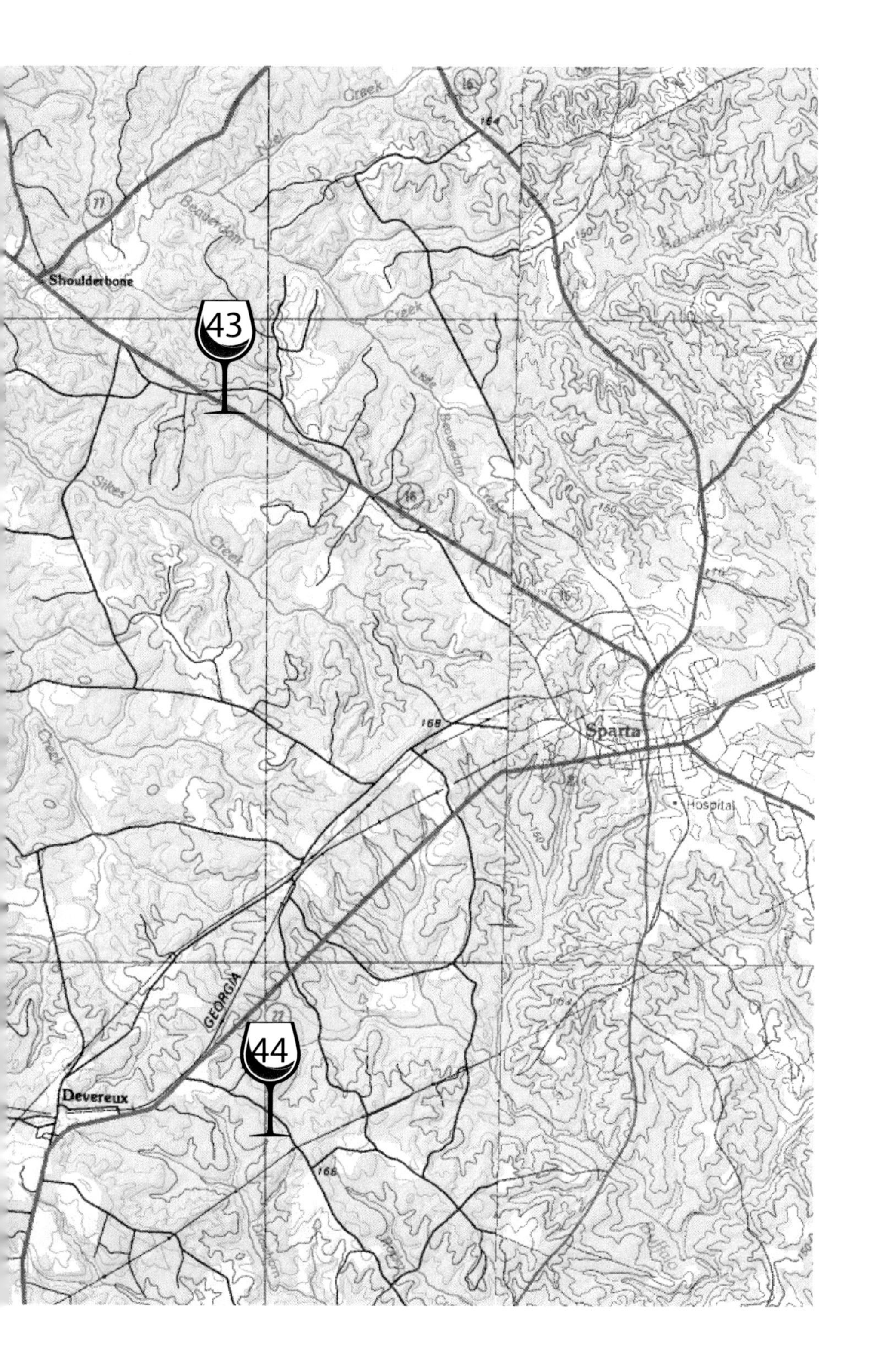
Shoulderbone
43
Sparta
Hospital
Devereux
44
GEORGIA

43

Cedar Green Vineyards

Family-Owned Plantation Now Producing Grapes and Wine

Bob was an electrical engineer with General Electric working closely with the US Navy, and Neile worked in the medical laboratories at the Centers for Disease Control. They enjoyed making wine as a hobby, which led to starting a small vineyard in 1995 at the Cedar Green Plantation. The plantation was built in 1795, and the family has owned the property for more than five generations.

There is a tasting room on location but by appointment only. They are most pleased with their July Cry white wine, made with Carlos, and their blackberry wine.

5115 Hwy 16, Sparta, GA 31087

Tasting room: At vineyard

Directions:
From Sparta
Take Hwy 16 NW 6.80 miles to intersection of Hunts Chapel Church Road.
Cedar Green Vineyards is just opposite.

Owners: Bob and Neile Weis
Winemaker/Vineyard manager: Bob Weis
Established: 1995

Altitude: 429 ft.
Hardiness zone: 7b 5–10 (F)
Soil: Sand, clay
Geographical coordinates: 33.331626, -83.067036
Vineyard acreage: 1 acre
Vineyard tonnage, 2016: 143 gallons
Varietal grapes: Carlos, .6 acres; Tara, .1 acres; Nobel, .25 acres; Alachua Muscadine, .5 acres. Blackberries are also grown on the property.

44

Courson's Winery

Family-Owned Land for Generations and Muscadine Is the Grape

Raymond's family has been on this land since 1842. His dad took over the property in 1972. The land has been muscadine country since its inception. Before his vineyard and winery ownership, Raymond served in the military and with the police as he transitioned into wines.

In addition to six or seven muscadine wines, Raymond grows and buys fruit and *Vitis vinifera* for twenty-three wines. The price range is $15 to $19. White Muscadine and Gran's Best, a late-harvest wine, are well crafted and excellent choices to taste when you are near Sparta.

2623 GA Highway 22, Sparta, GA 31087

Tasting room: At winery and the Red Door antique store
133 S. Wayne Street, Milledgeville, GA 31061

Directions:
From Sparta
Head south on Hwy 22 9.9 miles to winery and tasting room.

Owner: Raymond Reid Courson Jr.
Winemaker/Vineyard manager: Raymond Reid Courson Jr.
Established: 2002

Altitude: 593 ft.
Hardiness zone: 7b 5–10 (F)
Soil: Beach sand
Geographical coordinates: 33.179315, -83.077112
Vineyard acreage: 110 acres, 20 planted
Vineyard tonnage, 2016: 8.5 tons
Varietal grapes: Noble, 1 acre; Ison, 5 acres; Carlos, 7 acres; Darlene, 3 acres; Pam, 2 acres; Fry, .02 acres; Pineapple, 1 acre; Tara, 1 acre. Many vines are over seven years old, and they are blended.

Troup and Meriwether Counties each contain one vineyard winery between West Point and Warm Springs: River's Bend Winery and Vineyard **(45)**, and Warm Springs Vineyard and Winery **(46)**. West Point's annual rainfall is 52.1 inches.[1]

1 West Point, Georgia, Weatherbase by CantyMedia, accessed September 12, 2017, http://www.weatherbase.com/weather/weather.php3?s=722254.

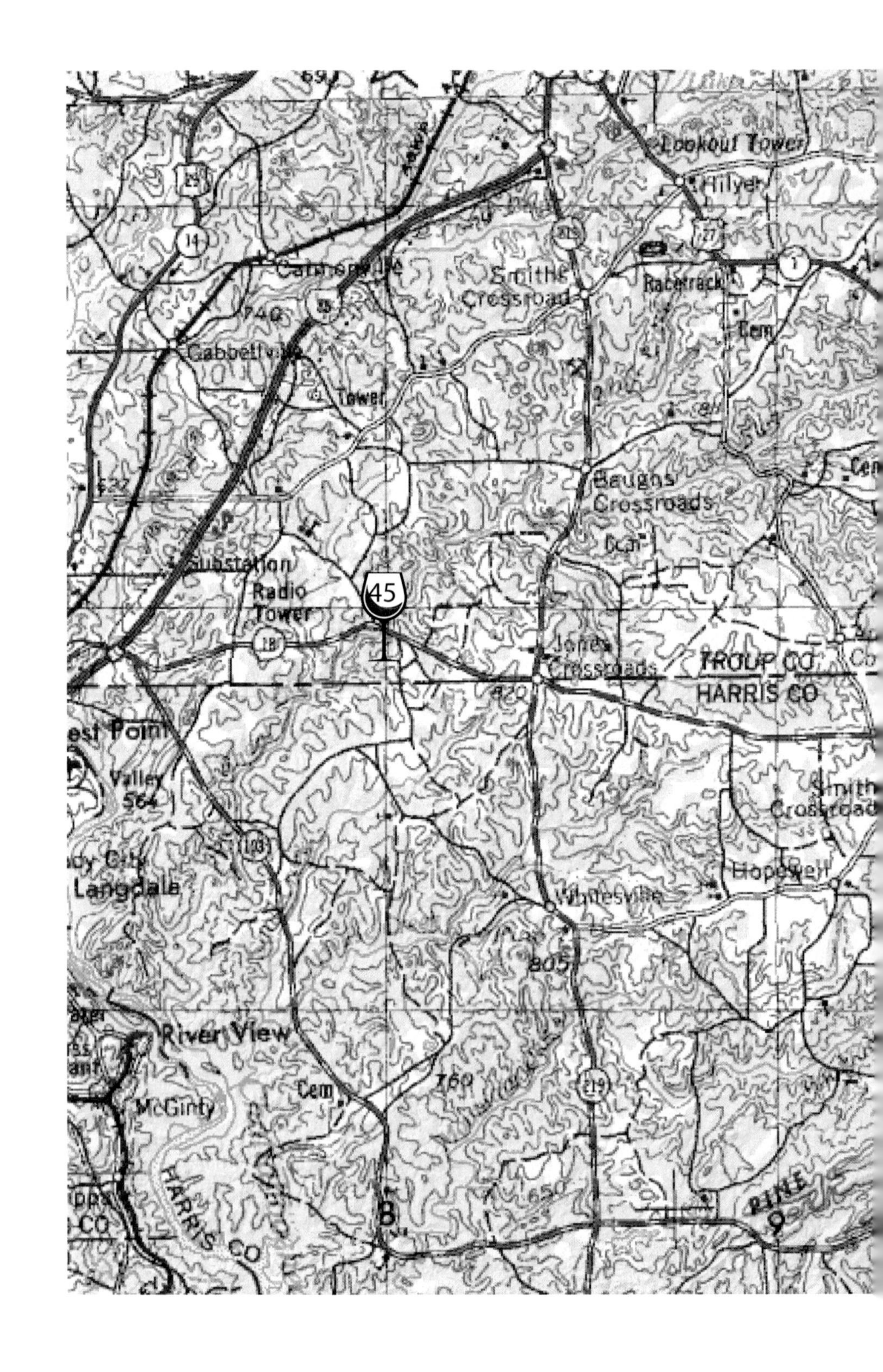

Lookout Tower
Hilyer
Smiths Crossroad
Racetrack
Cem
Gabbettville
Tower
Baughs Crossroads
Substation
Radio Tower
45
Jones Crossroads
TROUP CO
HARRIS CO
Valley
564
Langdale
Smiths Crossroads
Hopewell
Whitesville
805
River View
McGinty
Cem
760
HARRIS CO
650
PINE

Big Springs
Cem
Stovall
SEABOARD COAST LINE
Plant
TROUP CO
MERIWETHER CO
Durand
Crowder Crossing
Water
White Sulphur Springs
46
Little White Lookout
Pine Mountain
FRANKLIN D. ROOSEVELT STATE PARK
DOWDELL KNOB
1395
Gardens
Harris Co
Hog Gap
Pine Mountain Valley
Water
Cem
MOUNTAIN
OAK MOUNTAIN
Hamilton

45

River's Bend Winery and Vineyard

Winemaking Hobby Started Winery and Vineyard

DONALD BOUGHT TEN acres of property to establish his winery. They are currently producing ten wines using juice from California and selected grape juice from Georgia. Prices range from $13.95 to $16.95 with three fruit wines, Moscato, and six *Vitis vinifera* grapes. Donald turned a winemaking hobby into a vineyard and winery operation. He also grows blueberries.

692 Adams Road, West Point, GA 31833

Tasting room: At vineyard

Directions:
From I-85 exit 2
Go 4.4 miles east to Adams Road, then 1 mile on the left is the tasting room.

Owners: Donald Hughes and daughter Amanda Hughes
Winemakers: Donald Hughes and Amanda Hughes
Vineyard manager: Donald Hughes
Established: 2015

Altitude: 754 ft.
Hardiness zone: 7b 5–10 (F)
Soil: Loam, sand, and clay
Geographical coordinates: 32.891608, -85.085710
Vineyard acreage: 1 acre
Vineyard tonnage, 2016: None
Varietal grapes: Blanc du Bois, 1 acre; planted in March 2016.

46

Warm Springs Vineyard and Winery

Great Southern Hospitality in the Tasting Room with Free Samples

7227 Roosevelt Highway, Warm Springs, GA 31830

ED PURCHASED HIS fourteen acres of property and began planting two acres of muscadines in 2011 and 2012. Grape juice is purchased from other local Georgia wineries to make nine or ten different wines each year, with fresh blueberries in the summer.

All wines are offered free for sampling, and all wines are priced at $16. While the tasting room and production facility are in an old garage building, the joy of visiting with Ed is the delightful spirit the tasting-room staff provides the customer. Along with muscadine grapes, he is particularly pleased with his "Riverwalk," a dry muscadine blend with Norton grapes. A unique wine is Ed's Hotlanta, a sweet red wine infused with jalapeño, which sells at a record pace. In addition to visiting Warm Springs Vineyard and Winery, don't overlook the historical value the city of Warm Springs offers. Its "Little White House" served as a getaway for President Franklin Roosevelt.

Tasting room: At vineyard

Direction:
In Warm Springs
Go 1.4 miles north on Hwy 27.
Tasting room and winery are on the left.

Owner: Ed Rocereta
Winemaker/Vineyard manager: Ed Rocereta
Established: 2011

Altitude: 855 ft.
Hardiness zone: 7b 5–10 (F)
Soil: Loam, sand, and clay
Geographical coordinates: 32.9078846, -84.6949650
Vineyard acreage: 14 acres, 2 planted
Vineyard tonnage, 2016: 1,000 lbs.
Varietal grapes: Mixed muscadines, 2 acres.

(706) 655-2233

Chapter 16

Upper Coastal Plain Region

In the South, the lower and upper coastal plains combine to make this the largest geographical region within the state, covering almost 60 percent of Georgia. The soil is soft and sandy on limestone with some clay in the upper coastal plain with gentle slopes and better drainage than in the lower plain. There are ten wineries in this region with a few grower vineyards (grower vineyards sell their grapes to a winery).

In the upper coastal plain, there are six vineyards with five wineries: Tilford Winery and Farms **(47)**, Watermelon Creek Vineyard **(48)**, Paulk Vineyards, the largest vineyard within Georgia **(49)**, Still Pond Vineyard & Distillery, the second-largest vineyard in Georgia and the only winery with a distillery **(50)**, Farmer's Daughter Vineyards with a tasting room in Thomasville **(51)**, and RoseMott Vineyards at Gin Creek **(52)**. The first four vineyards grow 100 percent muscadine grapes. The final two vineyards produce American hybrids, with Gin Creek also growing muscadines. This is subtropical Georgia, with Tifton as the center to these vineyards. This area averages 47.3 inches of rain annually over 103 annual precipitation days.[1]

1 Tifton, Georgia, Weatherbase by CantyMedia, accessed September 12, 2017, http://www.weatherbase.com/weather/weather.php3?s=307890&.

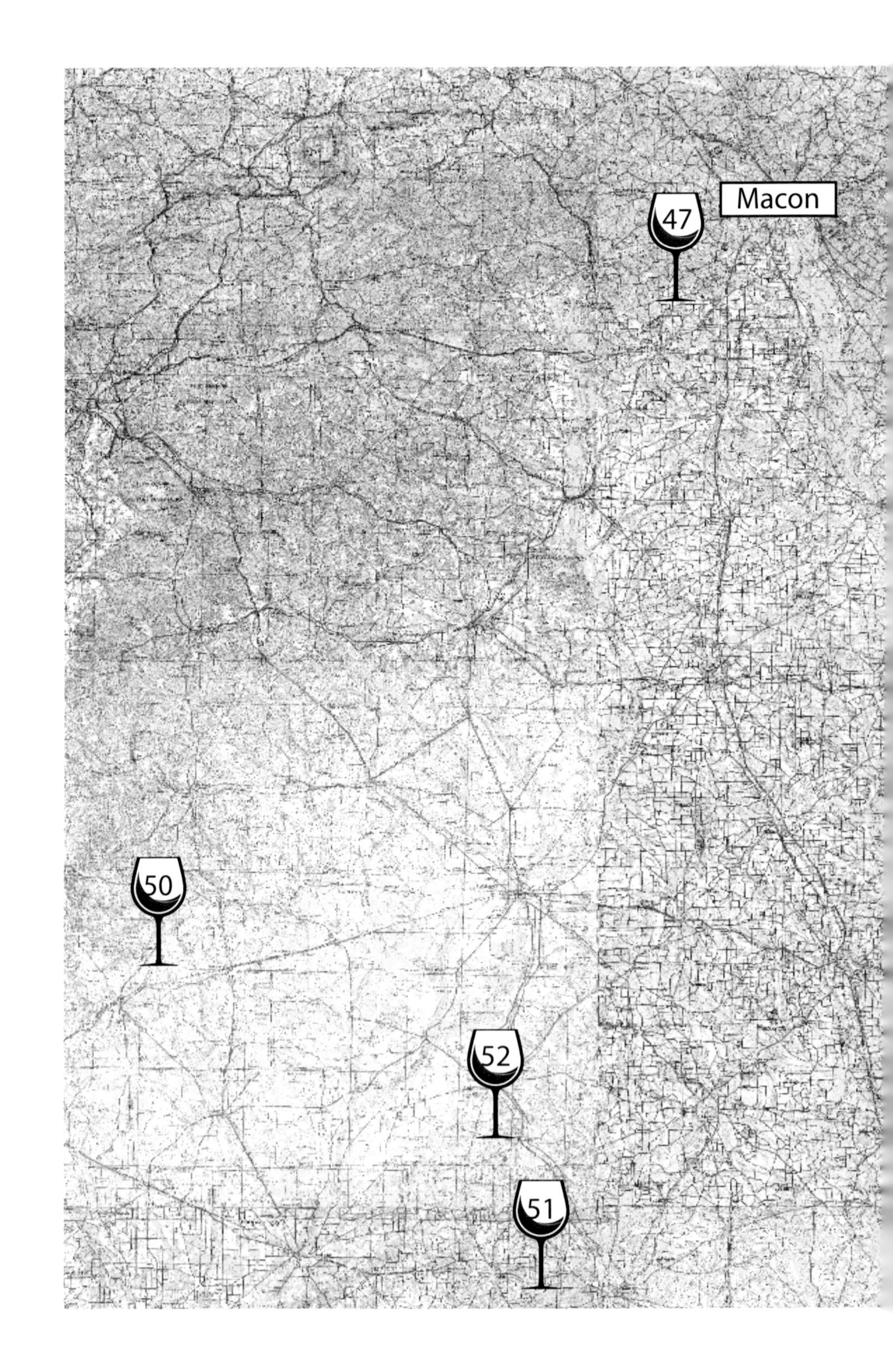
Macon
47
50
52
51

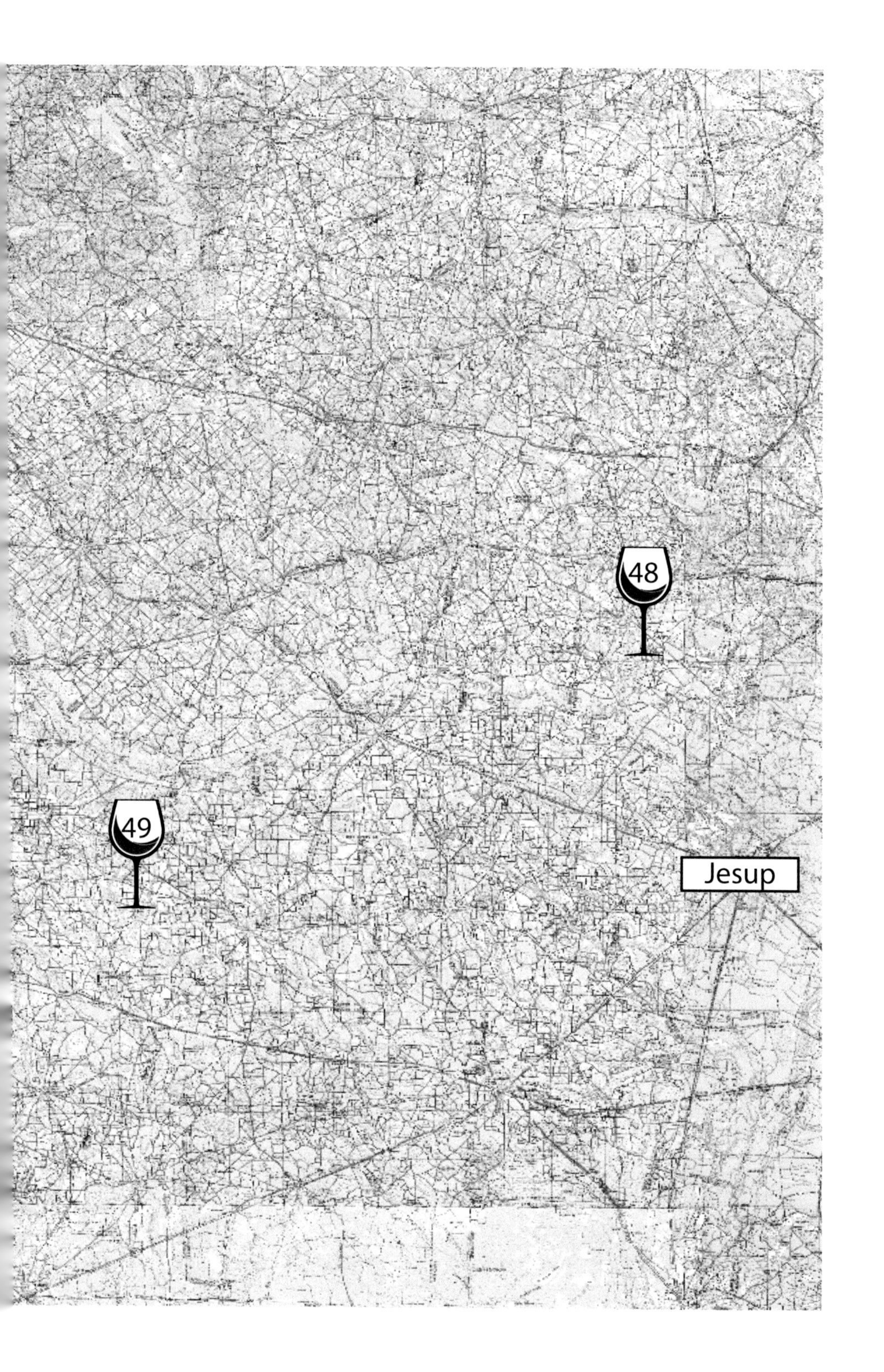
48
49
Jesup

47

Tilford Winery & Farms

Navy Veteran and Analyst at Warner Robins Operates Large Farm Winery

ROBERT SPENT TWENTY-TWO years in the naval reserve and concurrently forty-two years working at Warner Robins Air Force Base as a systems analyst. Robert started this vineyard in the city of Kathleen in 1996 while he was working at the air force base. Originally, Robert intended just to grow grapes on the five acres he started. In 2004, they became a farm winery. He grew up in Utica, Mississippi, with a family tradition of making muscadine wine. He was selected by Fort Valley State University in 2015 as their Farm Family of the Year. He is the first African American vineyard-and-winery owner in Georgia.

Robert produces fifteen wines, all selling from $12 to $15. He leases property from five growers but does all the planting and pruning himself with the support of his farm team. He grows all his cuttings for planting at the vineyard. He also produces fresh vegetables for the local market. All the wines are 9 percent alcohol by volume, and the Sweet Noble and Sweet Magnolia are two wines he recommends.

126 Berrypatch Lane, Kathleen, GA 31047

Tilford Winery

126 Berrypatch Lane
478-396-3025

Tasting room: At winery

Directions:
Take exit 142 off I-75.
Go east on Hwy 96 for 3.2 miles.
Turn south onto Lake Joy Road.
Go 1 mile.
Turn left onto Sandefur Road.
Go .8 miles.
Turn onto Berry Patch Lane. Winery on right 3 miles.

Owner: Robert Taylor
Winemaker/Vineyard manager: Robert Taylor
Established: 2001

Altitude: 370 ft.
Hardiness zone: 8a 10–15 (F)
Soil: Loam, sandy, clay
Geographical coordinates: 32.5298790, -83.6787700
Vineyard acreage: 45 acres
Vineyard tonnage, 2016: 8 tons
Varietal grapes: Noble, 15 acres; Magnolia, 15 acres; Carlos, 15 acres.

(478) 396-3025 / https://tilfordwinery.com/

48

Watermelon Creek

Family Land Provides Opportunity to Build Farm Winery

Charles and Deborah bought back his family land, which had been in the family since 1812, from a cousin in 2003. They produce ten wines in two series: Heritage and Whoopee. They support weddings and corporate meetings from the local communities. Charles makes his wine using his muscadine grapes supplemented by other Georgia grapes and fruits including peaches, black cherries, and blueberries. Given their location in southern Georgia, they see more visitors in the winter and the spring than in the hot summer.

Wine prices range from $14.99 to $16.99. Be sure to enjoy the Stafford's Ferry White, a dry Carlos muscadine, and Blu Passione, a dry, oaked, blueberry white made from Georgia blueberries. Be sure to check the labels and the bottles, as they are some of the best in the country. They are a winning team and well worth a side trip to a Deep South winery and vineyard.

2977 Mount Zion Church Rd, Glennville, GA 30427

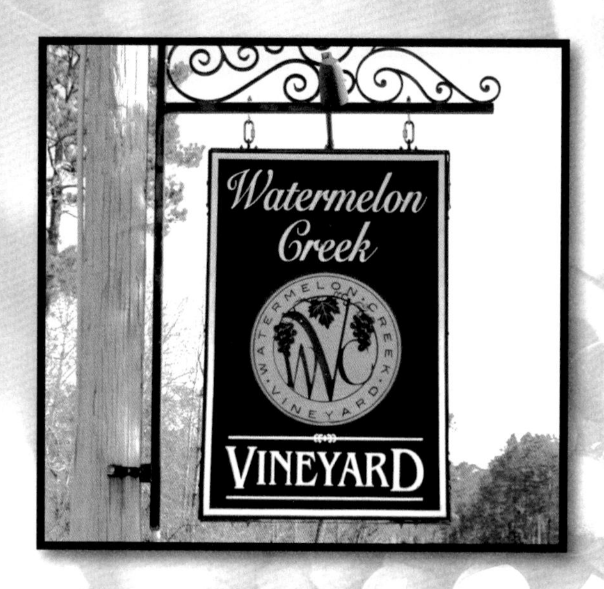

Tasting room: At vineyard

Directions:
Take Hwy 30 toward Glennville from Hwy 16.
Turn right onto 169 (exit 116).
Go 30 miles. Winery on right.

Owners: Charles and Deborah Tillman
Winemaker/Vineyard manager: Charles Tillman
Established: 2003 bought, 2007 planted, 2011 first harvest

Altitude: 141 ft.
Hardiness zone: 8b 15–20 (F)
Soil: Sandy, loam
Geographical coordinates: 31.940293, -82.020922
Vineyard acreage: 295 acres, 3 planted
Vineyard tonnage, 2016: 9 tons
Varietal grapes: Carlos and Noble (field blend)

49

Paulk Vineyards

Largest Muscadine Grower in Georgia Is Ready to Start Making Wine

In 2016 Paulk operated the largest muscadine-growing farm in Georgia. The family has been on the land for generations, with the first Paulks in the region arriving as early as 1782. The family land first planted muscadine in 1970 for fresh fruit. The family made the decision to become a farm winery in 2017, and they are already fully equipped to produce wine with presses, fermentation tanks, and a bottling line. As a farm winery, they will become one of the largest wineries in the state.

Paulk contributed 600 tons of juice for wine production in Georgia in 2016.

1786 Satilla Road, Wray, GA 31798

Directions:
From Ocilla, GA
Go south on Hwy 129 .5 miles.
Turn left onto Hwy 90.
Go 3.5 miles. Turn left onto Satilla Road.
Go 8 miles to vineyard.

Owner: Paulk family
Winemaker: Chris Paulk
Vineyard manager: Gary Paulk
Established: 1973

Altitude: 280 ft.
Hardiness zone: 8a 10–15 (F)
Soil: Sand and clay
Geographical coordinates: 31.547593, -83.080570
Vineyard acreage: 600 acres
Vineyard tonnage, 2016: Sold 200 tons of Noble and 400 tons of Carlos within Georgia
Varietal grapes: Noble, 100 acres; Carlos, 100 acres.

50

Still Pond Vineyard & Distillery

First Winery-and-Distillery Joint Operation in Georgia

In the 1960s, Charles Cowart's father began to plant muscadine grapes for fruit along with raising cattle on the family farm in South Georgia. Over time, his father and mother continued to plant muscadines, and today Still Pond is the largest farm winery in Georgia. When his father died in 1991, Charles Cowart returned to Arlington to manage the farm and vineyards. In 2003, they became a farm winery. His son, Charlie, and his wife are key contributors to the Still Pond team from planting to production. The family has 180+ acres under vine and are focused on producing a Still Pond brand using their muscadine grapes and a farmhouse brand of fruit wines.

The average price per bottle is $10, with their two late-harvest or dessert wines at $18. Be sure to try their Notchaway white, made with Carlos, and Plantation red, made with Noble.

In 2012, Still Pond Vineyards ventured into distilled spirits as the first winery in Georgia to do so. There were challenges, as Georgia laws were not well established for such an endeavor. I remember visiting with them when

1575 Still Pond Road Arlington, Ga 39813

they first started assembling their two Portuguese copper stills; little did they know then how hard acquiring state approval to operate would become. Two years later in 2014, they were able to produce both vodka and gin, which they must sell wholesale along with the brandy they make. But, the distilled-spirit laws may change in 2017. Unique to this winery and one other in Georgia, the tasting room is free.

> *If you are willing to come this far into South Georgia and Arlington, the least we can do is provide you a free tasting.*
>
> —Charles Cowart

Tasting room: At vineyard

Direction:
From Arlington
Go east on Hwy 62.
Travel 7.7 miles. Turn right onto Jones Road.
Travel 2.3 miles and turn right onto Still Pond Road.

Owner: Charles Cowart and family
Winemaker: Charlie Cowart (son)
Vineyard manager: Charles Cowart, Charlie Cowart
Established: 2003

Altitude: 213 ft.
Hardiness zone: 8a 10–15 (F)
Soil: Red clay, sand
Geographical coordinates: 31.4376255, -84.6161030
Vineyard acreage: 168 acres
Vineyard tonnage, 2016: 70 tons
Varietal grapes: Carlos, 100 acres; Noble, 10 acres; Magnolia, 15 acres; Fry, 6 acres; Early Fry, 2 acres; Higgins, 22 acres; Granny Val, 8 acres; Doreen, 6 acres; Red Gate, 8 acres; a muscadine field blend, 1 acre.

(800) 475-1193 / https://stillpond.com/

51

Farmer's Daughter Vineyard

Largest Farm in Georgia Growing Wine on Family Land

CLAYTON IS A third-generation farmer with a degree in agricultural economics from the University of Kentucky. The vineyard is on the part of the three-thousand-acre Hawthorne Farms that belongs to his family, and he operates. The farm and vineyards are near Pelham, Georgia, and the tasting room is just south in historic Thomasville in the center of town. Hawthorne Farms grows cotton, peanuts, and other row crops.

Renee handles all the sales and marketing for Farmer's Daughter. They produce six award-winning wines ranging in price from $20 to $35. Be sure to taste the Hellraiser, a crisp, fresh white wine using the Blanc du Bois grape, and the Knockout, using the Lenoir grape. Plan a weekend trip to Thomasville to enjoy the wine, shopping, and excellent Southern hospitality. Tallahassee, Florida, is just down the road from Thomasville. A great town to overnight in during football season.

2249 Highway 112, Pelham GA, 31779

Tasting room: Thomasville, GA

Directions:
Intersection of N. Broad Street and W. Jackson Street

Owners: Clayton and Renee Moss
Winemaker: Clayton Moss
Vineyard-and-farm manager: Randal Mercer
Established: 2015

Altitude: 183 ft.
Hardiness zone: 7b 5–10 (F)
Soil: Red clay
Geographical coordinates: 31.1525617, -84.2385057
Vineyard acreage: 9.5 acres
Vineyard tonnage, 2016: 16 tons
Varietal grapes: (First planting) Blanc du Bois, 6 acres; Lenoir, 3 acres; (second planting) Lomanto, .5 acres.

52

RoseMott Vineyards at Gin Creek

Family Land for Farm Winery and Significant Wedding Venue

Doug and Rich DeMott took the family land of one hundred acres and constructed a twenty-acre lake, forming a delightful setting for weddings. RoseMott Vineyards hosts about eighty weddings a year. Concurrently, they planted a twenty-two-acre vineyard with a mix of muscadines and hybrid grapes. The lake is surrounded by cottages to facilitate comfort, ease of access to the wedding venue, and Southern tranquility.

Rich passed away in 2015, and his son Max, a University of Georgia graduate and agricultural extension agent, returned to help with the vineyard. They typically make twelve different wines per year, usually dry, semisweet, and sweet, with prices ranging from $12 to $24. Two wines to enjoy are the Blanc du Bois and their strawberry wine made with fresh Georgia strawberries. Their cabins along the lake support wedding parties, but they are available for quiet family weekends, as well.

251 DeMott Road, Hartsfield, GA 31756

Tasting room: At vineyard (by appointment only)

Directions:
From Moultrie
Take Hwy 37 west 8 miles.
Turn south on Bay-Rockyford Road.
Go .3 miles to DeMott Road and the vineyard.

Owners: Doug DeMott, Max DeMott, and Kelli Williams
Winemakers: Doug DeMott and Joe Smith
Vineyard managers: Doug and Max DeMott
Established: 1999; opened 2009 for wine production and tasting

Altitude: 321 ft.
Hardiness zone: 8a 10–15 (F)
Soil: Clay and sand
Geographical coordinates: 31.186764, -83.932209
Vineyard acreage: 22 acres planted
Vineyard tonnage, 2016: 68 tons
Varietal grapes: Blue du Bois, 5 acres; Lenoir, 5 acres; Noble, 5 acres; Carlos, 5 acres; Lomanto, 1 acre; Darlene, 1 acre.

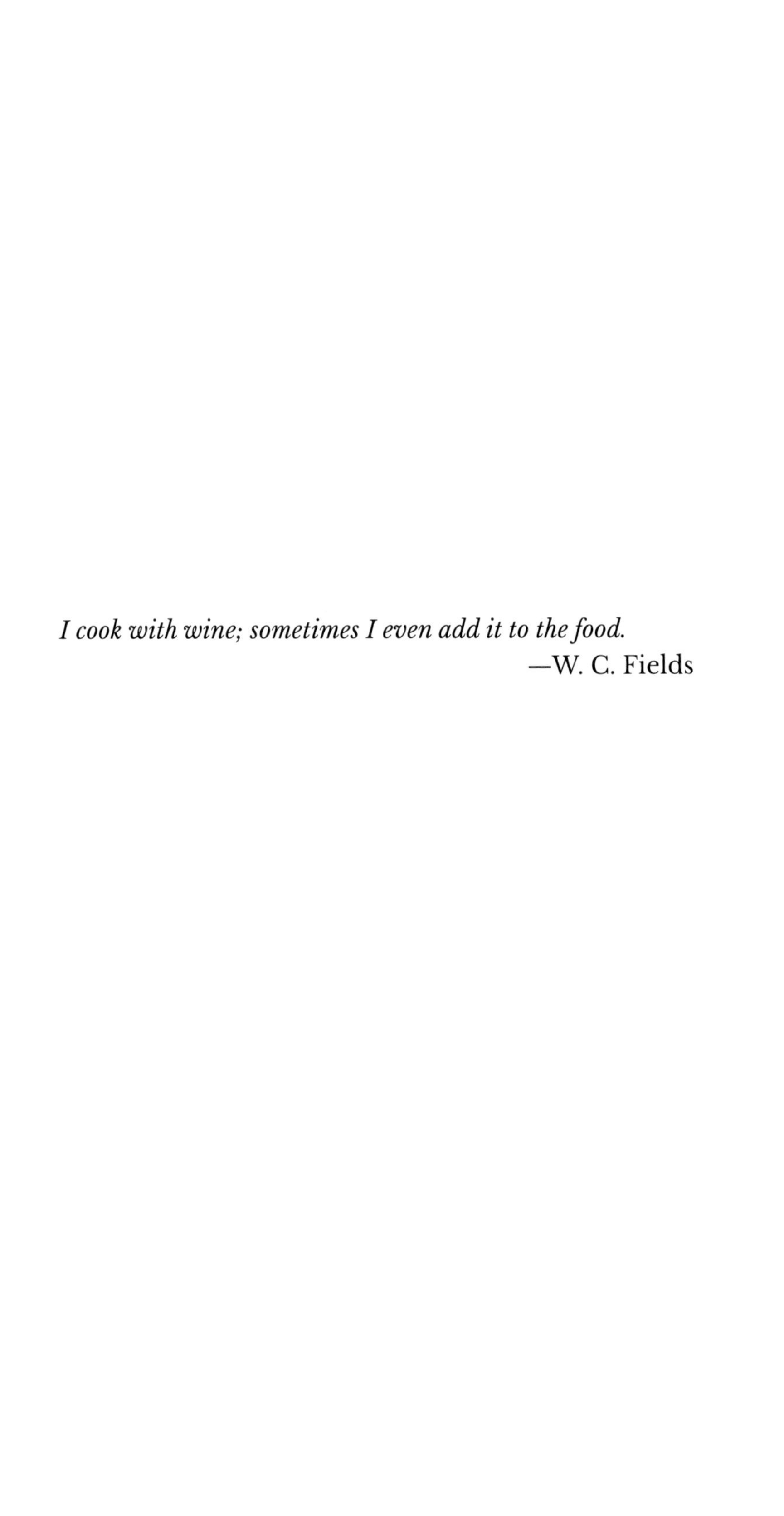

I cook with wine; sometimes I even add it to the food.

—W. C. Fields

Chapter 17

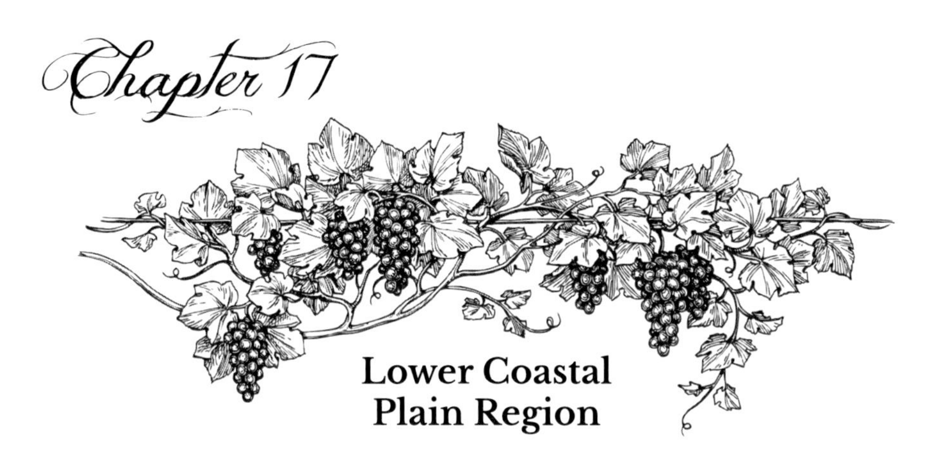

Lower Coastal Plain Region

The Lower Coastal Plain touches the Atlantic Ocean at sea level and contains the Okefenokee Swamp, the largest swamp in the United States, and seven hundred square miles nestled in the southeast corner in the Lower Coastal Plain. Rainfall is the primary source for water in the swamp.[1] The closest weather-monitoring station is Steven Foster State Park, which reports 47.4 inches in annual rainfall and 97.5 precipitation days.[2] Nashville, Georgia, home to Horse Creek Winery, receives 51.2 inches in annual rainfall and 104 days with precipitation.[3]

There are four vineyard wineries and one winery with a tasting room in the Lower Coastal Plain: Horse Creek Winery **(53)**, Bell Farms Rabbiteye, the largest blueberry winery in Georgia **(54)**, Butterducks Winery **(55)**, and Susina Plantation Winery **(56)**. In addition to the four vineyards and wineries, Frogtown **(6)** has a tasting room and 18.5 acres planted with muscadines near Hahira, Georgia.

---

1 Whit Gibbons, "Natural History of the Okefenokee Swamp," September 6, 2002, *New Georgia Encyclopedia,* http://www.georgiaencyclopedia.org/articles/geography-environment/natural-history-okefenokee-swamp.

2 Stephen Foster State Park, Weatherbase by CantyMedia, accessed September 12, 2017, http://www.weatherbase.com/weather/weather.php3?s=594966&cityname=Stephen-Foster-State-Park-Georgia.

3 Nashville, Georgia, Weatherbase by CantyMedia, accessed September 12, 2017, http://www.weatherbase.com/weather/weather.php3?s=732690&.

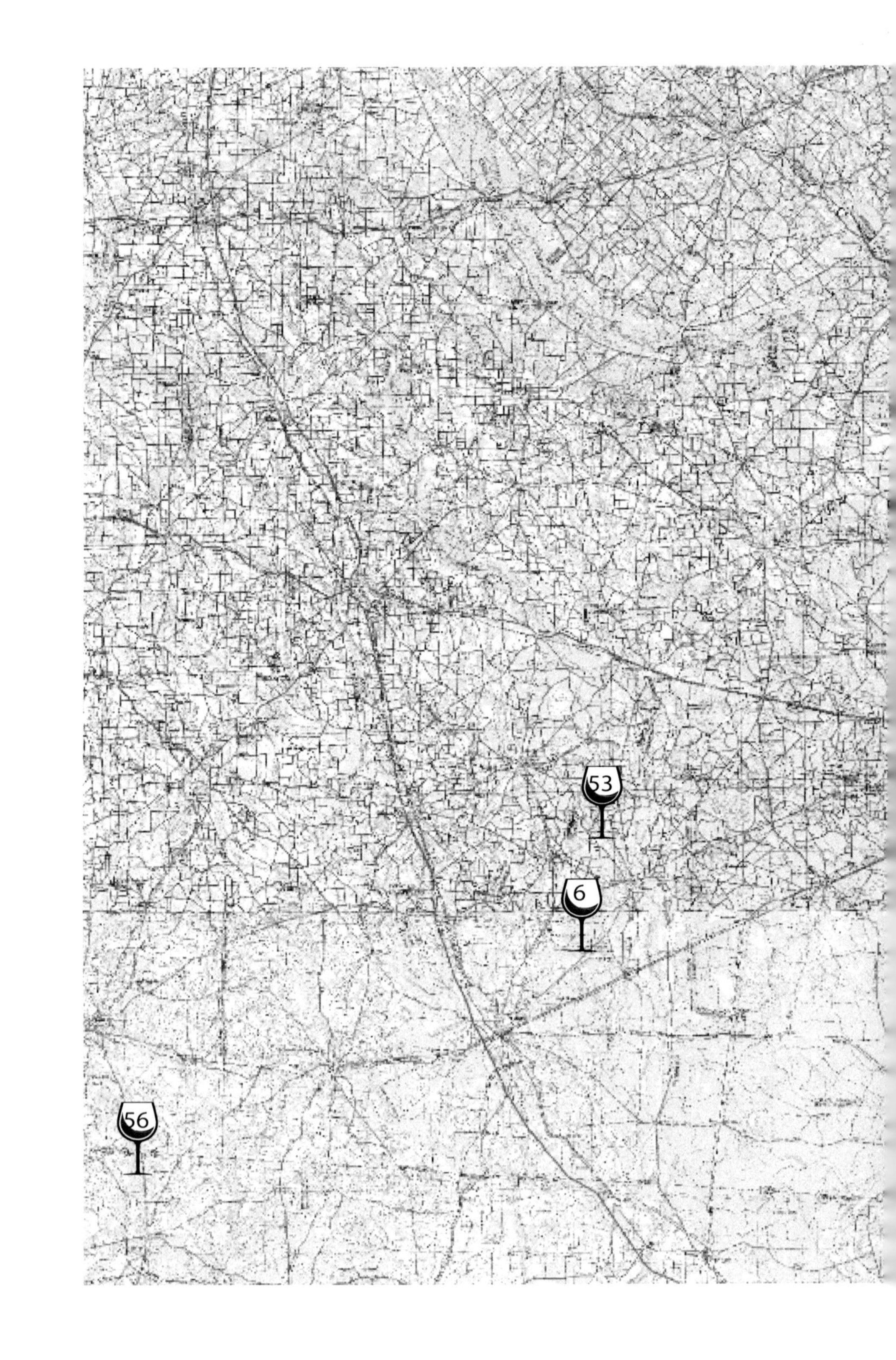
53
6
56

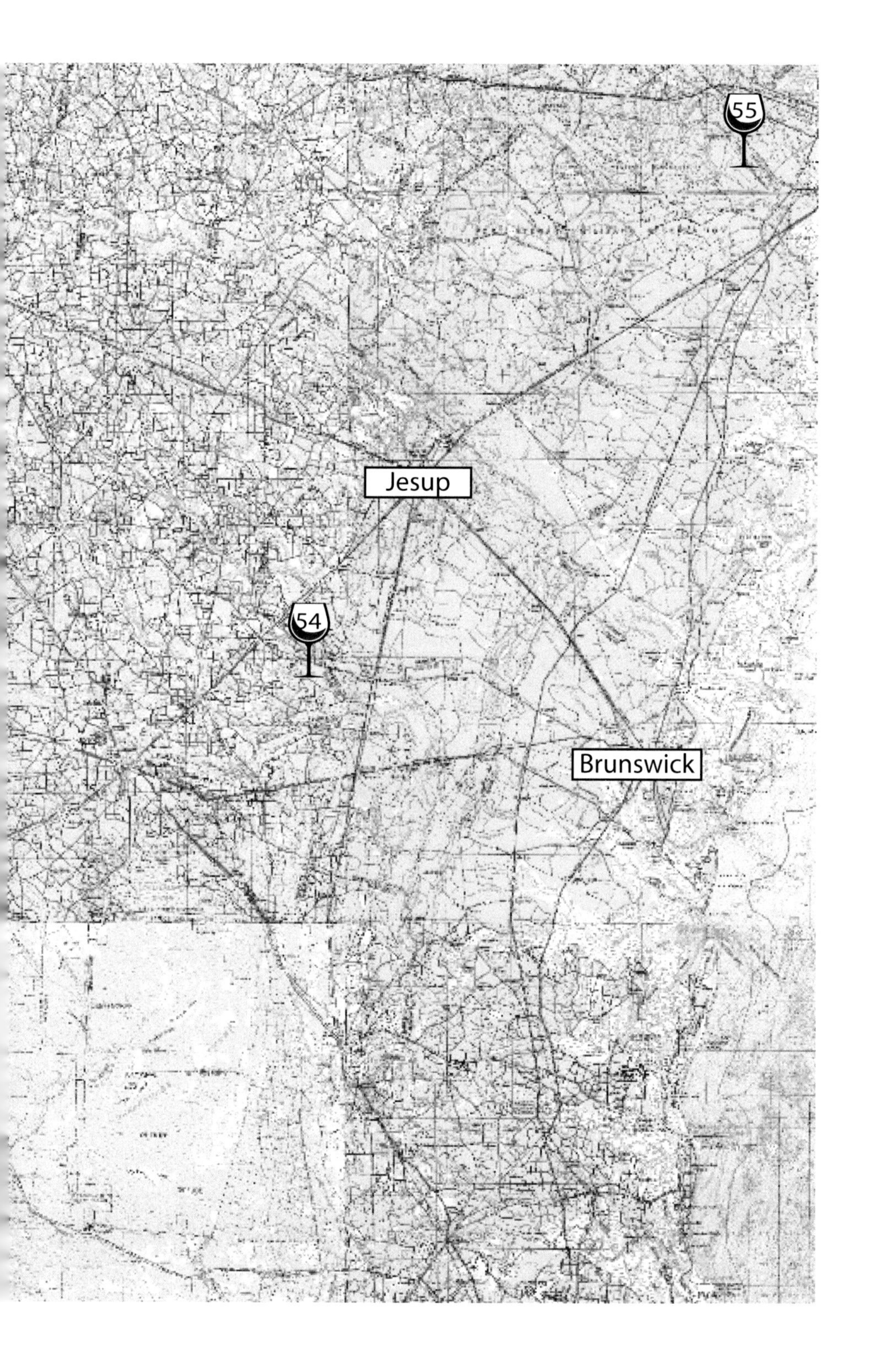
55
Jesup
54
Brunswick

53

Horse Creek Winery

Family Farmland Since 1938 Evolved into Vineyard and Winery

THIS FAMILY FARM has ventured far and wide in what it has grown or raised to include tobacco, cotton, timber, row crops, pecans, and livestock, with silage to feed cattle. Ed Perry served one year in the Georgia House of Representatives and then the remainder in the Georgia Senate from 1981 to 1992. He had a market for fresh produce with a local Harvey grocery, so he hedged his bets by planting both juice and fresh-fruit varietals of muscadine in 2008.

His goal now is to get out of the market for fresh grapes and focus on juice muscadines for wine. Ed makes twenty-five wines ranging in price from $11.95 to $18.95. Given so many choices to taste, be certain to enjoy the Ponderosa Gold, a 100 percent Darlene grape, and Big Red, a blend of Ison, Supreme, and Noble grapes.

2873 Hwy 76 West, Nashville, GA

Tasting room: At vineyard and in Sparks, GA
101 Rountree Bridge Road, Sparks, GA

Directions:
The Sparks tasting room is off exit 41 on I-75.
The Winery is 2 miles west of Nashville, GA, on Hwy 76.

Owners: Ed and Andrea Perry
Winemakers: Ed Perry, Drew Hancock, and Carlton Cotney
Vineyard manager: Drew Hancock
Established: Family land since 1938; planted grapes in 1992; opened winery in 2008

Altitude: 228 ft.
Hardiness zone: 8b 15–20 (F)
Soil: Clay, sand, pebbles
Geographical coordinates: 31.20057, -83.281276
Vineyard acreage: 40 acres
Vineyard tonnage, 2016: 53 tons
Varietal grapes: Supreme, 10 acres, with Ison pollinator; Darlene, 8 acres, with Ison pollinator; Early Fry, 6 acres; Late Fry, 10 acres; Pam, 10 acres; the last three are Ison and Granny Val self-fertilizing vines.

54

Rabbiteye Wine Bell Farms

One of the Largest Blueberry Farms in Georgia That Also Makes Wine

THIS IS A family operation, with Rusty and his sons actively working together to plant and harvest blueberries for both fruit sales and wine.

Bell Farms has been operational since 1979, and blueberry planting began in 1983. Rusty and his sons grow six varieties of Rabbiteye blueberry bushes. Currently, they produce three wines. Each bottle is 100 percent a single varietal. Brightwell is their dryer wine, Powderblue is semisweet, and Tifblue is sweet. All three have won awards for fruit wines. Blueberry farming, even in South Georgia, is high risk, as the plants are very sensitive to frost damage during flowering.

4331 Highway 32 Bristol, GA 31518

Tasting room: At vineyard

Directions:
From Bristol
Take Hwy 32 2.2 miles.
The farm is on the right.

Owner: Rusty Bell and family
Winemaker: Rusty Bell
Vineyard manager: Wil Bell
Established: 1979–1980; first planting 1983

Altitude: 142 ft.
Hardiness zone: 8b 15–20 (F)
Soil: Sand, clay
Geographical coordinates: 31.432918, -82.185001
Vineyard acreage: 187 acres blueberry; 125 in production
Vineyard tonnage, 2016: 150 tons
Blueberry plants: Brightwell, Premier, Climax, Tifblue, Powderblue, and Ochlockonee

55

Butterducks Winery

Butterducks Winery is a short drive from Savannah, Georgia. What started as a hobby has turned into a winemaking passion. Bill Utter's commitment to winemaking shows how important producing fine wines is to Butterducks. The winery currently produces twenty-eight wines, ranging from traditional Merlot and Chardonnay to award-winning fruit wines, at prices ranging from $10.95 to $20. All wines at the winery are made with whole fruit and grapes, and whenever possible, they are Georgia grown.

3332 Blue Jay Road, Guyton, GA 31312

Tasting room: At winery

Directions:
From junction Hwy 21 and I-95
Go north 7.55 miles and turn SW onto Blandford-Blue Jay Road.
Travel 7.4 miles to winery on right.

Owner: Bill and Barbara Utter
Established: 2006
Geographical coordinates: 32.230133, -81334681

56

Susina Plantation Winery

A Restored, Historic, Antebellum House Showcases Vineyards and Winery

SUSINA PLANTATION IS a private residence without a tasting room open to the public. This antebellum Greek Revival house is on the National Historic Register. Built by the famed Southern architect and Englishman John Wind in the 1840s, the plantation was purchased in 2000 by Randy and Marilynn Rhea from Atlanta. It then underwent extensive renovations to include adding a vineyard. John Wind's signature Rosetta flower carving remains on the front upper facing of the home.

Randy worked for Scientific Atlanta, then founded Eagleware-Elanix Corporation and Noble Publishing before moving to Susina Plantation. Randy plants a cross section of muscadine and Norton grapes. Five wines are produced and sold locally in and around Thomasville, Georgia, for $9.99. Two wines to look for when in Thomasville are Oh Susina, a sweet white muscadine infused with peach, and Plantation Red, a dry muscadine made with Ison and Noble with a touch of *Vitis vinifera.*

1134 Meridian Road, Thomasville, GA 31792

Tasting room: None available

Directions:
From Thomasville
Go south on Hwy 319 11.3 miles.
Turn west on Meridian Road.
Travel 2.2 miles. Plantation is on the right.

Owner: Randy Rhea
Winemaker/Vineyard manager: Randy Rhea
Established: 2001

Hardiness zone: 7b 5–10 (F)
Soil: Sand and loam
Geographical coordinates: 30.722451, -84.149520
Vineyard acreage: 3 acres
Vineyard tonnage, 2016: 8 tons
Varietal Grapes: Early Fry, .5 acres; Pam, .33 acres; Ison, .33 acres; Supreme, .33 acres; Noble, .33 acres; Norton, .33 acres; Tara, .25 acres; Black Beauty, .25 acres.

He looked as if he had been beaten to death with a wine bottle, but by doing it with the contents of the bottle.

—Richard Brautigan

Chapter 18

Grower Vineyards in Georgia

Beca Farms and Vineyards
402 Caldwell Drive, Cleveland, GA
Vineyard is 5 acres: Pinot Gris, 2.5 acres; Sauvignon Blanc, 2.5 acres. Owned by Beca and Greg Olson.

Berry Ranch
Ringgold, GA
Vineyard is 1.5 acres of Blanc du Bois. Owner is Jim Nichols.

Blue Mountain Vineyard
184 Turkey Hill, Dahlonega, GA
Vineyard is 3 acres: Traminette, 1.5 acres; Noiret, 1.5 acres. Jessica and Teddy Tardonias are owners. Tonnage in 2016 was less than one ton.

Cannady Vineyards
91 Mountain View Lane, Danielsville, GA
Vineyard is made up of 2–3 acres of Norton. Owner is Shelly Kennedy.

Just a Boy Vineyard

203 Broadus Road, Rome, GA

Vineyard is 1 acre: Blanc de Bois, .75 acres; Lenoir, .25 acres. Owners are Rick and Patti Causey. Tonnage in 2016 was 2.5 tons.

Milestone Vineyards

342 Luttrell Lane, Ringgold, GA

Vineyard is 2 acres: Norton, .75 acres; Chardonnel, .75 acres; Chambourcin, .75 acres. Owner is Lee Kay.

The Stack Farm

1309 Bethal Road, Tiger, GA

Vineyard has 5 acres planted: Norton, 2 acres; Lenoir, 1 acre; Viognier, 1 acre; Tannat, 1 acre; Petit Manseng, 1 acre. Owner is Bill Stack. Total tonnage in 2016 was 15.

Sweet Gum Hollow

2014 South Long Hollow Road, Trion, GA

Vineyard is (newly planted) 1.7 acres: Blanc du Bois, .8 acres; Chambourcin, .95 acres. Owner is John Harward.

The Vineyard at Hominy Creek

83 Hominy Creek Road, Carrollton, GA

Vineyard is made up of .75 acres of Chambourcin, Noiret, Cayuga White, and Vidal Blanc. Owners are Charlie and Eloise Cornell.

Seek more strength for weaker spine. No grape grows on sinner's vine.

—Munia Khan

Chapter 19

Georgia-Grown Varietals

THE DEFINITIVE REFERENCE for grape varietals within this chapter is drawn from *Wine Grapes,* a complete guide to 1,368 wine varieties, including their origins and flavors.

There are seventy-four grape varietals included in this chapter reflecting all the grapes growing in Georgia vineyards in 2016. Total grape acreage committed to wine production is 937.22 acres, to include fourteen acres of muscadine grapes not identified by varietal. I collected this information over eighteen months visiting every vine-growing location in Georgia.

Acreage counting is not an exact science; vineyard planting involves varietal, spacing, aspect, and trellis positioning. Accordingly, a vineyard owner may elect to plant 550 plants per acre (or some other number). In old wineries, which plant and replant varietals to fill sections damaged by Mother Nature or disease, they more often talk in acres planted. The newer growers establishing vineyards for the first time may relate better to the plant purchase count. I believe we are in a band of excellence with the numbers provided with a plus or minus range of 2 percent, or roughly nineteen acres.

Top-Fifteen Georgia Grapes Planted by Acre

Grape	Acres	*Vitis*/Hybrid
Carlos	256	*rotundifolia*
Noble	137	*rotundifolia*
Norton	37	*aestivalis*
Cabernet Sauvignon	35	*vinifera*
Merlot	32	*vinifera*
Magnolia	30	*rotundifolia*
Chardonnay	29	*vinifera*
Blanc du Bois	27	American hybrid
Cabernet Franc	25	*vinifera*
Higgins	23	*rotundifolia*
Chambourcin	21	French hybrid
Vidal Blanc	18.4	French hybrid
Lenoir	17.8	American hybrid
Supreme	15	*rotundifolia*
Traminette	11	American hybrid

Several grapes on this list are familiar to readers. Cabernet Sauvignon is the number-one red-wine grape consumed in North America. Merlot and Cabernet Franc are also well-known grapes originally from Bordeaux, France.

Chardonnay is the number-one selling white-wine grape in North America and is also a native French grape originally from an area between Lyon and Dijon. All these grapes are European or Old World grapes from the *Vitis vinifera* grapevine classification.

The other grapes are not as well known. Our two leading grapes by volume, Carlos and Noble, along with Magnolia and Higgins, are muscadine grapes native to North America from the *Vitis* family *rotundifolia*. These are not the muscadines early Georgia explorers would have observed. Carlos was bred in North Carolina State University's Agricultural Experimental Station in 1951, along with Noble in 1971.

Blanc du Bois is an excellent American-hybrid white grape produced by the University of Florida in 1968 as a highly drinkable wine grape with resistance to Pierce's disease and downy mildew, both of which thrive in Georgia's subtropical climate. Georgia has six-year-old vines producing this grape in 2016.

Chambourcin is a dark-purple French-hybrid grape developed in France in 1948. It is resistant to fungal disease, including downy mildew. It is an excellent blending grape but can be equally enjoyed as a single varietal.

North America is rich in native *Vitis* classifications. The following is a short guide to those growing in Georgia.

Vitis labrusca, the fox grapevine, is also known as the slip-skin grape, referring to the ease in which the outside skin can be squeezed and removed. Native to the eastern United States, the Catawba grows in Georgia for wine.

Vitis aestivalis, the summer grape, is native to the eastern United States. Norton is the best-known grape in this category and is grown in Georgia.

Vitis rotundifolia, or *Muscadinia rotundifolia,* the muscadine, is used for jams and wine and is native to the southeastern United States. Georgia is the largest producer of muscadine grapes in the world. According to varietal data and technical information drawn from the University of Georgia College of Agricultural & Environmental Sciences, twenty-four varietals grow in state vineyards and are used in winemaking.

The University of Georgia operates the oldest and largest breeding program dedicated to the breeding of muscadine grapes, a program that began in 1909.

Muscadine grapes, in general, are produced either for the fresh-fruit market or for juice and wine. There are overlaps with these cultivars; for example, the University of Georgia recommends Carlos, Doreen, Golden Isles, Magnolia, Noble, Regale, Sterling, and Welder as potential juice cultivars, while the University of Florida recommends Alachua, Carlos, Noble, and Welder. One is not more correct than the other. Each state has different climates and soil to contend with, and Alachua, for example, was developed at the University of Florida. Muscadine grapes, in general, range from Delaware to Florida and across the Gulf of Mexico region into Texas.

Muscadine grapes are either self-fertile or female. Self-fertile allows the grape to grow on its own, while female cultivars require fertilization from a self-fertile plant located within fifty feet of it. All the recommended juice cultivars are self-fertile. However, female cultivars can provide blended juice for wine production rather than going to fresh market.

The most prolific Georgia muscadine breeder is William G. Ison, the inventor and patent holder from Ison's Nursery in Brooks, Georgia. Bill developed muscadines for a patent from 1988 to 1995. Included among the grapes currently in production are Black Beauty, Darlene, Early Fry, Ison, Late Fry, Pam, Pineapple, and Supreme.

Vitis vinifera, the European grapevine, is native to the Mediterranean and Central Asia. Thirty-three varietals grow in Georgia vineyards with Cabernet Sauvignon, Merlot, Chardonnay, and Cabernet Franc providing the most acreage.

Alachua at Bottoms Nursery

Vitis rotundifolia, .3 acres are cultivated, .05 at Cedar Green Vineyards and .25 at Frogtown in Hahira, Georgia, in Lowndes County. Alachua is a self-fertile, purple grape developed at the University of Florida Agricultural Experiment Station by J. A. Mortensen and J. W. Harris. The grape was first established in 1976 to undergo testing. The grape provides high-quality juice for both fresh market and wine production. Only time will tell if this grape encourages added acreage in the state.

Albariño (ahl-vah-REE-nyoh)/Alvarinho at Ellijay River, 2016

This *Vitis vinifera* grape originated along the Spanish-Portuguese border. First mentioned in 1843, it is a white grape used to produce a high-quality, light body, fresh, crisp wine with citrus and peach aromas and flavors. In Georgia, .75 acres are planted, with .5 acres at Ellijay River and .25 at Debarge Vineyards and Winery in Walker County. Albariño is a delightful wine with aromas of grapefruit and apple blossom, similar in style to Viognier. My hope is these test plots prove beneficial and encourage additional acreage to develop in North Georgia.

Aromella from Cornell University

Aromella is an American hybrid grape developed at Cornell University in 1976. Its first wine was produced in 1983. It is a winter-hardy white grape with 1.1 acres planted in 2016 at Habersham Vineyards and Winery. The grape has yet to produce wine in Georgia. Cornell notes indicate the grape produces aromas and flavors of pineapple, honeysuckle, citrus, and floral muscat character. Tom Slick, Habersham's owner, is never reluctant to try new vines, and we should look forward to enjoying this new grape as wine in the next two years.

Barbera (bar-BARE-ah) at CeNita Vineyards, 2016

This *Vitis vinifera*, with Italian origins dating back to 1798, is a primary red grape in the Piedmont region in northern Italy. CeNita Vineyard is the only winery in Georgia growing this grape (.25 acres). Consider this a test site for this ripe, tangy grape with cherry and blackberry overtones. It is an excellent performer in Italy as a medium-body red wine with moderate tannin. The hope is that it will perform to the same high quality in Georgia. This picture was taken just at harvest in 2016 while the dry weather provided plump, hardy grapes. CeNita has two years of bottle experience with this grape, allowing it to age longer to soften the tannins. Perhaps some wines will be available in late 2017.

Black Beauty at Milnefarm
Photo by Produce Oasis

This *Vitis rotundifolia* has only .5 acres planted in South Georgia at Frogtown Vineyards in Hahira. Black Beauty is a pistillate, or female, cultivar. It produces an attractive, large, black grape. Berries are crunchy when ripe. Vine vigor and yield are moderate, and harvest is midseason. This grape was developed by William G. Ison in Georgia with the patent issued on July 16, 1991.

Blanc du Bois (BLAHNK du-bwah) at Rosemont Vineyards at Gin Creek, July 2016

This is an American hybrid developed at the University of Florida by John Mortensen in 1968. In Georgia, 26.9 acres grow. Vineyard producers include Farmers Daughter (6 acres), Gin Creek (5 acres), The Vineyards at Mill Creek (2.5 acres), Trillium (1.85 acres), Boutier (.5 acres), Feathers Edge (.75 acres), River Bend (1 acre), Big Door (4 acres), Little Vine Vineyards (2.2 acres), Just a Boy Vineyard (.77 acres), Berry Ranch (1.5 acres), and Sweet Gum Vineyards (.8 acres). There are several reasons Blanc du Bois has success. The grape is resistant to Pierce's disease, downy mildew, and is able to survive in the subtropical climate in the Piedmont and Coastal Plains regions. I enjoyed wine made from this grape from six-year-old vines at Gin Creek; it provides fresh, crisp citrus-fruit flavors in a dry wine that's best served chilled. This grape should continue to prosper and delight consumers across the state. At Gin Creek in Colquitt County, it grows well along with muscadine grapes, and is opening new vistas to grape growers in West and South Georgia.

Blaufrãnkish (blouw-FRANN-keesh) at Crane Creek, September 2016

Three acres of this *Vitis vinifera* grape grow at Crane Creek near Young Harris. This grape also goes by Blauer Limberger in Germany. Its native home is Austria, and appears as early as 1862. This is a vigorous red-wine grape that ripens late. The wine is a lighter red with noticeable acidity, with red-currant and blueberry aromas and flavors on the palate.

Cabernet Franc (cab-er-nay Franc) at 12 Spies, August 2016

This *Vitis vinifera* is an ancient grape that goes back perhaps as early as 1054, and is well known in the French Bordeaux and Loire regions. This grape is a Cabernet Sauvignon parent. Some scholars today believe the Basque country may be its real origin. Origin aside, the grape performs well on clay and sandy soil, producing small, black berries, and the wine is lighter and crisper than Cabernet Sauvignon. Most wines produced with this grape have a medium body with light fruit and pronounced tannin and acid, with blackberry and ripe strawberry aromas and flavors. In Georgia, it is a top-ten cultivar with 24.7 acres planted. The nineteen vineyards growing this grape include Crane Creek (1.8 acres), Hightower Creek (1.4 acres), Paradise Hills Resort (2.5 acres), Cavender Creek (.25 acres), Montaluce (.9 acres), The Cottage Vineyard (.6 acres), Three Sisters (3.9 acres), Frogtown (3 acres), 12 Spies (.34 acres), Stonewall Creek (2.5 acres), Ellijay River Vineyards (.25 acre), CeNita (1 acre), Debarge (.75 acres), Boutier (.25 acres), Sharp Mountain (1.75 acres), Yonah Mountain (1.75 acres), Habersham (.75 acres), and Engelheim (.5 acres). Cabernet Franc is used both as a single varietal or in red-wine blends. This grape should continue to be a cornerstone grape in North Georgia.

Cabernet Sauvignon (cab-er-NAY sew-veen-YON) at Habersham, August 2016

Vitis vinifera, an offspring from Cabernet Franc and Sauvignon Blanc, was recognized in Bordeaux, France, from as early as 1763. In Georgia, twenty-one growers produce this grape. They include Crane Creek (.2 acres), Paradise Hills Resort (.25 acres), Cavender Creek (1 acre), Kaya (3.5 acres), Frogtown (4 acres), Montaluce (1.5 acres), Three Sisters (1.05 acres), Stonewall Creek (.25 acres), Tiger Mountain (2.5 acres), Ellijay River Vineyards (.5 acres), Cartecay (2.5 acres), CeNita (.5 acres), Debarge (.4 acres), Boutier (.25 acres), Sharp Mountain (.75 acres), Fainting Goat (1.25 acres), Yonah Mountain (.75 acres), Serenity (1.2 acres), Habersham (6.3 acres), Wolf Mountain (3 acres), and Engelheim (1.5 acres). A full-body wine with noticeable tannins for longevity, its black fruit dominates both aroma and palate. In Georgia, it tends to be more fruit forward with black cherry and blackberry flavors dominating.

Carlos at Still Pond, August 2017

This *Vitis rotundifolia* was developed in 1951 by W. B. Nesbitt, V. H. Underwood, and D. E. Carroll at the Department of Horticultural Science at North Carolina State University. Carlos is the number-one muscadine wine–grape grown in Georgia at 256.1 acres. Primary used for white wine, Carlos is cold hardy and self-fertile with small, bitter, tough berries with bronze skin. Eleven vineyards produce this grape for dry, semisweet, sweet, and late-harvest wine production. Producers include Still Pond

(100 acres), Paulk (grower vineyard that committed 100 acres to juice in Georgia), Château Élan (23 acres), Tilford (15 acres), Courson's Winery (7 acres), Fox (2 acres), Gin Creek (5 acres), Frogtown in Hahira (2 acres), Currahee (1.25 acres), Feather's Edge (.25 acres), and Cedar Green (.6 acres). I drew out my tasting notes at Still Pond Vineyards with Notchaway white. It had a light, straw color and was brilliant and reflective with complex aromas including peach, melon, banana, yellow apple, and floral citrus blossom. On the palate, it is a full-bodied, sweet wine with tropical fruit flavors and a smooth mouthfeel with sweet fruit dominating this still wine. On the finish, lingering, sweet fruit flavors of peach and melon provide a pleasant experience. It is overall a well-crafted sweet white wine, typical for the Carlos grape. Serve chilled and enjoy on the back porch with fresh fruit, goat cheese, and peach cobbler.

Carménère (kahr-mhen-NEH-re) at Frogtown, September 2015

This *Vitis vinifera* is a French Bordeaux grape. Cabernet Franc is one parent first mentioned from the Gironde in 1783. There is one acre of this grape planted in Georgia at Frogtown. Carménère is a medium-bodied red wine with black plum, jam, and raspberry flavors with low acidity and light tannins. It is one of the six red grapes authorized in Bordeaux wines. Most often this grape is used as a blending grape.

Catawba (kuh-TAW-bah) at Hightower Creek, August 2016

Vitis labrusca Catawba is an American grape that may have crossed with another *Vitis*, becoming a hybrid. It was discovered as early as 1802 in North Carolina. In Georgia, the vigorous-growing vine is a late-ripening grape. There are 5.6 acres planted to include Crane Creek (3 acres), Cartecay (1.75 acres), Feather's Edge (.75 acres), and Hightower Creek (.1 acres). Wine from this grape is often considered grapy or foxy in taste with high natural acidity, making it suitable for sparkling wines.

Cayuga White at The Vineyard at Hominy Greek, 2016
Photo by Atwater Estate Vineyards

Cayuga White, an American hybrid developed at the New York State Agricultural Experiment Station in Geneva, was released in

1972 for planting. In Georgia, there is .15 acres at The Vineyard at Hominy Creek. Consider this a test plot to determine growing potential in Georgia. It is a white grape used to produce off-dry and medium-bodied wines.

Chambourcin (shahm-boor-SAN) at CeNita, August 2016

This is a French hybrid that became commercially available in 1963. In Georgia, there are 21.3 acres planted in ten vineyards: Crane Creek (5 acres), Odom Springs (2 acres), Frogtown (.5 acres), CeNita (1 acre), Debarge (.40 acres), Habersham (8.4 acres), Serenberry (.75 acres), Engelheim (1.5 acres), Milestone Vineyards (.75 acres), and Sweet Gum Hollow (.95 acres). It is a dark-skinned grape often used as a blending grape with aromas and flavors of black cherry, plum, and herbs. Crane Creek's Mountain Harvest Red is 100 percent Chambourcin—an easy drinking wine and typical for this varietal.

Chardonel at Crane Creek, September 2016

Released in 1990, this American hybrid is a white grape produced in New York State. In Georgia, there are 8.5 acres in five vineyards to include Crane Creek (3 acres), Paradise Hills Resort (2.5 acres), Debarge (.5 acres), Habersham (1.7 acres), and Milestone Vineyards (.75 acres). This grape is a Chardonnay and Seyval Blanc hybrid offering high acidity as well as aromas and flavors associated with Chardonnay citrus, tropical fruit, and yellow apple.

Chardonnay (SHAR-duh-nay) at Sharp Mountain, August 2016

A *Vitis vinifera* and ancient French white grape first mentioned in 1583 from the area around Lyon and Dijon, this is a principal grape in both Burgundy and Champagne. Chardonnay is the leading white grape consumed in the United States, and 29.2 acres are planted in Georgia in eleven vineyards. Vineyards growing the grape include Montaluce (1.7 acres), The Cottage Vineyard (1 acre), Three Sisters (3.3 acres), Frogtown (7 acres), Kaya (2 acres), Bear Claw (3 acres), Ellijay River Vineyards (.25 acres), Boutier (.25 acres), Sharp Mountain (.75 acres), Yonah Mountain (3.6 acres), and Habersham (6.3 acres). Chardonnay is a full-bodied white wine that can either be oaked or unoaked during the production process. In warm climates, the flavors and aromas are likely to be citrus, yellow apple, and pineapple. When oaked, Chardonnay picks up vanilla, cream, and nut flavors. We are likely to see more Chardonnay acreage added to Georgia vineyards.

Cowart at Bottoms Nursery

This Vitus rotundifolia is a self-fertile, purple grape. Cowart was developed and released in 1968 by B. O. Fry from the University of Georgia. Cowart is a fresh-market grape. The current acreage in Georgia is .25 in Frogtown Hahira.

Creek at Ison's Nursery

A *Vitis rotundifolia*, this grape is not patented. Creek produces a small, purple berry with high acid. The grape is a self-fertile varietal that ripens late in the season. There is one acre planted in the Frogtown Hahira vineyard.

Cynthiana/Norton at Little Vine Vineyards, August 2017

This *Vitis aestivalis* is a classic American red grape discovered by Dr. Daniel N. Norton in Richmond, Virginia, in 1820. This grape produces a medium- to full-bodied wine with aromas and flavors of blackberry, black cherries, spice, and earth. This high-acid and light-tannin grape can produce excellent dry red wine. It has become the state grape in Missouri. In Georgia, twenty-one vineyards produce 36.9 acres. Contributing vineyards include Crane Creek (6 acres), Hightower Creek (.01 acres), Odom Springs (2 acres), Cavender Creek (1 acre), Frogtown (3 acres), Three Sisters (5.5 acres), Stonewall Creek (1.5 acres), Tiger Mountain (2 acres), Cartecay (2.25 acres), Chateau Meichtry (1 acre), CeNita (.1 acre), Debarge (.75 acres), Boutier (2 acres), Montaluce (1.3 acres), Feather's Edge (1.5 acres), Trillium (.05 acres), Little Vine Vineyards (1.4 acres), Susina Plantation (.33 acres), Cannady Vineyards (2.5 acres), Milestone Vineyards (.75 acre), and The Stack Farm (2 acres). This grape should continue to rise in acreage over the next five years.

Darlene at Horse Creek, July 2016

This *Vitis rotundifolia* is a bronze, female grape. Darlene is another muscadine developed by William Ison in Georgia as a fresh-market cultivar. Darlene is planted in twelve acres at three vineyards to include Gin Creek (1 acre), Courson's Winery (3 acres), and Horse Creek (8 acres). The fresh juice from this grape, unfermented, is sweet, fresh, and crisp. Horse Creek's Ed Perry believes this grape makes a unique wine, and I agree. It is one of only four muscadines I have tasted that is 100 percent single varietal; the others are Carlos, Norton, and Ison.

Doreen at Gin Creek, July 2016

This *Vitis rotundifolia* is a bronze muscadine recommended as a juice cultivar for making wine. In Georgia, there are 7.25 acres planted in two vineyards: Still Pond (6 acres) and Frogtown Hahira (1.25 acres). Doreen is a self-fertile cultivar that produces a large crop of small to medium-sized berries. Harvest season is late. Doreen is one of the best cultivars for juice production.

Early Fry at Horse Creek, July 2016

This *Vitis rotundifolia* is a bronze female muscadine recommended as a fresh-market cultivar. In Georgia, there are 8.5 acres in three vineyards: Still Pond (2 acres), Horse Creek (6 acres), and Susina Plantation (.5 acres). It was developed by Bill Ison at Ison's Nursery. Early Fry produces high yields, and is cold hardy and an early producing grape. The grape is a blending grape with other muscadines when used as juice.

Fry at Still Pond Vineyard & Distillery, August 2017

This *Vitis rotundifolia* is a bronze female recommended as a fresh-market cultivar. In Georgia, there are 6.01 acres in two vineyards: Still Pond (6 acres) and Courson's Winery (.01 acres). Fry was released in 1970 by R. Lane, University of Georgia. Fry has set the standard for fresh-fruit quality for bronze muscadines. Most growers are quite familiar with this cultivar. Fry is famous for its large berry size and good flavor, even when picked immaturely.

Gewürztraminer (guh-VERTZ-tra-mean-er) at Sharp Mountain, August 2016

This *Vitis vinifera* has .75 acres in Georgia produced only at Sharp Mountain in Jasper, Georgia. This grape produces an aromatic wine famous in Alsace, France, and Germany for its rose-petal aromas, lychee-nut aromas and flavors, spice, and high alcohol. It is a mutation of Savagnin Rose, and was first mentioned in Europe in 1827.

Granny Val at Horse Creek, July 2016

This *Vitis rotundifolia* is a bronze, self-fertile muscadine with nine acres grown on two vineyards in Georgia: Still Pond (8 acres) and Horse Creek (1 acre to fertilize Pam). Granny Val is the heaviest-producing grape of all muscadines, and it was patented by Bill Ison at Ison's Nursery in Georgia.

Grüner Veltliner (GROO-ner FELT-lih-ner) at Crane Creek, September 2016

This *Vitis vinifera* is a white grape from Austria dating back to the seventeenth century. In Georgia, two vineyards produce this grape: Crane Creek (3 acres) and Ellijay River (.5 acres). The grapes are typically used to produce a full-bodied, dry wine. Zusa is a blended white wine from Crane Creek that uses this white grape in its blend. It tastes clean, fresh, and crisp, and is one of my favorite wines.

Herbemont at Little Vine Vineyards, August 2017

Much is written about the heritage of Herbemont, an American hybrid, although some of it is conflicting. Nicholas Herbemont from South Carolina was an active grower and champion for this grape beginning in 1811, hence the name.

The grape has a good balance of sugar and acid but requires the right conditions to grow. At one point, two vineyards in Georgia planted experimental plots in 2015 and 2016. Today, only one vineyard, Little Vine Vineyards, produces .05 acres. Herbemont himself used this grape to make a Madeira-type wine. I have yet to see this grape grow well in Georgia, or produce wine.

Higgins at Still Pond Vineyard & Distillery

Produced by M. Murphy and B. Fry, this *Vitis rotundifolia* is a bronze, female, fresh-market muscadine developed by the University of Georgia breeding program and released in 1951. Two vineyards plant the grape in 23.25 acres: Still Pond (22 acres) and Frogtown Hahira (1.25 acres). This grape is in the top-four muscadines produced in Georgia.

Ison at Susina Plantation, August 2017

This *Vitis rotundifolia* is a self-fertile, bronze grape. The plant was designed for late-season harvest and patented in 1995 by Bill Ison. The fruit is large and sweet when allowed to ripen fully.

Jumbo at Ison's Nursery

This is a female, black grape that requires pollination. Harvest early to midseason. The grape produces large fruit, and the vine is disease resistant and cold hardy. Good spice fruit flavor that produces quality juice. A long-lasting muscadine.

Late Fry at Horse Creek, July 2016

Late Fry is a self-fertile, bronze grape designed for late-season harvest by Bill Ison at Ison's Nursery. This delicious, large grape is cold hardy.

Lenoir/Black Spanish/Jacquez at Gin Creek, July 2016

An American hybrid, this grape's mixed heritage and multiple names have led to several hypotheses on its origin. The grape may have originated around the town of New Bordeaux near the Savannah River between South Carolina and Georgia. The grape was authorized for use in Châteauneuf-du-Pape until 1935 under the name Jacquez. It was widely grown in Texas to make communion wine, and grows well in Brazil. The grape is resistant to Pierce's disease but not particularly useful as a rootstock, as it has little resistance to phylloxera. The grape is often used for sweet, fortified wines and dry to semisweet red, still wines with intense dark-berry flavors. In Georgia, nine vineyards are growing this grape on 17.8 acres: Boutier (1 acre), Big Door (5 acres), Farmer's Daughter (3 acres), Gin Creek (5 acres), The Vineyards at Mill Creek (1.5 acres), Trillium (.05 acres), Little Vine Vineyards (2 acres), Just a Boy Vineyard (.25 acres), and The Stack Farm (1 acre). The grape's resistance to Pierce's disease and its ability to grow well in warm, humid climates have contributed to its success in the Piedmont and Coastal Plains regions. This grape has considerable potential for increased acreage within Georgia.

Lomanto at Big Door Vineyards & Winery, August 2017

Another American hybrid, this grape is a cross between Salado and Pense by the famous Texas hybrid master and horticulturist T. V. Munson. Pierce's disease–resistant and able to grow well in humid climates, it was introduced in 1902. It boasts black, thin skin with drought-resistant vines that provide a claret red juice and good acidity for dry, still winemaking. In Georgia, there are 5.75 acres grown in four vineyards: Big Door (4 acres), Farmer's Daughter (.5 acres), The Vineyards at Mill Creek (.25 acres), and Gin Creek (1 acre). This grape is gaining acceptance in the Piedmont and Coastal Plains regions of Georgia as an alternative to muscadine grapes.

Magnolia at Still Pond Vineyards & Distillery, August 2017

This *Vitis rotundifolia* is a self-fertile, bronze, midseason juice cultivar. Two vineyards grow this grape on thirty acres: Tilford (15 acres) and Still Pond (15 acres). Magnolia is a hardy, disease-resistant vine that produces white grapes. This grape is a good blending grape with excellent quality.

Malbec (MAHL-bek)/Côt at 12 Spies, August 2016

This *Vitis vinifera* is a red grape with 4.5 acres in Georgia in seven vineyards: Montaluce (.3 acres), 12 Spies (.25 acres), Stonewall Creek (1 acre), Tiger Mountain (.75 acres), Frogtown (1 acre), Yonah Mountain (.2 acres), and Wolf Mountain (1 acre). This grape originated in Cahors in Quercy, France, around 1761, or perhaps later where it is called Côt. Malbec is a dark grape with the potential to produce age-worthy wines. In early 2017, I tasted a 2008 Malbec from Tiger Mountain. My comments include aromas of blackberry, spice, cherry, and dried fruit, with violet, floral overtones. On the palate it is medium-bodied and balanced with a smooth mouthfeel and complex flavors of cherry, black fruit, and plum with hints of tobacco. It offered a long finish in which the fruit dominated the palate—an excellent, well-crafted wine. Today most wine drinkers are aware that Argentina is producing good Malbec, but in the right location in North Georgia, this grape is producing quality wine.

Marsanne (mahr-SAN) at Frogtown, August 2015

Vitis vinifera Marsanne originated in the Rhône Valley in France around 1781. In Georgia, only one vineyard is growing this grape—Frogtown with 1.25 acres. Marsanne is a white-wine grape often blended in the Rhône Valley in France. When young, the wine is crisp, fresh with citrus and peach aromas and flavors, and has a touch of honeysuckle and nuts. Blending Marsanne with two other Rhône white wines, Viognier and Roussanne, occurs frequently. Frogtown Cellar's MRV blend is an excellent example.

Merlot (mer-LOW) at Hightower Creek Vineyards, August 2016

A *Vitis vinifera*, the grape was first mentioned in 1783–1784 in Libourne in French Bordeaux. Merlot is widely used in Bordeaux and is the primary red blending grape on the right bank. In Georgia there are fifteen vineyards that plant this vine on 32 acres. Growers include Hightower Creek (.75 acres), Kaya (10.5 acres), Montaluce (1.7 acres), The Cottage Vineyards (1 acre), Frogtown (3.5 acres), Three Sisters (2.9 acres), Cartecay (1.75 acres), Ellijay River Vineyards (.5 acres), CeNita (.5 acres), Debarge (.1 acres), Sharp Mountain (.15 acres), Fainting Goat (.75 acres), Yonah Mountain (3 acres), Habersham (3.4 acres), and Engelheim (1.5 acres). Only Cabernet Sauvignon grows on more acres than Merlot. Merlot is a medium-bodied red wine with soft tannins and hints of raspberry, black cherry, and black currant. When aged in oak, the wine acquires hints of vanilla along with cedar if American oak is used. The wine can taste jammy when the grapes are grown in warm climates. Try the Three Sisters Merlot, which boasts flavors of light, black fruit and soft tannins with a pleasant mouthfeel and lingering finish.

Meunier/Pinot Meunier (muh-NYAY) at The Cottage Vineyards, August 2017

A *Vitis vinifera*, the grape is first mentioned in 1690 in France and is a key red grape in Champagne for making sparkling wine. In Georgia, only one vineyard grows this grape, The Cottage Vineyard, which has 1 acre. Meunier is a blending grape and a good grower in cooler regions. It is lighter red in color with a fresh acidity but not overly age worthy as a red wine.

Mourvèdre (moor-VEH-druh) Monastrell

Another *Vitis vinifera*, the primary name for this grape in Monastrell. It was first noted in Spain from 1381 to 1386 in Valencia. Today the grape is best known in Spain and Southern France. In Georgia, two vineyards grow Mourvèdre: Tiger Mountain (.5 acres) and Wolf Mountain (1 acre). Mourvèdre is frequently a blending grape, particularly in the Southern Rhône. The wine is garnet colored, tannic, and spicy with black fruit aromas and flavors. Mourvèdre makes good rosé wine.

Muscat (MUHS-kat) Blanc à Petits Grains

This *Vitis vinifera* is an ancient grape—Italian or Greek—first mentioned in Italy in 1304. However, the likely source is

Greece, assuming the Romans brought the grape into Italy and Southern France. The Cottage Vineyard grows .5 acres and is the only vineyard growing this ancient, white grape in Georgia. Small white berries characterize this grape, which is considered perhaps the best of the several Muscat varieties developed. Muscat produces dry, still wine, sweet wine, and sparkling wine.

Nebbiolo (neb-ee-OH-loh)
Photo by Hilloah Rohr

This *Vitis vinifera* is an ancient grape with origins in Italy around 1266. The grape is the foundation for Barolo and Barbaresco. In Georgia, one vineyard, Frogtown, grows .5 acres. Nebbiolo produces a full-bodied wine with cherry, anise, and raspberry aromas and flavors. A floral, violet aroma is also noteworthy. As the base for Barolo and Barbaresco, this grape produces wines with ageability, allowing tannins to soften.

Noble at Château Élan, 2016

Noble is a self-fertile, purple *Vitis rotundifolia* (muscadine) that is highly productive and is the primary grape used to make Red muscadine wine. Eleven vineyards plant 137.1 acres of Noble: Currahee (1.25 acres), Feather's Edge (1.25 acres), Gin Creek (5 acres), Frogtown Hahira (6 acres), Still Pond (10 acres), Château Élan (10 acres), Fox (2 acres), Courson's Winery (1 acre), Cedar Green (.25 acres), Paulk (100 acres), and Susina Plantation (.33 acres). Wines from this grape range from dry to sweet, typically having an alcohol level around 12.5 percent with RS 6 percent. It can be fresh and crisp. Enjoy this wine at Still Pond.

Noiret at Engelheim, August 2016

An American hybrid produced by Cornell University in 2006, Noiret is planted on only 2.5 acres in Georgia where it is grown in three vineyards: Chateau Meichtry (.5 acres), Engelheim (.5 acres), and Blue Mountain (1.5 acres). Noiret grapes produce red wines with soft tannins, and are fruit forward with raspberry and mint aromas along with hints of spice. There is a green-pepper, herbaceous aroma associated with this wine.

Pam at Susina Plantation, August 2017

This *Vitis rotundifolia* is a female, bronze muscadine with a late harvest. It is a fresh-market cultivar. In Georgia, there are two vineyards with 12 acres that produce this grape: Courson's Winery (2 acres) and Horse Creek (10 acres).

Petit Manseng at Frogtown, August 2015

A *Vitis vinifera*, this grape was mentioned in the Jurançon, France, in 1562. Petit Manseng was first introduced into Georgia by John Ezzard of Tiger Mountain from his friends at Horton Vineyards in Virginia. In Georgia there are eight vineyards that produce twelve acres: Cavender Creek (1 acre), Stonewall Creek (1 acre), Frogtown (1 acre), Tiger Mountain (1.5 acres), Cartecay (1.5 acres), Yonah Mountain (3.5 acres), Engelheim (1.5 acres), and The Stack Farm (1 acre). The grapes can produce either a dry or sweet wine with a naturally high acidity and aromas and flavors of fresh green apples, lemon, and lime. On the palate, it boasts a crisp acidity, and fresh fruit and citrus flavors dominate. The Tiger Mountain and Stonewall Creek Petit Manseng wines have received the best wine award for best Georgia-grown *Vitis vinifera* and overall best wine at the last two Georgia Trustees Wine Challenge.

Petit Verdot (peh-TEE vehr-DOH) at Frogtown, September 2015

Another *Vitis vinifera*, this grape's origin is in the Gironde region of Bordeaux, France, around 1736. The wines produced from this grape are dark red in color with bold tannins, and are used to make full-bodied, Bordeaux-type blended wines. In Georgia, six vineyards total four acres planted with Petit Verdot: Montaluce (.36 acres), The Cottage Vineyard (.5 acres), Frogtown

(1 acre), Stonewall Creek (.25 acres), Yonah Mountain (1.4 acres), and Wolf Mountain (.5 acres). This grape is in the Frogtown Personality red-wine blend.

Pineapple at Courson's, August 2017

This *Vitis rotundifolia* is a self-fertile, bronze grape which can be found in one acre at Courson's Winery. Pineapple, not surprisingly, is said to project pineapple aromas as a fresh-market cultivar. Pineapple was introduced in 1988 by Ison's Nursery in Georgia.

Pinot Blanc (pee-noe blahnk)
Photo by Wikimedia Commons

A *Vitis vinifera*, this grape is a mutation of Pinot Noir and produces white wine. Alsace has significant plantings of this grape. In Georgia, there is one vineyard, Three Sisters, with

1.6 acres. The grape is most often produced as a dry, still wine with apple, spice, and yeast aromas. On the palate its fresh, crisp acidity dominates along with apple and spice. The wine can be aged, and over time transforms into honey aromas and flavors. Pinot Blanc is good for making sparkling wine. The Three Sisters's excellent Georgia Cuvee, produced in the traditional method with secondary fermentation occurring in the bottle, contains Pinot Blanc, Chardonnay, and Pinot Noir grapes.

Pinot Grigio (pee-noh gree-joe)/Pinot Gris at Hightower, August 2016

A *Vitis vinifera*, this grape is a color mutation of Pinot Noir, producing a graying-blue grape used to make white wine. Pinot Gris was first mentioned 1283 in Burgundy, France. The Italians call this grape Pinot Grigio. In Georgia, five vineyards grow 4.8 acres: Hightower Creek (.75 acres), Montaluce (1.1 acres), Sharp Mountain (.2 acres), Engelheim (.25 acres), and Beca Farms (2.5 acres). The grape produces crisp, fresh, dry, and fruity wines with aromas and flavors of apricot, citrus lemon and lime, tropical fruit melon, and hints of yellow apple. Italy and the United States are the two largest producers. Hightower Creek produced their first full-bodied Pinot Gris in 2016. Enjoy as you travel.

Pinot Noir (pee-noe nwahr) at Sharp Mountain, August 2016

A *Vitis vinifera*, this is an ancient grape from the Burgundy region in France. The grape produces a light- to medium-body red wine with black plum, raspberry, strawberry, red cherry, and cranberry aromas and flavors. Two vineyards grow .25 acres: Sharp Mountain (.2 acres) and Three Sisters (.05 acres). Sharp Mountain's Pinot Noir is a light- to medium-body wine and remains the only Pinot Noir produced as a varietal.

Primitivo (pri-meh-TEE-voh)/Zinfandel/Tribidrag at Sharp Mountain, August 2016

This *Vitis vinifera* grape produces a medium-bodied red wine. One vineyard, Sharp Mountain, grows .25 acres. Zinfandel wine provides aromas and flavors of blackberry, strawberry, dried fruits, and spice with a range of alcohol levels. Sharp Mountain's Gris Rough uses this grape in a blend.

Redgate at Still Pond, August 2017

This *Vitis rotundifolia* is a self-fertilizing muscadine grape with a light- to dark-red color with large grape clusters. In Georgia, one vineyard, Still Pond, grows 8 acres.

Riesling (REES-ling) at Paradise Hills Resort & Spa, September 2016

This *Vitis vinifera* has origins in Rheingau, Germany, perhaps as early as 1348. It is a terrific white grape that has struggled to be productive in Georgia. One vineyard, Paradise Hills Resort & Spa, grows 2.5 acres. Riesling contains high sugar levels and lively acidity, producing a dry, semisweet wine and a late harvest.

Roussanne (roo-SAHN) at Frogtown, August 2015

This *Vitis vinifera* has origins in the Northern Rhône Valley since 1781. It is a white blending grape that is challenging to grow. It's typically used for blending with other grapes, like Marsanne. Roussanne is aromatic with good acidity. There is one acre of it planted in Georgia at Frogtown. The MRV at Frogtown contains Marsanne, Roussanne, and Viognier, much like white wines in the Rhône Valley. It is a full-bodied wine with enough structure and complexity to age.

Sangiovese (san-joh-VAY-zeh) at Sharp Mountain, August 2016

This *Vitis vinifera* most likely originates from Southern Italy. Today it is a dominant grape in Tuscany but grown throughout the world. Sangiovese grapes produce a medium-body red wine with blackberry, raspberry, and red currant aromas and flavors. In Italy, the grape produces Chianti, Rosso di Montalcino, and Brunello di Montalcino. In Georgia, five vineyards produce 6.5 acres: Kaya (2 acres), Montaluce (.8 acres), Sharp Mountain (.1 acres), Frogtown (3 acres), and Serenity (.6 acres). Try the Serenity Cellars Sangiovese as one example of how well this grape can grow and produce wine in Georgia.

Sauvignon Blanc (SOH-vihn-yohn blahnk) at Sharp Mountain, August 2016

This *Vitis vinifera* has origins in Loire Valley around 1534 with one parent likely being Chenin Blanc. It is a key white grape in the Loire Valley, although its best-known region is Pouilly-Fume. Sauvignon Blanc is a light-bodied wine with aromas and flavors of white peach, melon, lime, and grapefruit. Sauvignon Blanc is one parent of Cabernet Sauvignon. In Georgia, 3.8 acres grow at four vineyards: Sharp Mountain (.5 acres), Frogtown (.5 acres), Yonah Mountain (.33 acres), and Becca Farms (2.5 acres).

Sauvignon (sah-vah-NYAHN) Gris at Frogtown, September 2015

A *Vitis vinifera*, this grape is a mutation of Sauvignon Blanc with darker skins which can produce a more medium-body wine. One acre grows in Georgia at Frogtown.

Seyval Blanc (say-vahl blahnk) at Habersham, August 2016

This is a highly successful French-hybrid white grape produced by Bertille Seyve and Victor Villard in the midtwentieth century. Seyval Blanc was used to breed other grapes grown in Georgia to include Cayuga White and Chardonnel. Like Chardonnay, it has high acidity and can produce crisp, fresh, white dry or sparkling wines. In Georgia, six vineyards grow this grape on a total of 9.9

acres: Odom Springs (2 acres), Frogtown (.75 acres), Montaluce (1.38 acres), Chateau Meichtry (.5 acres), and Ellijay River (1 acre). Try Odom Springs Shortstop Seyval.

Southland at Bottoms Nursery

This *Vitis rotundifolia* is a self-fertile, purple grape with .25 acres grown at Frogtown Hahira. Southland is a fresh-market cultivar that can produce red wine. Most often, the juice from this grape is blended with other juices.

Sterling at Bottoms Nursery

Another Vitus rotundifolia, Sterling is a self-fertile juice cultivar that is bronze in color. Currently, only one vineyard, Frogtown Hahira, is growing this grape (.25 acres).

Supreme at Horse Creek, August 2017

A Vitus rotundifolia, Supreme is a female, purple, fresh-market cultivar. Three vineyards grow this grape—Frogtown Hahira (5 acres), Horse Creek Winey (10 acres), and Susina Plantation (.33 acres)—for a combined 15.33 acres. Supreme is a highly preferred black muscadine with a long shelf life for fresh-market cultivars.

Syrah (sih-RAH) at Cottage Vineyard, September 2016

This *Vitis vinifera* is a red grape with origins in the Northern Rhône, first mentioned in 1781. Two vineyards grow this grape in Georgia: The Cottage Vineyard (1 acre) and Wolf Mountain (1 acre). Syrah is enjoyed both as a 100 percent varietal and in blended wines. Syrah makes medium- and full-bodied wines with blackberry, blueberry, plum, tobacco, and chocolate aromas and flavors. Wolf Mountain produces two red-wine blends containing Syrah: Howling Wolf Red and Instinct.

Tannat (tan–nat) at 12 Spies Vineyard, August 2017

This *Vitis vinifera* is a red-wine grape first mentioned in 1783–1784 in the Madiran region of Hautes-Pyrénées in Southwest France. Tannat is a dark-red grape known for its firm tannin and high acidity. Spice, plum, and tobacco notes frame the aromas, while raspberry and plum dominate the wine's flavors. In Georgia, six vineyards grow this grape on a total of 8.6 acres: 12 Spies (.2 acres), Stonewall Creek (.2 acres), Frogtown (3.5 acres), Tiger Mountain (.75 acres), Wolf Mountain (3 acres), and The Stack Farm (1 acre). Tannat grows well in Georgia. Try the Frogtown Cellars or Tiger Mountain Tannat wines.

Tara at Susina Plantation in August 2017

This *Vitis rotundifolia* is a self-fertile, bronze muscadine grown in six Georgia vineyards—Currahee (1.25 acres), Feather's Edge (1 acre), Frogtown Hahira (.5 acres), Cedar Green (.1 acres), Courson's Winery (1 acre), and Susina Plantation (.25 acres)—for a total 4.1 acres. The grape ripens early and is well suited for making white wine.

Teroldego at Frogtown, August 2015

This *Vitis vinifera* is an ancient grape from Northeast Italy, first mentioned in 1480. In Georgia, two vineyards account for one acre: Frogtown (.5 acres) and Montaluce (.5 acres). A dark-colored wine with black cherry, plum, and smoke aromas, on the palate it boasts balanced acidity and good tannins. Oak barrels are used to age this wine.

Tourgia Nacional (too-REE-gah nah-syoo-NAHL) at Frogtown, August 2015

This *Vitis vinifera* is perhaps the most famous Portuguese red grape from the Dão region. It was first mentioned in 1822. In Georgia, this grape is grown on 8.2 acres scattered among five vineyards: Kaya (3.7 acres), Three Sisters (.5 acres), Frogtown (1.5 acres), Tiger Mountain (.5 acres), and Wolf Mountain (2 acres). In Portugal, the grape is used to make port. As a still wine, it can retain substantial tannins, which take time to mellow, with blackberry, cherry, spice, and floral aromas of violet. The grape blends well with other reds. Frogtown produces a Touriga Nacional with dark-cherry aromas and soft tannins.

Traminette (trah-men-ett) at Hightower Creek Vineyards, August 2016

An American hybrid first bred in 1965 by Herb C. Barrett at the University of Illinois, this grape has a complex family tree with many different *Vitis* including riparia, labrusca, vinifera, aestivalis, lincecumii, rupestris, and cinerea. The original intent was to develop a table grape with Gewürztraminer flavors. In 1996, the grape was released for public use. In Georgia, ten vineyards are growing this grape on a total of 11.3 acres, including Hightower Creek (.75 acres), 12 Spies (.2 acres), Stonewall Creek (1 acre), Serenberry Vineyard (.75 acres), Cartecay (2 acres), CeNita (.6 acres), Debarge (.25 acres), Engelheim (2 acres), Habersham Vineyards (2.2 acres), and Blue Mountain (1.5 acres). Cartecay Vineyards produces a 100 percent Traminette that is fresh and has crisp acidity with citrus, apricot, mango, and honey overtones. It is an increasingly popular white wine in Georgia.

Trebbiano (treb-bee-AH-no) at Sharp Mountain, August 2016

There are only .5 acres of this *Vitis vinifera* planted in Georgia at Sharp Mountain. The earliest mention of this grape is north-central Italy in 1303. Sharp Mountain blends this grape with Chardonnay to make a semisweet white wine. In Italy, this grape contributes a significant percentage of white-wine production with high acidity and relatively neutral flavors. In France, it is called Ugni Blanc and is used extensively for producing brandy in Cognac and Armagnac.

Vidal Blanc (vee-dahl blahnk) at Habersham in August 2016

This French hybrid, created in the 1930s for a variety, is well suited for cognac and ice wine. In Georgia, nine vineyards are growing this grape for a total acreage of 18.4. Those growing this grape include Crane Creek (4 acres), Odom Springs (1 acre), Montaluce (2.38 acres), Frogtown (.5 acres), Three Sisters (1.6 acres), Bear Claw (1.5 acres), Cartecay (2 acres), CeNita (.2 acres), and Habersham (5.2 acres). Crane Creek's 100 percent Vidal Blanc is a crisp, fresh wine with flavors of citrus, tropical and tree fruits, and has medium acidity. It offers a crisp and fresh wine.

Villard Blanc (vee-yahr blahnk) at Cornell University

A French hybrid popular in France in the 1960s when at its zenith, it is now more likely to be grown in the Northeast and Southeast United States. It is similar to Sauvignon Blanc with more neutral flavors. In Georgia, there are seven vineyards that grow this grape in 7.6 total acres. Those vineyards include Boutier (.25 acres), Big Door (1 acre), Habersham (5.2 acres), Engelheim (.5 acres), The Vineyards at Mill Creek (.25 acres), Trillium (.05 acres), and Little Vine Vineyards (.3 acres). Villard Blanc grows on a prolific vine and yields grapes that make a wine predominately showing citrus aromas and flavors.

Villard Noir (vee-YAHR NWAHR) at Crane Creek, September 2016

This French hybrid is grown in one vineyard in Georgia, Crane Creek, which plants this grape in 1.8 acres. Villard Noir is a late-ripening grape that requires a long growing season. Crane Creek produces a Villard Noir rosé wine that is light-bodied and refreshing with hints of caramel and toasted nuts.

Vignoles at Hightower Creek, August 2016

Vignoles is a French hybrid developed in the 1930s by J. F. Ravat. In Georgia, one vineyard, Hightower Creek, grows .5 acres. The Vignoles grape is an excellent choice for dry and semisweet wines. However, it is often a vital grape in producing late-harvest wines where Botrytis cinerea, or noble rot, has formed.

Viognier (vee-oh-nee-aye) at Sharp Mountain in August 2016

This *Vitis vinifera* is a French, white grape with origins in the northern Rhône Valley around 1781. In Georgia, there are eight vineyards collectively growing 10.25 acres. Producers include Cavender Creek (.25 acres), Frogtown (3.5 acres), Kaya (1 acre), The Cottage Vineyard (1 acre), Tiger Mountain (2 aces), Ellijay River Vineyards (1 acre), Sharp Mountain (.5 acres), and The Stack Farm (1 acre). Viognier buds early, risking late-frost damage. The grape produces a full-bodied white wine with tropical and tree-fruit flavors to include apricot, mango, and peach along with floral, honeysuckle aromas. This grape has not always been a consistent performer year to year. One year outstanding results were achieved, but the following year the wine produced did not have the same zest and complexity.

Welder at Bottoms Nursery

Henry Welder of Tavares, Florida, introduced this *Vitis rotundifolia* juice cultivar in 1972 since the grape's discovery in 1957. One Georgia grower, Frogtown Hahira, grows 1.25 acres. A self-fertile, bronze grape, Welder is a prolific, white grape cultivar with a high sugar content and flavors usually associated with grape juice.

Appendix A

Map of the Coastal Georgia Botanical Gardens (One-Acre Design)

PROPOSED TRUSTEES GARDEN

COASTAL GEORGIA BOTANICAL GARDENS

JUNE 18, 2014

CONCEPT A

SIX-FOOT TALL PALE FENCE

EVERGREEN HEDGE

TO GREAT LAWN

SEMI-FORMAL / SEMI-RUSTIC ALLÉE

SOUR ORANGES

TO FORMAL GARDEN

GRAPE ARBOR

GRAPE ARBOR

ENGLISH-COMMON FRUIT TREES

MULBERRIES

SOUR ORANGES

MULBERRIES

GRAINS/COMMODITIES

HERBS/MEDICINALS

GRAPE ARBOR

GRAPE ARBOR

KITCHEN GARDEN

TROPICALS

MEDITERRANEAN PLANTS

GRAPE TRELLISES

Although no historical drawings of the original Trustees Garden in downtown Savannah exist, we do have an idea of the plants and design thanks to historical letters between gardeners and the English trustees. Mulberry, citrus, fig, pomegranate, grape, apple, plum, indigo, hemp, flax, quinine, and olive plants were grown. While the eighteenth-century colonists underestimated the climate and soils needed for these novel crops, we can develop a sustainable garden with many of these plants thanks to better horticultural understanding after 280 years.

2 Canebrake Road
Savannah, Georgia 31419
Phone: (912) 921-5460

Picture by Coastal Georgia Botanical Gardens

Appendix B

James Edward Oglethorpe, Esq.

JAMES OGLETHORPE.

Picture copied from Harriet C. Cooper, James Oglethorpe: The Founder of Georgia, Illustrated *(New York: D. Appleton and Company, 1904), inside cover-page leaf.*

Inscription on Monumental Tablet in Cranham Church, England

"Near this place lie the remains of James Edward Oglethorpe, Esq., who served under Prince Eugene, and in 1714 was Captain-Lieutenant in the 1st troop of Queen's Guards. In 1740, he was appointed Colonel of a regiment to be raised in Georgia. In 1745, he was appointed Major-General; in 1747 Lieutenant-General; and in 1765 General of His Majesty's forces.
"In his civil station, he was very early conspicuous. He was chosen M. P. for Halsmere in Surrey in 1722, and continued to represent it until 1754. In the Committee of Parliament for enquiring into the state of the Gaols, formed Feb. 25th 1728 and of which he was chairman, the active and preserving zeal of his benevolence found a truly suitable employment, by visiting with his colleagues of the generous body, the dark and pestilential dungeons of the prisons which at that time dishonored the Metropolis, detecting the most enormous oppressions; obtaining exemplary punishment on those who had been guilty of such outrages against humanity and Justice, and restoring multitudes from extreme misery to light and freedom. Of these, about 700, rendered, by long confinement for debt, strangers and helpless in the country of their birth, and desirous of seeking an asylum in the wilds of America, were by him conducted thither in 1732.
"He willingly encountered in their behalf a variety of fatigue and danger, and thus became the Founder of the Colony of Georgia: which (Founded on the ardent wish for liberty). Set the noble example of prohibiting the importation of slaves. This new establishment he strenuously and successfully defended against a powerful invasion of Spaniards.
"In the year in which he quitted England to found this settlement, he nobly strove to restore our true national defenses by Sea and Land, A free navy without impressing; a constitutional militia, but his sole affections were more enlarged than even the term Patriotism can express. He was the friend of the oppressed Negro; No part of the world was too remote, no interest too unconnected or too opposed to his own, to prevent his immediate succor of suffering humanity. For such qualities, he received from the ever-memorable John, Duke of Argyle, and a full testimony in the British Senate to his military character, his natural generosity, his contempt of danger, and

his regard for the Publick. A similar encomium is perpetuated in a foreign language; and, by one of our most celebrated Poets, his remembrance is transmitted to Posterity in lines justly expressive of the purity, the ardor, the extent of his benevolence. He lived till the 1st of July 1785, a venerable instance to what a fullness of duration and of continued usefulness a life of temperance and virtuous labor is capable of being protracted. His widow, Elizabeth, Daughter of Sir Nathan Wrighte, Cranham Hall Essex, Bart., and only sister and heiress of Sir Samuel Wrighte Bart. Of the same place, surviving with regret (through with due submission to Divine Providence) an affectionate husband, after a union of more than 40 years, hath inscribed to his memory these faint traces of his excellent character."[1]

1 Harriet C. Cooper, *James Oglethorpe: The Founder of Georgia, Illustrated* (New York: D. Appleton and Company, 1904), 207–209.

Appendix C

Georgia Wine Producers 2016

Winery Members
12 Spies Vineyards & Farm, LLC
Cartecay Vineyards
Château Élan Winery
Crane Creek Vineyards
Engelheim Vineyards
Gin Creek Vineyards & Winery
Habersham Vineyards & Winery
Hard Press Beverages
Hightower Creek Vineyards, LLC
Horse Creek Winery
Little Vine Vineyards
Odom Springs Vineyards
Paradise Hills, Winery Resort & Spa
Serenberry Vineyards
Still Pond Vineyard & Winery
Stonewall Creek Vineyards
Sweet Acre Farms Winery
The Georgia Winery
Tiger Mountain Vineyards
Watermelon Creek Vineyard
Yonah Mountain Vineyards

Vineyard/Orchard Members
Buffalo Lick Vineyards
Fainting Goat Vineyards & Winery
Farmer's Daughter Vineyards
G. A. Graff & Associates Inc. (Blackjack Mountain Vineyard & Winery)
Just A Boy Vineyard
Squirrel Ridge Vineyards
The Stack Farm
The Vineyard at Hominy Creek
The Vineyards at Mill Creek/Uncorked on Main
Trillium Vineyard, LLC

Associate Members
Brett Huske, *Dalton Area CVB*
Christina Ernst, *VIP Southern Tours*
Clarks Wesley
Wayne Crawford
Doug Mabry, *The Vineyard and Winery Association of West Georgia*
Jane F. Garvey
Parks Redwine
Rachel A. Itle, *University of Georgia, Griffin*
Sandi Simpson, *Norton-Mountain Insurance, LLC*
Georgia Winegrowers Association of Georgia[1]

1 Georgia Wine Producers Members, Georgia Wine Producers, accessed September 13, 2017, http://www.georgiawineproducers.org/members/.

Appendix D

"Wayne on Wine" Guide to Enjoying Wine

Drink what you like and challenge yourself to experiment with new wines!

The Five S's: SEE, SWIRL, SMELL, SIP, and SAVOR

There are variations to this memory aid. A wine profile contains sweetness, acidity, tannin, alcohol, and body.

1. SEE

Using a white background and good lighting, tilt your glass to capture appearance, color, intensity, saturation, and hue at the glass rim and tears (tears, or legs, do not indicate quality).

Appearance:

- *Brilliant*: Sparkling clear.
- *Clear*: No visible solids but lacking sparkling clarity.
- *Dull*: A suggestion of haziness but without visible suspended material.
- *Cloudy*: Definitely hazy or hazing visible with suspended material.
- *Precipitated*: Observable deposit in wine but the wine is still clear.

Color:

- White Wines
    - *Light yellow/straw*: Almost watery. May be with or without a slight greenish tinge.
    - *Medium yellow*: Approaching the color of natural lemon juice.
    - *Light gold*: A full, rounded, dark-golden color (may indicate barrel aging).
    - *Amber/light brown*: A color fault usually the result of too much oxidation; older whites begin to turn golden in color.
- Red Wines
    - *Pink/rose*: Self-defined. Grenache Pink may have orange tint; with other pinks, this may indicate over-oxidation.
    - *Light red*: Deeper than pink; lighter than standard red.
    - *Medium red*: Decisively red but without purple tint.
    - *Dark red*: Very deep color, often with purple overtones.
    - *Tawny*: Tinged with brown; a sign of age or oxidation.

2. SWIRL

Sniff still wine once to obtain initial aromas. Then swirl to allow the wine to release aroma compounds into the air to boost detection (fruit, floral, esters) bouquet (fermentation, barrel, and bottle aging). DO NOT SWIRL SPARKLING WINE INITIALLY. Sniff, observe mousse and bubbles, then swirl as needed to capture aroma.

3. SMELL

Switch between smelling and sniffing and thinking about the aroma. To avoid overload while smelling, sniff your forearm to neutralize smells.

Aroma:

- *Varietal*: Has primary grape aroma.

- *Distinct*: Possesses uniqueness but not sufficient to identify the grape.
- *Vinous*: Smells like grape wine without distinctiveness.

Bouquet:

- *Cask-aged*: Retains a mixture of odors reflecting wine held in casks for a proper period; includes the sensation of oakiness.
- *Bottle-aged*: Retains rounded balance of odors brought about by continual maturation in the wine bottle (important to recognize; impossible to describe).
- *Off-odors*: Foreign to the ordinary smell of clean, sound wine.
    - Excess of sulfur-containing compounds: Winemaker used too much sulfur.
        - *Hydrogen sulfide*: Possesses the so-called "rotten egg" smell.
        - *Sulfur dioxide*: Has an overpowering smell, clearly suggesting sulfur.
        - *Mercaptans*: Has smell described as "garlicky" or "skunky."
    - Off-odors resulting from the action of lactic acid on the developing wine.
        - *Mousey*: Sharp, strong smell brought on by the action of unwanted lactobacilli (once the wine is swallowed). The cause is lactic-acid bacteria formed by yeasts. Not detected by smell.
        - *Butrytic*: Similar to the smell of rancid butter.
        - *Acetic*: The wine vinegar odor.
        - *Lactic*: Sometimes described as a "sauerkraut" smell.
    - Other off-odors
        - *Moldy*: A readily recognized fault. An aroma is suggestive of rotten fruit or wood.
        - *Raisiny*: An aroma of raisins or overripe grapes.
        - *Woody*: Odor suggestive of wet wood (a trace of this smell—mainly oak—is wanted in an

excellent red wine. It is an off-odor only when it is obviously apparent).

- *Corky*: A smell resembling dampened or moldy cork.

4. SIP

Spit as needed when tasting various wines. Check the following:

- *Acidity*: As grapes ripen they become less acidic.
- *Flat*: Possessing so little acid as to be hardly apparent.
- *Tart*: Having a pleasant amount of acid; lively on the tongue but not overly so.
- *Acidy*: Having unwarranted acid content. Very sharp on the tongue.
- *Sweetness*: Comes from the presence of sugars (glucose and fructose) in the wine. With glycerol contributing to the sweet taste, acidity and astringency interact with the sweet impression.
  - *Bone dry*: No sweetness. Most brut Champagne, Chablis, Sancerre-Sauvignon Blanc, and Chianti Classico are examples.
  - *Dry*: Possessing no apparent sweetness; most Chardonnay and 85 percent of red wines.
  - *Medium dry*: Barely noticeable sweetness; Riesling, Viognier, Merlot, and Pinot Noir.
  - *Medium sweet*: Sweetness but subdued; some late-harvest white and red; late-harvest Zinfandel and Muscadines.
  - *Sweet*: Unquestionably sweet; botrytized wines, white, some Muscadines.
  - *Very sweet*: Fortified wines and some late-harvest wines
- *Body*: Body in wine can be measured only in the mouth. Essentially, a body is the feel of the wine as it is swished about in the mouth. It is almost impossible to describe. Recognition of body only comes with experience.
  - *Light- or thin-bodied*: Lacking a sense of viscosity; watery. Think skim milk.

  - *Medium-bodied*: Possessing noticeable viscosity in the mouth. Think 2 percent milk.
  - *Full-bodied*: Having a great feel of viscosity. Think whole milk.
- *Bitterness and astringency*: Though altered by other factors—mainly sugar—wine tastes smooth, rough, puckered, or bitter in part because of the kinds of tannins it possesses. With age, astringency declines, but bitterness seldom disappears. A wine whose taste is like caffeine or quinine is not, nor will it become, a good wine, and should be described as bitter.
  - *Smooth/soft*: Without irritating astringency.
  - *Slightly rough/very rough*: Describing increasing degrees of astringency.
- *Tannin*: Exclusive to red-wine textural astringent taste; provided by grape skins, seeds, and new wood barrels.
- *Flavor*: Trying to relate it to a grape variety. Alcohol is also part of wine's flavor.
- *Varietal*: Possessing an ability to bring to mind the taste of a particular grape, thus clarifying or confirming a previously made nasal determination.
- *Age*: Wine age may be discerned by vigilant tasting, though age for a specific wine depends both on whether it is red or white and the varietal. See aging chart for examples. Consider acquiring several bottles you intend to age, and taste one every several years in the aging window suggested.
  - *Young*: Fresh, commonly limited in bottle bouquet, sprightly and fruity.
  - *Mature*: Has sufficient age to have captured its various components into a whole.
  - *Aged*: Possessing a softening balance due to cask and bottle maturation based on winemakers' choice.

Taste-Odors

- *Fruity*: Freshness, tartness with a fruit-like impression on nose and palate.

- *Stemmy*: Idea of bitterness; most often a result of fermentation in the presence of grape stems.
- *Gassy*: Slight amount of dissolved carbon-dioxide gas that pecks the tongue; still wine.
- *Metallic*: Tastes like zinc or copper.
- *Spoiled*: Having a less-than-good taste resulting from spoilage or oxidation; old wine.
- *Fresh*: Fruitiness and needed tartness.
- *Clean*: Bacterial and wine processing–defects free.
- *Tired*: Lacks freshness, fruitiness, and aroma; telling of overly processed wine.
- *Well balanced*: Component elements in relation to one another that the total imprint is pleasant; think taste buds (sweet, sour, bitter, and salty).
- *Unbalanced*: Excessive amount of flavor or component to the point where the palate impression is one of taste conflict.
- *Coarse*: Tannins are gritty on the palate like sandpaper.
- *Harsh*: Odor or taste in which acidity or astringency is disproportionate.
- *Foxy*: Having the aroma and flavor of Concord or other Labrusca grapes.
- *Hot wine*: High alcohol and noticeable when tasting.
- *TCA (or 2, 4, 6 trichloranisole)*: The unpleasant-smelling, musty compound associated with corked wine or more common cork taint.

5. SAVOR

Did you enjoy what you were tasting? Can you savor the moment? How would you improve the wine? Great wines have complex aromas and bouquets, excellent structures, are well balanced, have a pleasant mouthfeel, a long finish, and the wine is varietal or blend-typical. Often, well-aged red wines are soft with highly integrated tannins. In white wine, expect notable structure with integrated acidity. The wine is balanced.

Wine Temperature for Serving

Sparkling wines and sweet wines	45°–50° F	7°–10° C
Dry white and rosé table wines	50°–60° F	10°–15° C
Light-bodied red table wines	55°–65° F	13°–18° C
Full-bodied red table wines	62°–68° F	17°–21° C

Store wine in a cool, dark place with no vibrations. For sparkling wine, store standing or flat.

Note: Sparkling wine may taste better if served at 50–55° F. I prefer drinking sparkling wine in a white-wine glass to better appreciate the aromas and flavors.

Wine Education and Wine Facts

One acre of land averages:

- 5 tons of grapes = 10,000 lbs.
- 13.5 barrels of wine = 59 gallons ea., or 797 gallons of wine
- 3,958 bottles of wine, 25.6 oz. ea.
- 15,940 glasses of wine, 6.4 oz. ea.

One case of wine contains:

- 12 x 750 ml bottles, or 24 half bottles
- 30 lbs. of grapes
- 307.2 oz. of wine
- 48 glasses of wine (6 oz. ea.) or 61 glasses of wine (5 oz. ea.)

One 225-liter Bordeaux barrique barrel of wine contains:

- 740 lbs. of grapes / 59 gallons (1 gallon = 3.785 liters) (1 liter = .198 gallons)
- 24.6 cases of wine (12 x 750 ml bottles)
- 297 bottles of wine
- 1,485 glasses of wine (5 oz. ea)

One bottle of wine contains:

- 750 ml of wine
- 2.4 lbs. of grapes (39 oz.)
- 25.6 oz. of wine
- 4–6 glasses of wine (12 pours if tasting 2 oz. or at 5 full glasses if tasting 5 oz. on average when entertaining)
- 750 calories on average
- 12–15.5 alcohol by volume for average still wine

Wine Bottle Sizes

187.5 ml Piccolo or Split: Typically used for a single serving of Champagne.

375 ml Demi or Half: Holds one-half of the standard 750 ml size.

750 ml Standard: Common bottle size for most distributed wine.

1.5 L Magnum: Equivalent to two standard 750 ml bottles.

3.0 L Double Magnum/Jeroboam: Equivalent to two Magnums or four standard 750 ml bottles.

4.5 L Rehoboam (still wine): Equivalent to six standard 750 ml bottles.

6.0 L Imperial/Methuselah: Equivalent to eight standard 750 ml bottles or two Double Magnums.

9.0 L Salmanazar: Equivalent to twelve standard 750 ml bottles or a full case of wine!

12.0 L Balthazar: Equivalent to sixteen standard 750 ml bottles or two Imperials.

15.0 L Nebuchadnezzar: Equivalent to twenty standard 750 ml bottles.

18.0 L Solomon/Melchior: Equivalent to twenty-four 750 ml bottles

30.0 L Melchizedek/Midas: Equivalent to thirty 750 ml bottles.

General Tasting Order for Wines

- White before red
- Dry before sweet
- Young before old
- Modest before fine

- Light-bodied before full-bodied
- Light, young red before full-bodied, sweet wine
- Taste in related groups when possible

Aging Guidelines

Provided by Jancis Robinson (master of wine) and author experience

Wines with little aging potential

- German QBAs
- Asti and Moscato Spumante
- Rosé and blush wines
- White Zinfandel
- Branded wines such as Yellow Tail
- European table wine
- American jug and box wine
- Inexpensive varietals
- The majority of Vin de pays
- All Nouveau wines
- Vermouth
- Basic Sherry
- Tawny Ports
- Muscadine
- Albariño

Wines with aging potential

- Botrytized wines (5–25 yrs.)
- Chardonnay (2–6 yrs.)
- Riesling (2–30 yrs.)
- Hungarian Furmint (3–25 yrs.)
- Chenin Blanc (4–30 yrs.)
- Semillon (6–15 yrs.)
- Cabernet Sauvignon (4–20 yrs.)
- Merlot (2–10 yrs.)
- Nebbiolo (4–20 yrs.)

- Pinot Noir (2–8 yrs.)
- Sangiovese (2–8 yrs.)
- Syrah (4–16 yrs.)
- Zinfandel (2–6 yrs.)
- Classified Bordeaux (8–25 yrs.)
- Grand Cru Burgundy (8–25 yrs.)
- Tannat (4–12 yrs.)
- Spanish Tempranillo (5–10 yrs.)
- Gewürztraminer (3–10 yrs.)
- Cabernet Franc (5–10 yrs.)
- Amarone (10–20 yrs.)
- Grenache (5–10 yrs.)
- Carménère (5–10 yrs.)
- Oaked Chardonnay (5–8 yrs.)
- Sauternes (10–20 yrs.)
- Petit Manseng (4–6 yrs.)
- Champagne top houses (25–30 yrs.)
- Sparkling wine (2–7 yrs.)
- Barbera (5–10 yrs.)

Appendix E

Glossary

American Viticultural Area (AVA): A delimited grape-growing region having distinguishing features as described in the Code of Federal Regulations. These designations allow vintners and consumers to attribute a given quality, reputation, or other characteristic of a wine made from grapes grown in an area to its geographic origin. The establishment of viticultural areas allows vintners to describe more accurately the origin of their wines to consumers and helps consumers to identify wines they may purchase.

Farm winery: A winery which makes at least 40 percent of its annual production from agricultural produce grown in the state where the winery is located on premises, a substantial portion of which is used for agricultural purposes, including the cultivation of grapes, berries, or fruits to be utilized in the manufacture or production of wine by the winery, or is owned and operated by persons who are engaged in the production of a substantial portion of the agricultural produce used in its annual production.[1]

Grower vineyard: A vineyard that grows grapes and sells those grapes uncrushed to a winery for wine production that is

1 Department of Revenue, "Farm Winery (Out-of-State)," Georgia.gov, accessed September 13, 2017, https://dor.georgia.gov/farm-winery.

either sold by the winery or sold back to a tasting room with the producer's label.

Grower vineyard and tasting room: Purchases crushed or uncrushed grape juice, produces grapes, and produces wine at another winery and sells the wine as a satellite of another farm winery.

Phylloxera vastatrix: A yellow-colored species of root louse indigenous to southern North America and the Mississippi Valley. Phylloxera feeds on vine roots and leaves, causing rot and plant death. This louse exported on plants from the United States to England devastated the vineyards of Europe in the late-nineteenth century, forcing replanting on American rootstock, which is resistant to the pest. The louse remains active today in most vineyard areas of the world and in Georgia.[2]

Special-event wine auction: Permit issued to a bona-fide nonprofit civic organization authorizing the auction of wine-sealed containers only for a period not to exceed three days. No more than six permits may be issued in any one calendar year. The permit is only valid for the place specified in the permit and it must be lawful to sell alcohol in that place. This guideline is to assist you in the preparation of a State of Georgia Special Event Wine Auction License application that is submitted electronically at the Georgia Tax Center.[3]

Tasting room and winery: Purchases grapes (crushed or uncrushed), produces the wine, and sells the wine out of its tasting room or other distribution location.

Winery: Any maker, producer, or bottler of an alcoholic beverage, and in the case of wine, any vintner.[4]

Wine special-order shipping: Any shipper that is also a winery that is authorized to make direct shipments of wine to consumers

---

2 Tom Stevenson, *The New Sotheby's Wine Encyclopedia* (New York: DK Publishing, 1997), 21.

3 Department of Revenue, "Special Event Wine Auction," Georgia.gov, accessed September 13, 2017, https://dor.georgia.gov/special-event-wine-auction.

4 Department of Revenue, "Winery (Out-of-State)," Georgia.gov, accessed September 13, 2017, https://dor.georgia.gov/winery.

in this state. A special-order shipping license shall only be issued to a winery upon compliance with all applicable provisions and upon payment of the license fee designated. A special-order shipping license shall entitle the winery to ship wine upon order directly to consumers for personal or household use in this state without designating wholesalers. It is not a requirement for the winery to be licensed in the state in order to apply for a special-order shipping license in the state.[5]

5 Department of Revenue, "Wine Special Order Shipping (In-State)," Georgia.gov, accessed September 13, 2017, https://dor.georgia.gov/wine-special-order-shipping.

Appendix F

2017 Georgia Trustees Wine Challenge Results

Note: An asterisk (*) indicates the grapes are in part or in whole not Georgia-grown.

Gold Medals

Cartecay Vineyards

2015 (Traminette, Estate, Georgia)

Chateau Meichtry

2017 “George’s Cuvee” red proprietary blend (Norton and Noiret)

City Winery

2016 “Gone with the Vine” (Vidal Blanc, Three Sisters Vineyards) **Oglethorpe Award for Best Wine from Georgia-Grown Grapes, Best Dessert Wine**

Ellijay River Vineyards

2016 (Albariño, Estate, Georgia)

Georgia Winery

2016 Chattanooga Blush rosé proprietary blend (Cayuga, Concord, and Niagara*)

Gin Creek Vineyards and Winery (2 Golds)

NV (Lenoir, Estate, Reserve, Georgia) **Thomas McCall Award for Best American Hybrid Grape Wine, Best Georgia Red Overall**

NV “South Peach” propriety blend (Carlos and Peach)

Habersham Winery

2014 "Creekstone" (Chambourcin fortified, Stonepile Vineyards) **Best Fortified Wine**

Still Pond Winery and Distillery (2 Golds)

NV "Notchaway White" (Carlos, Estate, Georgia) **Ison Family Award for Best Muscadine Wine**

NV "Notchaway Red" (Noble, Estate, Georgia)

Stonewall Creek Vineyards & Winery

2016 (Norton, Stack Farm Vineyard)

Sweet Acre Farms Winery

2016 "Bramblin' Sam" proprietary fruit wine (blackberry and apple)

Tiger Mountain Vineyards (2 Golds) **Colonel William Stephens Award for Winery of Distinction**

2016 (Petit Manseng, Ezzard Vineyard) **Gay Dellinger Award for Best Vinifera Wine, Overall and White**

2016 Rosé (Ezzard Vineyard, Cabernet Franc) **Best Rosé Wine**

Urban Tree Cidery

NV "Wild Buzz" Cider (Golden Delicious apples) **Best Hard Cider**

The Viking Alchemist Meadery

"Bliss" Wildflower Mead (sweet honey wine*) **Best Mead**

Vineyards at Mill Creek

2016 (Lenoir, Estate, made at Horse Creek Winery)

Silver Medals

Big Door Vineyard (3 Silver) (made at Horse Creek Winery)

2016 (Blanc du Bois, Estate)

2016 "Gold Lace" (Blanc du Bois and Carlos)

2015 "Perfect Evening" red blend (Lenoir and Noble)

Boutier Winery (3 Silver)

2014 "Villardonnay" (55 percent Villard Blanc, 45 percent Chardonnay, Estate)

2014 "P. Victor Boutier" (Pinot Noir*)

2015 "Caberana" (45 percent Cabernet Sauvignon, 55 percent Cynthiana, Estate)

Butterducks Winery (2 Silver)

2015 (Viognier)

2014 "Brass Duck Red" (Cabernet Sauvignon and Merlot*)

Cartecay Vineyards (2 Silver)

2014 (Cabernet Sauvignon, Estate)

NV "Chimney Red" (Merlot, Chambourcin, Traminette, and Vidal Blanc)

Cavender Creek Vineyards (2 Silver)

2015 (Cabernet Sauvignon, Estate)

2015 "Blackjack" (80 percent Norton, 15 percent Lenoir from The Stack Farm, and 5 percent Cabernet Sauvignon, Estate)

CeNita Vineyards and Winery

2015 (Chambourcin, Estate)

Crane Creek Vineyards (2 Silver)

NV "Sweet Sally" (Catawba, Estate)

2015 "Brasstown Red" (Noiret, Estate)

Farmer's Daughter Vineyards

2016 "Bombshell" (Blanc du Bois, Pelham Vineyard)

Georgia Winery

2015 (Concord*)

2016 (Muscadine, Estate)

Gin Creek Vineyards and Winery

NV "Moscato" (Muscat*)

Habersham Winery (4 Silver)

2016 "Creekstone" (Chardonnay, Stonepile Vineyards)

NV "Scarlett" (Chambourcin, Cabernet Sauvignon, Merlot, Seyval, and Chardonnay)

NV "Georgia White Muscadine" (Stonepile Vineyard)

2016 (Traminette)

Horse Creek Winery (3 Silver)

NV "Traveler" (Pam, Perry Vineyards)

NV "Jockey" (79 percent Pam, 30 percent Carlos, semisweet, Perry Vineyards)

NV "Winnersville White" (79 percent Pam, 30 percent Carlos, sweet, Perry Vineyards)

Kaya Vineyard & Winery

2015 (Merlot, oak-aged, Estate)

Little Vine Vineyards (4 Silver)

2015 (Blanc du Bois, Estate)

2015 "Maddie's Rose" (Lenoir and Blanc du Bois, Estate)

2015 (Lenoir, Estate)

2015 "Sophie's Sweet Lenoir" (Lenoir, Estate)

Mercier Orchards

2016 "Old #3" cider (Gold Rush apples, Estate)

Monks Meadery

"Stigmata" Mead (honey wine blended with hibiscus, rose, elderflower, and hops)

Odom Springs Vineyard (2 Silver)

NV "Sharptop Seyval" (Seyval Blanc, Estate)

2016 "Homemade Sin" (Chambourcin, Vidal)

Sharp Mountain Vineyards

2016 "Etowah" (Merlot, Cabernet Sauvignon, Estate)

Still Pond Winery & Distillery (2 Silver)

NV "Plantation Red" (Noble, Estate)

NV "Confederate Peach" (Carlos, Magnolia and Peach, Estate)

Stonewall Creek Vineyards & Winery

"Yukari" rosé blend (Cabernet Sauvignon, Petit Verdot, Cabernet Franc, and Malbec, Estate)

Susina Plantation Winery (3 Silver)

2016 "Oh Susina" (Carlos and peach flavor, Estate)

2016 "Crisp" (white wine and apple flavor*)

2015 (Scuppernong, white muscadine, Estate)

Sweet Acre Farms Winery (6 Silver)

2015 (Carlos, Still Pond Vineyard, rooster label)

2016 "Medium White" (Carlos, Still Pond Vineyard, goat label)

2016 "Peachy Keen" (peach fruit wine, Jaemor Farms, rum barrel–aged from Richland Distillery)

2016 "Sweet Ass" (strawberry fruit wine, donkey label)

2016 "Quittin' Time" (Carlos, Still Pond Vineyard, and lemon*)
2016 "Sweet Nectarine" (fruit wine, Jaemor Farms, cow label)

Tiger Mountain Vineyards
2014 (Tannat, Ezzard, and Dr. Apple Vineyards)

Urban Tree Cidery (4 Silver)
NV "Classic" (cider, apples*)
NV "Original" (cider, apples*)
NV "Barrel-aged" (cider, apples*)
NV "Granny Drop" (cider, Granny Smith apples)

The Viking Alchemist Meadery (2 Silver)
NV "Ethereal" Mead (wildflower honey wine)
NV "Antinomy" Mead (wildflower honey wine)

About the Author

Wayne Crawford was a regular US Army officer for twenty-seven years in the infantry. With multiple military tours overseas, he acquired a passion for wine and wine writing. Wayne has lived in Georgia for over twenty years and spent the last eight years writing a wine column for Big Canoe's *Smoke Signals* newspaper in North Georgia. He is a French-wine scholar and certified specialist of wine, and he frequently judges wine competitions in the South.